Fashioning Models

Fashioning Models
Image, Text and Industry

Edited by
Joanne Entwistle and Elizabeth Wissinger

London • New York

English edition
First published in 2012 by
Berg
Editorial offices:
50 Bedford Square, London WC1B 3DP, UK
175 Fifth Avenue, New York, NY 10010, USA

Berg is an imprint of Bloomsbury Publishing Plc.

Library of Congress Cataloging-in-Publication Data

Fashioning models : image, text, and industry / edited by Joanne
Entwistle and Elizabeth Wissinger. — English ed.
p. cm.
Includes bibliographical references.
ISBN 978-0-85785-310-3 — ISBN 978-0-85785-311-0 —
ISBN 978-1-84788-155-7 — ISBN 978-1-84788-154-0   1. Models
(Persons)   I. Entwistle, Joanne.   II. Wissinger, Elizabeth.
HD8039.M77F37 2012
338.4'774692—dc23   2012013129

British Library Cataloguing-in-Publication Data

A catalogue record for this book is available from the British Library.

ISBN 978 1 84788 155 7 (Cloth)
978 1 84788 154 0 (Paper)
e-ISBN 978 0 85785 310 3 (ePDF)
978 0 85785 311 0 (epub)

Typeset by ApexCovantage LLC, USA.
Printed in the UK by the MPG Books Group

www.bergpublishers.com

For Ann and Paul (J. E.)
For Cassielle (E. W.)

Contents

List of Illustrations

Acknowledgements

J. E. As with all academic books, this one has been a long time in the making, although for all sorts of personal reasons, it took even longer than normal! I am extremely grateful for Betsy's hard work throughout the whole collaboration but especially at the very end when, due to a sudden health crisis, I had to step back completely and she had to take on the entire thing at a very critical stage. I also wish to thank our excellent contributors for their hard work and unending patience as the book made its slow progress. Our contributors were always prompt with drafts and responsive to comments and this made the process far easier than it might have otherwise been. We would also like to thank Eileen Cadman for her help preparing the manuscript and for her incredible attention to detail. I am, as always, eternally thankful to Don for not only his professional advice and support, but his care and loving support while also keeping the 'home fires burning'. This book is dedicated to my parents whose tireless love and care has always been a bedrock of stability and support throughout my life, but never more so than during stressful months of illness and treatment.

E. W. First of all, I would like to thank my co-editor, Jo, for her tireless cheer and endless resources of energy, without which this project would not have gotten off the ground. I will remember fondly our virtual collaboration punctuated by intense, in person, work sessions when one or the other of us could get across the pond. I am also grateful to Don Slater not only for his brilliant collaborative contribution to this volume, but also for letting Jo go so many times, holding down the fort and caring for kids, while she was either away in New York, or busy at home as we feverishly worked at the kitchen table, her desk, or wherever we found space for two computers and a lot of energy and excitement. My heartfelt gratitude also extends to Kristin Miller, whose vast organizational skills, kindness and willingness to not only track down resources, but to also be a sounding board for ideas, consistently made her research assistance both a joy and also a necessity that I miss to this day. Thanks also to the institutional support of the Andrew W. Mellon Fellowship in the Humanities, the BMCC/CUNY Faculty Development Grant for supporting the writing of some sections of this book and the PSC CUNY Research Award Grant, without which I would not have been able to afford Kristin's consummate skills. For her assistance in connecting me to modelling professionals for portions of my research presented here, a huge thanks goes to Renee Torriere. I am also grateful to Sage publications for allowing me to reproduce the article, 'Modeling Consumption: Fashion Modeling Work in Contemporary Society,' which appeared in the *Journal of Consumer Culture*, 9/2: 273–96. Thanks too are in order to Dan Cook for giving us the opportunity to present ideas in a conference setting which ultimately germinated into the core of this book. We are also grateful to our authors for their fine scholarship and collegiality. And finally, I have to thank Patrick; he knows the reasons why.

Contributors

ELSPETH H. BROWN is an Associate Professor of History, and Director of the Centre for the Study of the United States, at the University of Toronto. She is the author of *The Corporate Eye: Photography and the Rationalization of American Commercial Culture, 1884–1929* (Johns Hopkins, 2005) and co-editor of *Cultures of Commerce: Representation and American Business Culture, 1877–1960* (Palgrave, 2006) and *Feeling Photography* (Duke University Press, forthcoming.) Brown has published work in *Gender and History*, *Journal of American History*, *Enterprise and Society* and *Photography and Culture*, among others. Her current research is a book-length history of the commercial modelling industry in the twentieth-century United States.

JOANNE ENTWISTLE is Senior Lecturer in Culture, Media and Creative Industries at Kings College, London. She completed her PhD at Goldsmiths College and her early research focuses on fashion, gender and the body. More recently she has been examining the fashion industry as an aesthetic market. Her publications include *The Fashioned Body: Fashion, Dress and Modern Social Theory* (Polity, 2000) and *The Aesthetic Economy of Fashion: Markets and Value in Clothing and Modelling* (Berg, 2009) and *Body Dressing* (edited with Elizabeth Wilson, Berg, 2001).

LAILA HAIDARALI is Lecturer in the Department of History at the University of Essex in England. Before assuming this post in September 2009, Laila held the Inaugural Postdoctoral Fellowship in African American Studies in the Department of History at Case Western Reserve University in Cleveland, Ohio. Laila is currently working on her first book manuscript, tentatively entitled *Brownskin Woman: Sex, Colour, Beauty and African American Womanhood*, 1920–1954. Her first publication 'Polishing Brown Diamonds: African American Women, Popular Magazines and the Advent of Modelling in Early Postwar America' appeared in the *Journal of Women's History* (2005) and later was reprinted in the fourth edition of *Unequal Sisters: A Multicultural Reader in U.S. Women's History* (Routledge, 2007).

MARGARET MAYNARD is an Associate Professor and Honorary Research Consultant in the School of English, Media Studies, the University of Queensland. Her research interests are dress, identity and global consumption, with particular expertise in Australian dress. Recent publications include 'The Mystery of the Fashion Photograph', in *Fashion in Fiction: Text and Clothing in Literature, Film and Television*, edited by Peter McNeil, Vicki Karaminas and Catherine Cole (Berg, 2009) and 'What Is Australian Fashion Photography? A Dilemma', *Fashion Theory* (2009). She is the editor of *Volume Seven: Australia, New Zealand and the Pacific Islands*, for the *Berg Encyclopedia of World Dress and Fashion* (2010).

ASHLEY MEARS is Assistant Professor of Sociology at Boston University. She completed her Ph.D. from New York University and was a visiting fellow at the Centre for Gender Studies at the University of Cambridge. Her research focuses on the intersections of culture, markets and inequalities. In her first book, *Pricing Beauty: The Making of a Fashion Model* (University of California Press, 2011), she examined the backstage production of the 'look' in New York and London fashion markets. She is currently researching international model scout networks as a way to understand global flows of culture.

STEPHANIE SADRE-ORAFAI is Assistant Professor of Anthropology at the University of Cincinnati. Her research focuses on transformations in contemporary US racial thinking and visual culture through the lens of expert visions within and beyond the fashion industry. She has published essays on casting and model development and is beginning work on a comparative project on image and knowledge production practices in fashion and criminal justice.

DON SLATER is Reader in Sociology at the London School of Economics. His research focuses on information technology and development (e.g. *New Media, Development and Globalization*, Polity, forthcoming) and on issues of culture and economy (e.g. *Consumer Culture and Modernity*, Polity, 1997; and *The Technological Economy*, with Andrew Barry, Routledge 2005).

PATRÍCIA SOLEY-BELTRAN is Honorary Member of the Sociology Department, Edinburgh University. Her research focuses on feminist theory (e.g. *Transexualidad y la Matriz Heterosexual: Un Estudio Crítico de Judith Butler*, Bellaterra, 2009; ' "Having Words for Everything": Institutionalising Gender Migration in Spain (1998–2008)', with Dr. Gerard Coll-Planas, *Sexualities*, 14/3, 2011; and *Judith Butler en Disputa: Lecturas Sobre des la Performatividad*, editor with Dr. Leticia Sabsay, Egales, 2012), and on sociology of the body and fashion (she is currently working on a popularizing book weaving academically informed critical reflections with her personal experience as a professional model).

ELIZABETH WISSINGER is an Associate Professor of Sociology at the City University of New York, at the BMCC campus in Manhattan, and recipient of a

Mellon Fellowship with the CUNY Graduate School's Center for the Humanities. Her recent work on fashion modelling has appeared in *Ephemera: Theory and Politics in Organization*, *Journal of Consumer Culture* and in *The Affective Turn: Theorizing the Social* (Duke University Press, 2007). She is currently working on a book about the contemporary ramifications of modelling work in the USA (New York University Press, forthcoming).

Introduction

Joanne Entwistle and Elizabeth Wissinger

Why an academic book on fashion models? What can we learn from scholarly analysis of such cultural ephemera? Indeed, what, if anything, can we say about fashion models beyond the obvious and oft-made tabloid/newspaper points about their supposedly 'unhealthy' size or decidedly problematic status as iconic female role models? This book, we hope, answers some of these questions by analysing the cultural appeal and significance of models. While we cannot dismiss the column inches models now command in newspapers and magazines, there is more to fashion models and modelling than the sensational stories we read about in the popular press. Moreover, it is this very fascination with models as popular cultural entities that demands a more thorough, scholarly analysis because, despite their apparent triviality, models actually occupy an interesting and influential place within the social world. By examining the fashion model as contemporary figure, and the practices of fashion modelling as contemporary image industry, there is much to be discovered.

This collection explores how models have been integral to the development of modern consumer culture, and as such, have become a barometer of the current state of attitudes towards women, race and consumerism. From the 'long-stemmed American beauties' celebrated in the 1920s by the first American model agent John Robert Powers selling soap to the masses, to the hyper-marketing campaigns fronted by the supermodels of the 1980s, models have played a critical role in shaping how commodities are sold to us. Captivated by images and lifestyles of fashion models in sleek and glossy photographs and on the runways and catwalks of the fashion capitals, on the one hand, we are simultaneously repelled by images of the often extreme aesthetics of jumbled limbs and gaunt faces embodied by super-skinny 'waif-like' models. Consequently, models have become antagonistic and even repellent or at least uneasy characters in a moral drama about modern womanhood. Despite (or perhaps because of) these mixed messages, fashion models have an enduring appeal in contemporary visual culture.

The voracious consumption of stories and images of models thus articulate not only a fascination with the seemingly glamorous lifestyle of models, but also the apparent dark underside of the industry. When Kate Moss was caught on a mobile camera allegedly snorting cocaine, the images flashed around the world and caused widespread debate and controversy about models' behaviour and lifestyle. Models have also been at the centre of controversies concerning the female body, such as the outcry against the 'size zero' aesthetic, which has been condemned and vilified in the world's press in recent years. When a twenty-two-year-old model died after stepping off a runway during a fashion week in Montevideo, South America, in 2006, count-less press conferences, and everyone from media pundits, bloggers and international newspapers, jumped at the chance to cover a story that not only stirred outrage, but also afforded the opportunity to display provocative pictures of suffering young women. The vitriolic rhetoric surrounding the tragedy, coupled with the deaths of two other models (Hennigan 2007), spurred the organizers of Madrid's Fashion Week to ban models with a height-to-weight ratio—or BMI—below 18 (Klonick 2006). Milan quickly followed suit, with a code of conduct 'to protect young models vul-nerable to anorexia and exploitation' (Duff 2006). While the UK and USA did not exactly ban skinny models, the amount of controversy demanded action, and head fashion organizations in both countries issued guidelines and called for training in-dustry personnel to recognize signs of bulimia and anorexia (Wilson 2007; Thorpe and Campbell 2007). There were even two 'body image summits' in the UK. As these examples demonstrate, images and stories of fashion models consist of moral dramas that focus attention on their bodies as in some way excessive, abject, as well as desirable. These fixations have produced wave after wave of 'moral panics' about models' 'effects', from fears about their supposed influence on the rise in eating disorders among young women, to concerns as to the possible promotion of a hedo-nistic, drug-taking lifestyle.

To situate models within modern-day dramas of femininity also requires us to consider how modelling has become an idealized occupation for girls and young women; the new 'Cinderella' offering the promise of a fairytale fantasy life of glam-our and adoration. One way in which this lifestyle is sold to young girls is through the 'reality TV' formats that flood the international TV channels and which promote the modelling life. Whereas once girls and women could only consume images that models produced—in advertisements and fashion editorials—they are now in a po-sition to consume the lifestyle 'backstage' through such formats as *America's Next Top Model*.

For all these reasons, fashion models have become the focus of a number of pop-ular, often quite sensational books, such as *Model: The Ugly Business of Beauti-ful Women* (Gross 1995), and *Catwalking: A History of the Fashion Model* (Quick 1997), a grand retrospective museum exhibition (*Model as Muse* at the NYC Metro-politan Museum of Art), and recent filmic exposés, as well, such as the film *Picture Me* directed by fashion photographer Ole Schell and former fashion model Sarah Ziff (2009). This interest has been met, in recent years, by growing scholarly interest. Academic work in this area explores the complex nature of models and modelling from a range of disciplinary perspectives and examining an ever-widening spectrum of issues including representation, labour, gender, race and ethnicity. It is worth revisiting some of this work in this Introduction, as it is the intellectual context within which our book is embedded and responding to.

Making Sense of Fashion Modelling

Much research on fashion model imagery has been generated within social psychology and is linked to existing work within this discipline on either cultural definitions of attractiveness and/or the effects of media representations on women. Often the two are linked so that images are measured against, or in some way linked, to the prevalence of eating disorders (see for example Morris et al. 2006; Prabu et al. 2002; Sypeck et al. 2004). While there may be some merit in exploring these connections, the social psychology literature is fraught with problems and we have a number of reservations about such an approach. For one thing, the methodologies used to measure the effects of images are problematic. It might be legitimate to do a content analysis of fashion models in women's magazines that shows increasing thinness, but quite something else to read a correlation from this with the increase in disturbed eating patterns among American or European women. There may be a correlation, but not one that can be simply 'read' from media images alone. That said, the alternative method, of interviewing women about their consumption of such imagery, is also riddled with methodological problems, not least the fact that when subjects are prompted by researchers to read images in an interview, their responses do not replicate the usual ways in which images in fashion magazines might be read *in situ*. It is also apparent that while thinness has become a cultural obsession and eating disorders more widely diagnosed, the more pressing problem in much of the Western/Northern world, and increasingly in newly developing countries in the South as well, is that of obesity among children and young people. This significant issue is not addressed by those wanting to demonstrate a causal link between images of fashion models and eating disorders or the rise of body dissatisfaction, possibly because this anomalous data does not fall within their research agenda or line of sight. We suggest that this omission throws up some serious questions about the nature of our modern Western obsession with models, media and thinness. Why are academics, along with many journalists, so concerned with thinness and intent on dropping the problem at the doorstep of the fashion industry or model agency? What is it about thinness that is so compelling? Do we need to question our obsession with images of young thin women, as opposed to the obese? Fashion models are the obvious place to look and an easy target for our fears and desires about the female body.

More fruitful avenues of enquiry into the place and significance of fashion models can be found within a wide spectrum of cultural and historical analysis. Within a cultural historical perspective, models have been examined as exemplars of twentieth-century Fordist aesthetics (Evans 2001, 2003, 2005, 2008), or in terms of their role within the emerging consumer markets of that century (Brown 2011). So for Evans (2008: 255), the early fashion model shows demonstrated a modernist concern with the machine-like locomotion of the body, such that they sail down the catwalk in repetitious motion, not unlike 'cogs' in a 'machine'. The fashion show in turn served to promote the aesthetics of modern dress, with designers like Jean Patou and Coco Chanel designing for a modernist body that was streamlined, 'functional and anti-decorative,' which the fashion show models disseminated through shows in salons and later in department stores. Models' animation and object-like status are significant themes here. The use of the term *manikin* is itself telling of the 'slippage between animate and inanimate' that Evans describes when describing how fashion models and dummies can be interchangeable (2003: 172). *Mannequin* (or *manikin*) actually was a term originally used to describe early fashion models themselves, only later transferring to the inanimate shop window dummy, as Brown (in this collection) shows.

The object-like nature of models that haunts many of the contemporary debates about them has its origins in even earlier forms of fashion dissemination. As Evans (2003: 173) notes, fashion dolls wearing the latest creations of their day were popular playthings of wealthy women in the seventeenth and eighteenth centuries. As 'living dolls', the earliest fashion models were problematic figures—beautiful cogs—to use Evans's analogy—in the capitalist machinery (see also Evans 2000: 103). They were pure image—on stage or, later in images, as photographic modelling developed in the twentieth century—and did not speak to or come back at the audience. The assumed passivity of the fashion model, given this movement between animate and inanimate object, may partly explain some of our complex relationship with model imagery. That is to say, we tend to see models as more or less passive 'victims' of the fashion system. Certainly early feminist attacks on sexism in advertising tended to think so. Though not attacking the models themselves, the sexually attractive model in the advertisement was the symbol of the latent, or blatant, sexism of capitalism. The perception of models as 'dumb' or mute objects has been a common theme in scholarly work on visual culture. As numerous scholars have argued (Berger 1972; Mulvey 1975, 1988), women have long been the object of aesthetic contemplation, caught within 'the gaze', mute and without subjectivity and this would extend, inevitably, to those women—models and actresses—who largely populate the visual arena.

This is not to say that models always *are* dumb and mute; indeed, If we consider the labour involved in producing images, models can and do play a role in the co-production of the photograph, to some extent, as has been examined by Maynard (1999) who disputes the perception of models as mute putty in the photographer's hands and gives some agency to the models themselves as co-creators of the image. Still, even when creatively active in the production of the image, models have less control over the terms under which they are represented and, in this respect modelling practices have been read critically as producing gendered femininity and, in addition, reproducing racial and classed identities (Brown 2011; Goffman 1979; Mears 2008; Sadre-Orafai 2008; Soley-Beltran 2004, reprinted in this book). As these authors argue, modelling does more than service the capitalist imperative to sell us things; modelling practices shape our understandings and ways of seeing identities. Through the selection of particular body types—tall, thin, mostly white but sometimes exotically 'other'—gendered, racialized or nationalized identities are packaged in the images together with the commodities themselves. Further, as other studies of modelling practices show (see Neff et al. 2005; Wissinger 2007a,b, 2009, reprinted in this book), models come to literally model contemporary consumption and feed the image of the model 'lifestyle' that in turn feeds into wider consumption practices.

Indeed, it would seem that modelling work itself, while only performed by a minority of people, exemplifies wider trends in freelance and project-based work evident in other cultural industries (Grabher 2002; McRobbie 2002a,b; Gill 2002) and throws light on the difficulties of such seemingly glamorous work. In some recent scholarly papers on modelling there has been an explicit attempt to understand this industry through the actual processes and practices and the forms of embodied labour demanded. Here the concern has been to understand the specific nature of labour inside this highly volatile, unstable industry. The precarious nature of the industry, with its ever-fluctuating demands and inexplicable shifts in client and consumer tastes, fuel the working practices inside it. As Godart and Mears (2009; see also Mears 2010) argue, these ever-fluctuating industry demands also serve to reproduce existing aesthetic standards that favour the ever-prevalent white/thin version of femininity, often criticized by scholars, as a way of managing 'risk'. Wissinger (2012) corroborates this, finding that industry gatekeepers' appeals to 'aesthetics' mask discriminatory tendencies they blame on 'the market', tendencies that shift this need to manage risk more heavily onto the shoulders of black models.

In the face of massive uncertainties and very little control—as models and their bookers never know in advance what castings will result in jobs and what clients will book them—models attempt to effect some control through various forms of bodily investment. This precariousness has implications for the identity narratives of models (Parmentier and Fischer 2007) that may have wider application to understand other, similarly desirable yet also unsustainable career paths. Where conventions of work tend to reproduce very exacting aesthetic standards, these are inevitably going to take their toll upon the body/mind of the model who has to work hard (by not eating, or by exercising, or simply by smiling and being 'friendly') to gain and maintain work in the industry. As Entwistle and Wissinger (2006) argue, the responsibility of success appears to fall upon the 'enterprising' individual model's shoulders to manage the body/ self effectively in the form of 'aesthetic labour'. Similarly, Mears and Finlay (2005) develop an account of 'bodily capital' and 'emotional labour' to analyse how models attempt to manage the uncertainties of work and use such things as 'charm' to try to win over a potential client. That this labour is gendered and the particularities of how male and female models 'do' gender is very apparent in Mears's (2008) analysis of how modelling disciplines the body of the female model and this 'doing' of gender, she argues, is 'paradigmatic of women's general compulsion to regulate and discipline their bodies in pursuit of a prescribed and yet elusive feminine image' (2008: 430).

In contrast to the focus on female models, male models have warranted considerably less attention and yet they provide intriguing insights into what happens when men perform such nontraditional 'feminine' work—of posing, looking good and selling their appearance—in what is a female-dominated industry that pays women considerably more than men. The challenges this work poses to hegemonic masculinity is captured in Entwistle's (2004) account of male models in London and New York. She describes how the apparent 'femininity' and the assumed homosexuality of the occupation is not only a threat to their masculinity and produces 'macho' attempts to reclaim it, but is also a taken-for-granted aspect of the work that leads to strategic performances of 'camp', if the model wishes to score a job with an assumed gay client. In Mears's (2011) treatment of the subject, the focus of attention is the way in which the gendered nature of the work and the assumptions built into it about the inappropriateness of modelling as work for men produces men's 'worthlessness' within the industry. This translates into lower pay all round for the same work performed by female models and is an accepted 'fact' that goes unchallenged by models and model bookers.

For a fuller picture of the demands of this industry beyond the models themselves, it is necessary to examine the work of model agents or 'bookers' (Entwistle 2002, 2004, 2010; Godart and Mears 2009; Mears 2010) who help shape model 'looks' and develop strategies to counter these uncertainties and manage the inherent 'risk' of work in such an industry. As this research shows, these 'cultural intermediaries' (Bourdieu 1984) are part of a larger 'network' inside the fashion industry which includes not only model bookers but the clients who purchase model looks—fashion photographers, fashion editors and designers. This network of relationships inside fashion is also described in Aspers's (2001) scholarly study of the market in fashion photography in Sweden. The bookers' work of calculation is key to stabilizing models' careers and helping secure their identity and value across this network, and their selections are undoubtedly performative. While they may talk as if 'the look' of the moment is somewhere 'out there' or in clients' hands, their work of selection and calculation in fact goes some way to producing the look.

A different line of enquiry is taken by Wissinger (2007a,b) who attempts to situate modelling work within a broader account of fashion modelling within contemporary consumer capitalism. She argues that part of modelling work involves channelling 'affect' both in person at castings and in the image, which places emphasis upon the model's ability to understand and translate the very nebulous and highly unstable demands of the industry. For Wissinger, 'immaterial' and 'affective' labour would seem to be particularly effective within contemporary image-driven consumer capitalism. As she puts it, modelling work not only sells products, but also calibrates bodily affects, often in the form of attention, excitement or interest, so that they may be bought and sold in a circulation of affects that plays an important role in postindustrial economies (2007b: 251).

As this growing body of scholarly work highlights, modelling work is complex and not without contradictions. It's glamorous and well paid, but also irregular, unstable and demands more than turning up on time and looking pretty as one common perception suggests. We do not wish to over-state the claim that models have an especially hard time worthy of our sympathy—though there are aspects of their work that should, quite rightly, concern us, especially the working conditions of very young models who are often preyed upon by older men and may not be well looked after by their agency. That said, it is an obvious thing to state but models are frequently privileged, elite workers whose pay (sometimes) reflects this. However, what does emerge from a more thorough analysis of their labour and the industry practices, which we have briefly outlined above, is that the image models project is a long way from the reality of life in this industry and, while this image—depicted in magazines, newspapers and reality TV modelling shows—is worth investigating as indicative of trends in the consumption of celebrity lifestyles and perhaps the nature of modern obsessions with physical appearance, there is much we can learn by going 'behind the scenes' as well.

The Scope of *Fashioning Models*

Building on this growing body of literature, this volume attempts to look at modelling from both angles—the 'front-stage' images created by it and their place within historical and contemporary culture, along with the 'backstage' nature of modelling as work. In drawing together academics from different scholarly backgrounds—history, sociology, cultural studies, gender studies—this collection allows the authors to explore models from a range of perspectives that embrace current concerns surrounding aspects of visual culture, gender, sexuality and the body.

One of the strengths of this collection is this very interdisciplinary and multi-method approach. Chapters collected in Part I have developed out of intensive and thorough archival work, while other chapters in Part II derive from in-depth fieldwork inside the industry and, in the case of Mears's and Soley-Beltran's chapters, from direct experience working as a model. Another strength is the book's international focus. With chapters on modelling in America (Brown, Haidarali and Wissinger), Australia (Maynard) and Japan (Mears), this edited collection offers contrasting accounts and different histories of modelling. The specificities of different national market characteristics inform Mears's account of her experiences in Japan, while the particularities of Australia's rather marginal position vis-à-vis Europe and America is a concern in Maynard's chapter, as well as the ways in which modelling practices informed debate about a distinctive 'Australian' national type. Bringing some of the scholars in this expanding field of analysis together for the first time, *Fashioning Models* sheds light on the place of the fashion model, so inextricably linked to modernity, and, in doing so, examines a number of contemporary themes that resonate around this alluring figure.

The book opens with a theoretical and methodological treatise on how to understand and analyse the fashion model in contemporary culture. In recent years there has been considerable debate in the popular press and within scholarly work on the significance of model imagery, as somehow effecting a 'bad' influence upon us—or, more correctly, 'them', since the presumed 'victims' of these supposedly bad images are more often than not girls and young women. Entwistle and Slater take on this wide-ranging literature and try to develop a more nuanced and insightful account of models' cultural impact. Drawing on the work of Lury (2004) and also McFall (2004), they develop the concept of the model as brand as a way of understanding how models circulate and gather meaning across multiple locations. Thinking about models as brands, they argue, avoids some of the pitfalls and limitations of earlier attempts to understand models which tend towards looking at either the images or 'realities' of modelling as work, and thus fall on one or the other side of the simple dichotomies between representation/reality, image/materiality. The problem with the image-led focus is that it is too often reductive, concerning the 'impact' or 'influence' of particular model images that ignores the dynamic nature of images and image production and consumption. More recent accounts of modelling work, while valuable, 'bracket out' the image/representation issue to focus on the modelling practices inside the fashion industry and so cannot account for the wider 'influence' and circulation of models outside it, even while acknowledging that models' work reaches outside through their representation. Adopting a more actor-network analysis, as Lury does in her analysis of the brand as an 'event', enables a much more fluid and more nuanced account of the 'flow' of models—from 'real' spaces of production and work through to images consumed in the market beyond—which avoids the simple dichotomies of earlier work. Like Lury's notion of the brand, models are not fixed and finite objects, but mutable objects that 'travel' (literally and figuratively) and whose qualities are temporally and spatially calculated and constantly in flux as they are picked up and 'read' by consumers.

In contrast to this theoretical chapter, the remaining chapters of the book are either historical or empirically based, examining specific instances of models and modelling practices. Part I of the book examines some historical dimensions of modelling as it emerges in the early- to mid-twentieth century, while the chapters in Part II examine different dimensions of contemporary modelling, largely focused on the labour involved in modelling.

Fashion Modelling and the Rise of Consumer Culture

First, no account of fashion modelling can do it justice unless it seeks to situate it within broader transformations in capitalist commodification and consumer culture.

Modelling work is inextricably linked to the development of modern consumer culture: as markets opened up and the range of commodities expanded over the pre- and postwar period, this has been met with an expansion in the modelling industry, with more models required to render these things desirable. While some elements of the early history have been examined, for example the relationship of fashion modelling to characteristics of twentieth-century modernity, as discussed in Evans's (2005, 2008) account above, there remains much more historical work to be done to unearth the specific histories of fashion modelling and its connections to the development of modern consumption and forms of representation. The chapters in Part I therefore examine some elements of this history and show how modelling parallels and informs some important twentieth-century developments.

Elspeth Brown's chapter examines the early origins and history of modelling in America specifically as a response to the move within print advertising towards photographic-based illustration and the emergence of an expanded market for advertising models. Focusing on key agencies established in New York City, from the John Powers modelling agency of the 1920s to Eileen Ford who opened the Ford model agency in 1947, Brown traces the rise of the model agency from its infancy to the Second World War era. In doing so, she also charts how modelling informed the standardization of ideal beauty 'types' in the context of racial formation, class mobility and Americanization in the first half of the twentieth century. This history is significant, anticipating the later transformation of the American economy after the Second World War, which ushered in a new era of mass consumption and commercial modelling. The ways in which the early model agencies selected and shaped models, in terms of an Anglo-Saxon ideal, are also examined, and this chapter prefigures some later discussions and debates, popular and academic, about the whiteness of fashion modelling and foregrounds debates that continue in other chapters in the book.

Indeed, it is this immediate postwar history that is picked up in Laila Haidarali's chapter, which is concerned with the emergence of black models. While Brown foregrounds the racialized nature of early fashion modelling which purveyed a particularly Anglo-Saxon form of ideal beauty, Haidarali's chapter examines the work of African American female models, and the ways in which model work was viewed by, and presented to, diverse African American audiences in the immediate postwar era—during the nine- or ten-year period between 1945–1954. She argues that as modelling advanced new tenets of gendered self-presentation, the work of the female model helped reanimate representative understandings of African American womanhood at home and abroad, often doing so through the employment and display of 'Brownskin' womanhood. This worked to secure an image of 'race womanhood' that announced heterosexual appeal, feminized deportment and dress, and urban middle-class status through the access to consumer goods. Despite the conservative definitions of feminized beauty and heterosexual appeal, the image of the 'Brownskin' model challenged white representations of African America. Here the image of 'Brownskin' femininity is complex and contradictory: at once libratory in its redress of racist stereotyping, and confining in its narrow dictates of racialized gender expectations, this postwar visual discourse allows us to glean some understanding of an era when African America begin to visualize a different public racial representation. She questions to what extent this remains true of contemporary African American models, such as Tyra Banks.

The focus of this history—of modelling and the rise of consumer culture, and the commodification of particular body types—shifts its attention to Australia in Margaret Maynard's account of the development of Australian fashion modelling in the pre- and postwar period. The question for Maynard is: how did photographic modelling function in Australia, where a nexus between couturiers, high society and numerous glossy magazines did not exist quite as it did in say the USA or France? In answering this, she focuses on the differences in the Antipodean market, such as the availability of technology, the different kinds of clientele and retailing in Sydney and Melbourne, local climatic conditions, tastes and types of model. She argues that there is little doubt that isolation and a small population were key defining factors inhibiting fashion publishing, modelling and the related quality garment industry until the 1960s. As with Brown's and Haidarali's chapters, Maynard's also demonstrates how the model becomes a figure upon which much is projected, not least ideas and ideals of femininity. As Maynard argues, Australian media before the mid 1940s had been embroiled in persistent discussions about what constituted female attractiveness, initially in relation to national characteristics defined as the 'Australian Girl'. However, postwar, this debate was to splinter. What emerges at this time is public discussion embroiled more broadly in notions of women's appearances and comportment, where local fashions and models stood in relation, often unfavourably, to those of Europe or the USA. The mix of criticism and praise for appearances of Australian women is part of a paradox that runs through other aspects of local history, with a self-conscious sense of inadequacy that is, perhaps, she argues, a characteristic of provincialism.

A slightly different line of enquiry is pursued by Soley-Beltran who examines not only the historical rise of fashion models, but questions how models literally model femininity. Soley-Beltran's chapter addresses the ways in which models' 'glamour' is constructed; first through a historical account of modelling and the ways in which layers of meaning have been spun around models to create a persona that can sell us stuff, and secondly through first-person accounts of the profession from models themselves, including the author herself, whose personal stories belie the very glamour they help to produce. As she argues, the model's body is an artefact in every sense of the word—an object, work of art and manufactured article or relic—that is the result of 'a careful construction of their social personas and visual representations'. The work that goes into producing the glamorous representations of our contemporary visual culture entails real bodies and selves whose embodiment is captured and translated into two-dimensional images by a whole visual machinery. This would not be a problem in itself: Western/Northern life has long been captured by the camera, and we are all caught up in visual representations in such things as our family album. The problem, as Soley-Beltran argues, is with the layers of meaning that are spun around models as they become embodiments *of* something else, be it race or ethnicity, national ideals of beauty or ideals of femininity. The effort to *be* something—an icon of one sort or another—is felt by models most acutely in their accounts of alienation from their constructed persona, but the effects are felt more widely, as the ideal of glamour comes to be desired in and of itself. We are all, theoretically at least, caught up in the illusion of glamour sold to us by models.

Fashion Modelling as Work

As already acknowledged above, one area of fertile research on models has been scholarly examination of the modelling industry that attempts to understand fashion modelling as *work*. This key theme runs through the chapters in Part II and is developed in different ways in each of the chapters gathered here. Modelling arguably represents a glamorization of flexible, temporary and contract work, making it seem desirable, especially to young people, while hiding its numerous drawbacks. As a form of commodification, since models themselves are commodities who sell their bodies in a highly uncertain market, analysis of modelling work reveals how idealized forms of beauty are manufactured through image-making, and how bodies are gendered, raced and sexualized in the process. These issues are taken up in this collection in a number of ways.

Sadre-Orafai's chapter on reality TV modelling show *America's Next Top Model* (*ANTM*) goes some way to highlighting something of the visual machinery that goes into producing fashion models. With such shows aiming to show modelling for what it is—an industry demanding bodies to perform in particular ways—she argues that this format foregrounds the production practices that go into creating aesthetic performances, over and above the contemplation or aesthetic evaluation of the performances themselves. She suggests that such shows (and these are numerous, of which *ANTM* is only one example) have expanded the definition of fashion commodities to include not only fetishized objects alienated from their production, but also the lifestyles and labour of fashion producers themselves (other similar reality shows have focused on designers, such as *House of Style*, *MTV 1989* or *Project Runway*). The format of such shows seemingly exposes the labour and 'effort' involved in fashion modelling, as opposed to the aesthetic evaluation of the model's appearance per se, although this is still a feature. However, while this would appear to be in line with feminist and liberal critiques of the disjuncture between ascribed and achieved status—what Douglas Mao has phrased 'the labor theory of beauty' (2003)—Sadre-Orafai suggests that these shows actually reinforce structural hierarchies and inequalities. However, these are effectively 'hidden' behind apparently neutral terms like *evidence*, *effort* and *the market* and *trends*. Recourse to such terms, she argues, not only masks discriminatory judgement processes, but also reinforces durable theories of visibility, personhood and authenticity.

There is, of course, no question that such shows do not represent the 'real' world of fashion modelling—and the models themselves rarely go on to 'make it' as top models. They are fictitious accounts, and while some industry insiders may make an appearance, by and large these programmes stand outside the mainstream fashion modelling world. They nonetheless demonstrate the current contemporary concern with models and modelling as a form of work, and one that is especially appealing to young girls. If nothing else, such shows are a testament to the enduring appeal of the fashion model and, even while they are a step or two removed from the realities of the industry, they highlight the fact that behind the images, modelling is *work*; real labour that taxes body, mind, emotions.

For an insider look at the realities of modelling as work one can turn to Ashley Mears's chapter. A former professional model, Mears describes, in close ethnographic detail, the demands of this work as experienced from the specific market location of Japan. In her account as a *gaijin* model (i.e. a Western model), Mears attends to a little-known element of the global modelling market—the Tokyo market. This is, she notes, a crucial economic part of the modelling industry, though it receives little attention by academics or the general public. Western models go to Japan to make money, not to appear in prestigious fashion campaigns and editorials and the images will not be placed in their European book on their return. In her chapter, Mears describes in detail the structural and cultural differences that bring models to Japan and examines how these forces shape a model's experience of the work, from the navigation of uncertainty, body consciousness, and language barriers, camaraderie and competition, and homesickness. What is perhaps striking about her chapter are the ways in which the problematic gendered and sexualized nature of the work, exacerbated by the language and cultural differences, is managed on a daily basis through the ongoing efforts of the models themselves. As such, her account highlights some of the emotional labour involved in modelling and goes some way to filling the gap in the research on models that tends to see them as passive screens upon which hopes, desires or fears are projected. In her account, models are active agents in the work process despite their largely futile attempts to gain some control over their work.

Placing modelling work within the structure of branding, Wissinger takes up this theme, arguing that modelling work is far more complex than just smiling for the camera. Wissinger claims that models not only model products, they frame consumer experiences and encounters with commodities in the selection, styling and dissemination of the images in which they appear. By examining models' self-commodification as forms of aesthetic, entrepreneurial and immaterial labour, Wissinger suggests that these practices of compulsory image management and socializing glamourize the 'model life' and so play into processes used to brand and sell different types of urban space, as well as commodifying the very experience of being 'in fashion'. As such, Wissinger paints a picture of modelling work that involves not only posing for photographs or walking runways, but also the hard work of producing the image of living the 'model life', thereby modelling a lifestyle that is then packaged and sold to consumers as an experience that can be had for the price of their attention.

Continuing this exploration of the model 'brand', the final chapter in this section and of the entire book takes a view from further inside the fashion industry. Here the editors enter into a discussion with four model agents whose combined work and influence spans three decades and across the two important fashion cities of London and New York. In this discussion, the agents describe some of the key changes that have taken place since the 1980s, a moment when the whole 'supermodel' phenomenon began apace and a time when we saw an expansion in the number of model agencies globally. The discussion covers the 'rise and fall' of the supermodel phenomenon: today, the supermodel who became a 'household name' and earned millions a year has become almost extinct. While many of the older supermodels are still working in 2011 (Giselle or Kate Moss, for example), a number of significant developments have served to undermine this phenomenon and reduce the likelihood of new supermodels being formed in their image. These conditions are explored in detail in the chapter. They include, in particular, the increasing quantity of images across more media with the expansion of new markets in products and the opening up of the former Soviet bloc and China, the rise of the Internet and the incredible expansion of model agencies across the globe. There are, quite literally, more models working today than ever before and thus the competition between models and between model agencies is tougher than ever. Models now command lower fees for jobs and enjoy even shorter careers as the whole system has 'speeded up' with everyone seeking to find, and then replace, the next 'new face'. While distinctive local markets in major fashion cities still exist, the conglomeration of fashion houses internationally and the increasing extension of high fashion into more cities across the world, with more and more 'scouting' (i.e. talent spotting) going to the farthest corners of the world, means that modelling today is a truly global phenomenon. Fashion models move around the globe, spending portions of time in different cities, and model agencies now have their offices in numerous fashion cities. We have come a long way since John Powers in the 1920s.

Conclusion

Fashion modelling today has extended its reach and influence from the early days when mannequins were required to parade on the shop floor. The fashion model today is the ultimate contemporary worker. One could argue that despite being an exotic and rare creature, the model is paradigmatic of working life in the early twenty-first century: a freelance, flexible, aesthetic worker who sells body and soul in the demanding and increasingly unpredictable labour markets of modern capitalism. We suggest that models provide an interesting perspective from which to examine the modularities of modern capitalism; the adaptations to new markets, the subtle shifts in representation and transformations in markets and working practices. We offer this collection of essays to readers interested not only in models and modelling, but also in understanding the nature of contemporary society and consumer culture.

We realize, too, the limitations of this book. While we have striven to produce a definitive account of fashion modelling from the current wave of scholarly work in this area, we concede that no single book could possibly cover the entire fashion modelling world or history. There are notable absences: we have nothing specifically on modelling in any of the four major fashion cities—London, New York, Milan and Paris—although the former two cities formed a component in both editors' own empirical work. Indeed, we might also have commissioned essays on newly emerging fashion cities, such as Istanbul or Delhi, and on the specificities of new, non-Western modelling practices. We do not have anything on the system of 'scouting' for new models, a phenomenon that is now a major factor in the ongoing success of many major fashion model agencies. These topics are absent in our account, however, largely because we have not seen any scholarly work being undertaken in these areas. We hope that this collection of papers spurs further work and helps to promote more empirical investigation to fill these gaps. In fact, we would be delighted if this book inspires and encourages more scholarly exploration of the rich and far-reaching topic of fashion modelling.

–2–

Models as Brands: Critical Thinking about Bodies and Images

Joanne Entwistle and Don Slater

Introduction

How should critical social thought think about fashion models? This, a key question of this entire collection, is our concern in this chapter. As noted in the Introduction, models are already the object of considerable academic and popular concern (e.g. Bordo 2003; Mears 2011; Wolf 1990), largely framed in terms of either (or both) the vulnerability of the model's body (anorexia, sexual exploitation, commodification) or the vulnerability of (particularly female) viewers to the 'impact' of the images models appear in, involving restricted constructions of gender and embodiment (e.g. traditional gender roles, sexualization, valorization of body types that are hyperbolically white and skinny). The contentiousness of models and their images is crystallized in recent waves of panic over 'size zero' models focused on the apparent 'influence' of skinny models on impressionable young women (Shaw 1995), though this continues a longer tradition of concern over representations of women that is periodically targeted on more specific pathologies such as eating disorders (Orbach 1993).

What interests us in this chapter is the extent to which critical and political concern about models revolves around the issue of representation and the way representations are produced, circulated and read. Clearly, models are employed to produce images, and these images are encountered by people in various texts (magazines, television, websites). And we can agree that in some sense 'representations matter', including representations of models. They have certainly mattered to feminists and media scholars for some time: As Gill (2007: 7) notes, 'feminist analyses of the media have been animated by the desire to understand how images and cultural constructions are connected to patterns of inequality, domination and oppression'. Yet the question remains as to *how* to connect these things up? And whether a connection between images and effects is the best way of formulating just what we are trying to connect up? Is the *image* of the model the best focus for getting to grips with the socio-political significance and consequences of all this intensive work on bodies?

Indeed, recent work on modelling itself—to some extent represented in this book—has been organized around a quite different research agenda: there has been a focus on the 'real' model body and on working practices inside the modelling industry (Entwistle 2002, 2009; Mears 2008, 2011; Mears and Finlay 2005; Mears and Godart 2009; Parmentier and Fischer 2007; Wissinger 2007b, 2009). Here it is the working models themselves and not their representational bodies that are analysed, with the focus on the model's labouring body, working economically, emotionally, aesthetically, under determinate and fluctuating conditions of employment and contract. The contrast between these two approaches is great indeed. In the former, the model's body seemed irrelevant—no more than a kind of raw material that was virtually undetectable, and analytically insignificant, under the layers of air-brushing, studio effects and now photoshopping. This older view presumed a dichotomy between real and represented bodies that current research refuses. The current literature, by contrast, testifies to the ways in which the model body is configured within extended networks; from the model agency, through the various agencies that assess, measure, style and photograph the model body. In these accounts the real and the represented model body are not usefully distinguishable. The central category of 'the look' is crucial here. The look is what model agents commodify and sell to clients, and combines the model's physical self and the photographs he or she appears in. It is therefore materialized in various ways—in the body of the model, how he or she presents himself or herself and how he or she is photographed. It goes without saying that all models are 'photogenic' but that is only the start of it; models have qualities they 'project' in an image, an 'individual' look that is appropriate for particular sorts of clients and markets, as calculated by their model agent or 'booker', and then 'read', evaluated and further calculated by photographers, fashion stylists, editors and a host of other industry players. Thus the stuff of feminist and other critical enquiry—model/fashion images—is the result of varied and complex processes of calculation and mediation.

However, the mediations do not stop within the processes of production, within the agencies that have been studied. The look is constructed and sustained across myriad social settings and processes, all of which combine symbolic and material processes: for example the integration of a model's look within larger branding practices; its placement within editorial work in magazines and other media; the orientation of consumers to the look not simply through the consumption of the model's image, but, *inter alia*, through dress and shopping practices, lifestyle and leisure choices and talk about style within social encounters. And of course this wider circulation and construction of the look loops back on the model and his or her career and body work, with countless intermediaries recalibrating or requalifying the body in relation to the dispersed practices in which it is implicated.

That is to say, we have a warrant for thinking about the social significance or effects of modelling not as something to do with the power of images and the ways they are read, but rather—by extending outwards, into 'the social', the logic of current research on the models' labour—as a matter of concrete practices which include, but cannot be reduced to, exposure to images of models. And we develop this line of inquiry by extending the notion of 'the look'. The premise of this chapter is that 'the look' is a very different object of research from 'images' and 'representations'. The latter terms point us, politically and critically, to address the encounter between a signification and a subjectivity, a text and a mind, in order to find what used to be called ideology or cultural constructions—the way identities are moulded through codified meanings. The 'look', by contrast, is not (just) an image: it is an object of calculation, something continuously worked upon, moulded, contested, performed, something that is identifiable out there in the world (we *know* Kate Moss as 'a look' across countless manifestations), and yet is constantly de- and re-stabilized in new forms. Much of this chapter is devoted to arguing that we can best bring out the analytical (and critical/political) potential of the notion of 'the look' by developing it in terms of recent theorizations of 'the brand' (notably those, such as Celia Lury's (2004, 2009) and Liz Moor's (2003, 2007), that are connected, in mediated ways, to Actor-Network Theory (ANT) and to the work of Michel Callon).

In this chapter, we want to develop this account of the model as a brand. The model brand is enacted in and through specific objects, actions and signs, but is always a kind of moving assemblage of all of them, something they all both perform and are performed by. The object which is passed from production to consumption, from fashion industry to consumers, is not representations that then have independent impacts on those subjects that read them; rather, diverse and overlapping production and consumption processes participate in the construction of the brand as an 'event'—an object in time—that involves objects, practices, agents and images. Reducing all this to 'representations' and readings is to miss most of the landscape of social consequence that we need to engage with if we are to understand the issues that initially motivated interest in models: how modelling is 'connected to patterns of inequality, domination and oppression' that Gill points us to.

Our chapter is divided into three parts. We firstly summarize our problems with 'impacts and influences' approaches to models that focus on images and representations rather than broader forms of practice. Secondly, we develop the idea that the crucial notion of 'the look' can be extended through an analysis of the model as 'brand', in the sense that Lury defined it. Lury's conceptualization of the brand as event and as interface focuses our attention on the way in which the model's look is assembled across a range of different practices. Although we can abstract the look as a text to be interpreted, it is—like the brand—an entity that is dispersed across a broad social field. Pursuing this methodology involves moving from a focus on the 'internal' world of modelling as one site of calculation and construction to look at the wider practices in which a look circulates.

Models—we want to argue—are complex objects whose meanings are actively constituted in multiple locations. They are also objects widely dispersed so that the meaning of the model is never captured in any one location; moreover, that meaning cannot be reduced to the real body of the model, or to the surface of the text/image, or to the various investments made in images through media commentaries, critiques or other multiple readings made by any number of possible audiences. Like the brand, the model is enacted in too many locations to have the meaning contained in any one location. Once we begin to think about models in this way, in terms of multiple locations—from model agency, to fashion magazine and reader engagement—the distinctions between real/representation, material/immaterial break down and we can begin to think about models and their 'influence' in more complex and comprehensive ways. In Part Three, we map out this analysis in more detail and examine it further through the ANT-derived idea of 'attachment'.

I. Models and Meanings

We start by colouring in our claim that the critical and political significance of modelling has been largely tied to the question of representations and their impacts; and that, therefore, critical engagement with modelling generally starts with a separation between body and image, production and consumption, and with the separating out of a critical social moment: the 'impact' or 'effect' of an encounter between, for example a young woman and a picture. While we develop this description specifically through a discussion of images of models, it should be clear that this story is part of a wider one that we will not address explicitly: modern social and cultural theory has been characterized by persistent recourse to textual analysis, involving claims that the underlying structures of meaning (e.g. ideology, myth, sign values) that can be read off/into texts are also socially effective and consequential (subjectivities are constituted, interpellated, constructed in and through representations). The vaunted transitions (after the 1980s) to more ethnographic cultural studies and to assertions of active and creative agency have only broken with this agenda to the extent that they have given up the language of 'readers' and 'texts', and this has never been entirely complete or convincing.

Firstly, it is wise not to forget the very crude and explicit versions of effects study that have been conducted over the past century and which are still produced on a huge scale. For example a large and expanding literature within social and clinical psychology has tried to measure the effects of looking at model images on the body satisfaction or self-esteem of readers—usually young adolescent girls or college students (Ahern et al. 2008; Ashmore et al. 1996; Foley Sypeck 2004; Shaw 1995). The idea of such effect is still pursued in some mass media research that similarly seeks to measure how images of fashion models influence young girls under laboratory-style conditions (e.g. David et al. 2002; Reaves and Bush Hitchon 2004). While such 'effects' research has been long discredited within cultural (and most media) studies for failing to understand the complexities of reading and our relationship to media, there persists a powerful desire to attribute specific social effects to specific images as discrete variables—the 1970s/1980s debates on pornography and rape are clear illustrations of this. This has directly instrumental value for policy and regulation, for pressure groups and for everyday political contest. Hence, despite the intellectual weakness of this sort of research, it frequently escapes the clinical laboratory and infects media interpretations of media imagery. So, for example when the British Medical Association reported in 2000 that there was a link between 'unrealistic' images of fashion models and a rise in instances of eating disorders, it is widely reported as 'Models link to teenage anorexia' with calls to the fashion industry to behave more 'responsibly' and produce more 'realistic' images of women.

The media frenzy was particularly acute when, in 2006, models Luisel Ramos from Uruguay and Brazilian Ana Carolina Reston died of complications due to anorexia and a panic about 'size zero' models ensued. Even while the complexity of eating disorders was also being explained by some clinicians as a complex blend of genetic and environmental factors (Conniff Taber 2006), the crude causal connection of model image to detrimental 'effect' remains firmly established in the mainstream media. Leaving aside the complex issue of how we should actually account for anorexia or bulimia, the fact remains that images of models are an easy target for social comment and criticism to the point where this media furor has real world 'effects' itself. Governments, for one, take notice: after similar size zero anxieties in 2000, the then Labour Women's Minister, Tessa Jowell, gathered together a 'body summit' to try to understand the problem and directly address the fashion industry and continued to discuss how to address the problem right through to 2007. Meanwhile, organizers of Madrid fashion week went as far as banning underweight models, following the 'size zero' panic in 2006.

Secondly, apart from the more crude effects research, the desire to 'blame' images of fashion models for reproducing culturally harmful ideas about the body is evident in both popular and academic feminist critiques of images of women, developed over several decades. In a more considered assessment of anorexia and the female body, Orbach (1993: 16) is careful to situate media images within a fuller account of the anorexic's relationship to the body, acknowledgeing that the influences stem from two features: how a woman believes she 'compares with the magnified images of women that surround her on billboards and on television, in movies, magazines and newspapers', and her early childhood experiences. Yet, as she notes, media images still do their work on the psyche and the woman 'cannot always cast off those incessant images . . . that get under her skin' (1993: 16). The woman is, she argues, 'receptive to the messages proclaiming her body' (1993: 16). Similarly in a more popular version, Wolf argued that the 'beauty myth' perpetuates the tyranny of women's body maintenance, so much so that it constitutes a 'third shift' of labour after work and domestic care that is every bit as enslaving to women as those were construed in second-wave feminism. Although not the sole target of her critique, prevalent images of slim, sexy and young models are partly held to account. Bordo's (2003) analysis is much the same: women's self-perception is shaped through engagement with media images of beauty in ways that are unrealistic and unhealthy. Again, it is the images of fashion models, so central to selling us stuff in consumer capitalism, that are targeted.

In contrast to earlier feminist and structuralist critiques of the image as ideologically structuring gendered subjectivities, poststructuralist approaches in the mould of Foucault appeared to move beyond the image, placing in the centre of analysis discourses that are enunciated as part of disciplinary or governmental practices rather than textual structures. Such 'technologies of gender' (de Lauretis 1989) are material means for organizing subjectivity in specifically gendered forms, and partly through a specific labour on the body. For example Bartky (1988) analyses the disciplining of the female body in relation to standardized requirements but acknowledges that while older forms of discipline had a singular authority—the school or prison system for example—'The disciplinary power that inscribes femininity in the female body is everywhere and nowhere; the disciplinarian is everyone and yet no one in particular' (1988: 103). Bartky continues, 'discipline can be institutionally unbound' (103) and this is 'crucial to a proper understanding of the subordination of women' (103).

The vagueness of this quote rather gives the game away: while an attempt is made to ground the process of gendering in specified practices, the latter are really merely an instantiation of something already bigger and more organized—an ideological structure that Bartky can't locate anywhere 'in particular' because it is 'unbound'. This is still more clear in Butler's work: model images would correspond to the endless reiteration of a heteronormativity, an overarching law or code that 'matters'—i.e. is both consequential, and produces specific material/bodily forms. Practices appear not as proper mediations but as mere conduits or materializations, occasions for the eternal recurrence of the ever-same codes. Indeed, in a common methodological move, representations are read 'symptomatically'—they are analysed not as specific mediations in their own right but as evidence of wider constructions of gender that they simply reflect and reproduce. The focus might move from specific texts (as in Orbach) to iterated codes but something very similar is going on: representations are placed at the centre of a fairly standard account of the reproduction of normativity, or socialization. None of these authors would explicitly argue that there is a straightforward 'effect' from looking at images, but rather invoke the idea of an all-pervasive cultural context within which these images work, albeit incrementally and insidiously, to produce their 'effect'; as Hollows and Moseley (2006: 4) note, 'From this perspective, the popular was seen as a site for the cultural reproduction of gender inequalities.'

Although proclaiming to be a more nuanced account of power that works not directly *on* us but through various 'capillary-like' actions and subtle investments of self, such accounts still don't tell us very much about *how* this power works. In particular, what is lacking is an understanding of *attachment*. How do images of beauty/fashion models call upon us? Older models of 'ideology' are often overtly or implicitly dismissed in this analytical framework, yet they come close to, while not stating, that images 'hail' us, but without a proper account of *how*. If these representations are 'technologies of gender' (de Lauretis 1989) that are performative (Butler 1993) in some way, we still need an account that moves from the text/image and into everyday practice; that is to fully account for how 'socially constructed ideals of beauty are internalised and made our own' (Gill 2003: 104). To repeat: to say that we deeply internalize media images does not grasp *how* this happens. By what mechanisms and practices are we able to take on images in this way and incorporate them into practice? And we can't get at that 'how' if we isolate a subjective moment of 'reading', a disembodied and disembedded encounter between minds and images.

There are in fact several assumptions that need explication here: First, there is the assumption that there are macro or transcendent cultural logics that are evidenced in specific texts or discourses. Second, there is the assumption that what is important about any specific practice is the flow of these already assumed meanings through them, and therefore the extent to which subjectivities are moulded in relation to overarching ideological structures. And third, there is the extremely underdeveloped connection between macro ideological structures and the effects they are presumed to secure through texts or discourses. When you come down to it, imitation (Orbach) or repetition (Butler) do not provide very compelling ways of thinking about the place of modelling in our lives or politics.

Finally, there is another and more practically political problem with equating the 'social effects' of modelling with the impacts of an image or a discourse: it is all too easy to treat these effects as 'externalities', as unintended consequences of market processes that are part of neither the production calculations nor the pricing of economic goods. Seen from the standpoint of producers, model images are not produced *in order to* reproduce gender; there is only the delimited commercial aim of selling clothes or cosmetics. What emerges from the model's labour is an image which then circulates into 'the social', at which point it is taken up in terms of the lifeworld of consumers who are moulded or disciplined by these images, are worked on or work upon themselves. Hence, in this view, there is a radical discontinuity between how modelling is produced and 'what it means', and a deep methodological divide between how we should research its production as opposed to its consumption. All that emerges from the modelling industry are images, which then circulate within an amorphous and entirely separate cultural and psychological space and are therefore to be analysed in terms of an entirely different logic. We then either study modelling images as material, commercial practices *or* as ideological ones, but not both (Slater 2011).

This separation has a long history: for example advertising has always claimed to 'just sell things', and not to have responsibility for 'wider social impacts', unless that responsibility is enforced on the industry by regulation (as in the case of say tobacco advertising or selling alcoholic goods to minors). As Latour (2007) argues in posing the question of the construction of the political, we need to be very careful in formulating just how things become 'matters of concern', in what form they get structured as objects of political action and therefore how our social scientific accounts of things like model bodies can enter into the way that politics is framed. More bluntly: can we restate the relationship between modelling and young women not as an externality (the impact of an image on a mind, the logic of an overarching 'culture') but as internal to the construction of the modelling body itself, as a process that is distributed across a much wider but very densely interconnected social field? The idea of the 'brand' seems to offer just that possibility.

II. Brands as Assemblages

In this section we want to argue that it would be fruitful to think of the model neither as an image (a representation that circulates and has effects) nor a real body (the labouring model). Instead, following a number of currents in contemporary thought about cultural industries—loosely connected to Actor-Network Theory in the main— we propose that we need to think about the model as a different kind of object or thing, as an 'assemblage' composed of heterogeneous elements—images, practices, relations, settings—that is dispersed over time and space. This can sound almost mystical but the intention is utterly practical: the new research on modelling thinks in terms of very concrete and researchable networks and practices of calculation; but can we extend this grounded research outwards to address the wider 'meaning' or 'impact' of modelling, which has, till now, been treated rather *more* mystically, in terms of encounters between subjectivities and representations?

We have glossed this way of thinking in our title by arguing that we should anal- yse 'models as brands'. This is not to say that models are always literally brands (though, in the case of celebrities and supermodels, they may well be). Rather, recent work on brands, particularly Lury and Moor, has asked us to think about the kinds of objects that circulate in commercial cultures, and to make our methodological strate- gies appropriate to the kinds of objects we are actually studying. More specifically, the brand notion elaborated here helps makes sense of 'the look', which has emerged from current research as a central category in understanding modelling. Consider- ing the model as brand addresses to 'the look' the fundamental question, what kind of object is this? And the answer it gives is not 'an image' or 'a representation'. To understand this theoretical and methodological 'move' we need to briefly outline this approach to the brand and how it differs from conventional understandings of brands.

The Brand—What Kind of Object Is It?

What kind of 'object' is a brand? Typically, we might want to start from what it is not. Conventionally, the brand is a sign, a logo, a 'brand name' as a mark of origin and identity. However, identifying brand with sign is inaccurate, even for its origins in the 1880s (or before, in the commercial practices of Wedgewood in the 1780s

(McKendrick 1959/1960; McKendrick et al. 1983)): brand names and logos were only one aspect of a revolutionary innovation of numerous interlinked practical and material devices: a company didn't simply slap a sign/logo on a product; firms first had to divide bulk commodities into individual goods (such as sacks of undifferentiated flour that became small packages of 'Pillsbury' in the late nineteenth century) by packaging them and giving them standardized prices; by creating systems of quality control to ensure homogenous goods; by setting up retail distribution networks including sales forces that could ensure that everyone was selling 'the same thing' across increasingly dispersed geographical markets. Behind the later notions of 'brand identity' and 'brand personality' were diverse techniques for connecting and interrelating circulating goods within an integrated commercial apparatus. Moor, for example, properly emphasizes that design was probably more central than advertising to the evolution of branding—the very ability to attach an identifying mark to a good already required and presupposed major surgery on the body of the good itself (and its packaging), and the credibility of the logo depended on the stability and durability of the designed object itself.

This is obviously a far cry from the way in which many academics and marketers understand a brand. The conventional view is that brands are largely semiotic constructions, signs that derive their meanings within language-like codes, that secure much of their power from their articulation with deeper and more pervasive semiotic structures ('myths', 'ideologies', etc.) and which are themselves part of a general transition from a more material to a more cultural economy (for a critique of this view see Slater 2002b). We can thank Barthes and Baudrillard for this approach, and more recently Holt (2002, 2004, 2006) approaches the brand solely as a structure of meaning that is aligned with broader cultural myths and with the reading strategies of consumers. There is barely a word to be heard about the broad range of relations, the huge assemblage of practices, through which relations between goods and signs are established, stabilized and exploited.

On the other hand, if the brand is not simply a sign, it is also not straightforwardly a thing or object. But, then, *no* object is 'simply' an object in the sense of a thing-in-itself with intrinsic properties or qualities, or in the sense of a brute materiality as opposed to a sign. ANT has been (in)famous for dissolving all objects into the networks that format and sustain them. Lury (see also Slater 2002b) uses the example of a car: the thing we call a car comprises a multitude of heterogeneous elements that include engineered parts, techniques of assemblage, skills, rules and practices of car use, forms of regulation, interlocked systems and infrastructures (e.g. oil supply and distribution chains, road and traffic systems, etc.), linguistic and visual codes. Specifying a car is an—in principle—endless business; I am only able to say unproblematically that 'I am going to buy a car' because this multitude of elements has been (provisionally) stabilized into an identifiable entity. And of course there are numerous actors (designers, marketers, consumers, regulators, roads, oil supplies and so on) that are continuously, and sometimes intentionally, destabilizing this thing called 'a car', or trying to restabilize it in new forms (as part of the very idea of innovation or competition) (Slater 2002a).

The brand is an object in precisely this sense—a dispersed and mutable yet identifiable and calculable thing. It is objective in the sense of having a social facticity (we can recognize and identify a brand and act rationally in relation to 'it' as something out there in the world). Lury actually characterizes the brand as 'an event', in a philosophically technical sense derived from Whitehead: rather than trying to reduce the brand to objective properties, we can keep in view the constantly emergent qualities of the brand; whatever it is emerges at particular moments from the constellation or assemblage of things that make it up—the brand is best thought of as something that happens or occurs, rather than something that 'is'.

Finally and crucially, as a social object, the brand doesn't quite belong to anyone but exists in its own right across social networks. This seems paradoxical: on the one hand, brands are meant to be the asset of firms who claim ownership over this intellectual property and seek to valorize that property in terms of notions like brand equity and brand asset value; on the other hand, the brand is meant to construct identifications or even 'community' across a wide social field, embracing consumers, subcultures and communities. In fact, in a strong sense the brand is really 'out there', an object in the world, acted upon by a wide range of actors (marketers, brand consultants, different types of consumers, different types of media, governmental regulators, lawyers, etc.). The idea that a brand like Nike 'belongs' to Nike in anything more than a legal sense raises issues that cannot be resolved in the abstract but rather require real empirical investigation (what control over its brand does Nike really exercise and to what extent can any firm really steer a broad cultural process like a brand; what does Nike do to the brand in the process of trying—always incompletely—to 'own' it?). That is to say, the brand cannot be reduced to any of the actors who have an interest in it; the brand is in some respect 'out there'—has an objectivity or facticity—for each of them (though all will understand the same brand quite differently); and the extent of any actor's control over 'it' is an empirical matter, not something to be specified theoretically (e.g. as a competition between sociological accounts that privilege consumer agency versus those that assume considerable producer power). Lury interestingly uses the metaphor of the brand as an 'interface': it is a space that is inhabited by heterogeneous agents, through which they transact very disparate kinds of information.

Let us now apply this way of thinking about objects, derived from the brand, to modelling. Our link is the notion of 'the look'. Modelling is a commercial practice that commodifies the model's embodied self and delivers it to clients in the form of a 'look'. The look is more than the sum of the physical parts that make up a body or an image; it is a 'certain something'—an ineffable magical quality that the old-fashioned notion of 'charisma' or 'charm' goes some way to capturing—that is conveyed in the photograph and on the runway. Model bookers select, promote, manage and help to shape the model's look through physical and embodied techniques—advising them to lose weight or cut their hair, for example—as well as managing their 'book' of images, constantly editing it to ensure the 'right' (i.e. most prestigious and best) pictures go in it. In shaping all aspects of the look, bookers thereby shape their career, making calculations as to what 'look' they embody and whether that look is 'editorial' or 'commercial' and how best to market this look which is constantly reconfigured as the model moves through a network of other mediators—designers, stylists, fashion editors and—we need to add—consumers of very diverse sorts.

Much like the idea of a brand, 'the look' can summarize what is actually produced and sold through modelling, and how a great deal of fashion production, selling and consumption is organized. Firstly, the overall look—like the brand—stands above individual goods or images yet provides a kind of container which can include all the images of a model. It is a kind of meta-commodity, a logic that makes sense of past and future jobs, and allows them to be narrated and produced as a career, across time and across contracts. This has prompted work on the forms of calculation and labour by which a look is produced in and through the model's body as it traverses extended social networks.

Hence, the 'look' is not just a product or commodity but also an organizing concept; indeed, in conventional marketing terms it is a 'product concept' (Slater 2002a): that which is sold to clients is a thing with certain defined properties, and to produce that thing requires material and intellectual labour to design, define, shape, present and promote it. The product concept marshals, disciplines, integrates and conceptualizes a considerable range of heterogeneous practices towards the production of a stable and consistently identifiable object. In the case of the model, bookers, stylists and the model himself or herself work on the model's body, movement, attitude, dress, portfolio, social life (Wissinger, this volume), selection of jobs and so forth, to effect an assemblage of qualities. This bundle of qualities is objectified as a 'look' in the model's portfolio or book, which is also yet another tool for constructing that look: the model's look—a kind of commercial narrative of the self (Giddens 1991)—orchestrates a consistency across space (jobs, book, images) and time (career, the shifts of fashion and fashion looks) such that the model can be deemed useful, distinct, a good fit with an identifiable range of commercial requirements. Like the brand, the look is therefore a kind of container that can encompass and interrelate a number of products—the model's look must be identifiable enough to make clear his or her use-value or market niche and to give him or her a 'brand identity' (all these images come from *him* or *her*, from the same person), but flexible enough to attach the same model to a range of uses, to not overspecialize the look to a narrow or too ephemeral market segment—no model or booker would want to be merely this season's model. Moreover, this also means that the model is— complexly—both a brand in his or her own right and something to be submerged or integrated within the brand he or she advertises.

So, like the brand, the look is a heterogeneous assemblage of elements that we can follow outwards from the model through a wide range of relations and practices, and it labels an object that is dispersed through the processes by which it is 'qualified'. This notion of 'qualification' is borrowed from Callon and Cochoy (see for example, Callon et al. 2005), and—in relation to models—is developed by Entwistle (2009) to describe the way qualities are attributed to commodities that are remoulded and reconceptualized, and describes how particular sorts of qualities are attributed to something—the model's look—and are constantly tested by others and, if 'found', requalified. This renders the look an object of calculation and strategic action: like the brand, the look conceptualizes the model in terms of market relations and that conceptualization is the logic through which the model's body and labour are moulded in a coherent direction. Like the brand, the look is clearly the object of calculation for producers (models, bookers, clients, media) and could be treated as somehow 'theirs', their property, their commodity with the implication that the look is what they actually produce rather than—as in the idea of a product *concept*—that which they are aiming at, intending, that which organizes their actions but not necessarily their outcomes. The look clearly exists in many contexts, each of which constitute it: in the inter-relations in a studio between stylists, models, photographers, clients; in magazine and other media as representations that are consumed in countless situations by diverse consumers. In fact, the look—like Lury's brand as event—is a thing suspended across time, space, relations. It cannot unproblematically 'belong' to the moment of production because it also lives in consumer relations, or in high street showrooms, where it becomes an object that, say, bookers have to treat as external and given. In fact, the very word *look* has an ambiguity that makes the point: it refers both to this model's look and to this year's look or this season's look.

However, the central point to make about 'the look', like the brand, is that it is clearly not reducible to either image or materiality (and therefore its distribution across social networks cannot be treated reductively as a matter of either 'intertextuality' or market relations). We mean this in at least two senses: firstly, concretely, the construction and stabilization of looks involves a vast range of practices, including ones that focus on representation, and we cannot usefully separate out specific practices or products that are purely 'representational'—the look is a truly heterogeneous assemblage. Secondly, even in everyday language 'the look' (like the brand) does not normally refer to an image or even to a series of images. When we refer to Nike, we do not only have in mind a swish logo, or a shoe, or the value of 'just doing it'. Rather, in the conception outlined here, what we have 'in mind' are the qualities which are emergent from an exceptionally complex apparatus, extended over time and space, and the shapes and arrangements in which they are (temporarily) stabilized. The look or brand in this sense come close to the idea of 'aesthetic form' (as Riles (2000) defines this term, following Bateson): the sensuous form or shape taken by information.

III. Impacts and Emergence

If we study models as if they were brands, in the sense outlined above, then we will analyse the model's 'look' as a particular kind of social object: a (temporarily) stabilized assemblage of things, signs, practices and so on. How does this view change anything? Above all, how does it help us reformulate the question of the 'social impacts' of modelling, of its cultural or political significance? One answer to this question is rather simple: if the product of modelling—'the look'—cannot be reduced to a representation, then the 'impacts' of modelling cannot be studied in terms of consumer encounters with images. Indeed, it is impossible to find a naturally occurring instance of this event (an occasion that is simply a meeting between a reading mind and a fixed text). Rather what we are asked to look at are the ways in which different kinds of people are incorporated in networks of circulation, and how they are attached to the objects and qualities that emerge in these networks.

Production and Consumption

One problem, as we have already intimated, is the conventional distinction between the production and consumption of modelling: once separated, all that seems to connect them is the image, a complete and finalized object that the consumer encounters in isolation (normally described with the metaphor of 'reading'). As in Hall's (1980) 'encoding/decoding' model, there seem to be entirely different and separated conditions of production and consumption. This analytical model has generally left us with a stark, either/or choice, fought over through several decades of cultural theory, between asserting that what the producer puts into the image is determining, or that consumers have great or total autonomy in producing their own meanings.

By contrast, Wissinger (2007a: and this volume) provides us with a vivid account of how impossible it is to fit modelling into this analytic: in extending the aesthetic labour approach, Wissinger looks at the extent to which the model's look and value is constructed across her own field of leisure, consumption and sociality—in the clubs she attends, the places she schmoozes, the way she appears at every moment of her day. The construction and stabilization of the look extends across places, practices and mediations of these through press, TV, word of mouth, YouTube (consider here the importance of paparazzi); the replication of lifestyles through new wannabee businesses and venues and so on. The models' labour includes all that goes into producing and living a fashionable life, for real, always dressing right, being seen at the right places with the right people (cf. du Gay 1996). The production of an integrated look as the logic of her career extends across the social landscape. Like the celebrity, the model is 'always on', and everything she does (potentially) has implications for her look. By the same token, the model's participation in a wider scene is part of the construction of the scenes themselves, including forms of consumption, style and look:

> By engaging in practices that create a 'scene' that appears glamorous or fashionable and thereby generates publicity, workers in the modeling industry help produce a 'common framework' in which goods have value, where getting into the hot nightclub or

restaurant, or having the 'it' bag or shoes, or reading and blogging about these practices, will be a meaningful experience, creating a sense of belonging, or being part of, a fashionable life. (Wissinger 2009: 287)

If, then, we treat models as if they were brands in the sense of objects that are suspended—unstably—across a messy and undifferentiated terrain, then we simply cannot restrict research to the movement of one kind of object—the image—across the production/consumption divide. The model's 'leisure' and the places she frequents, the way these are designed, how they are used in practice, and how they are mediated through media and word of mouth are all interconnected such that we can think of the model and the club as part of one socio-technical apparatus that sustains 'the look'. The elaboration and extension of the look is carried out through the multiple and heterogeneous connections that link producers and consumers. That these connections will include the representations that models actually get paid for is obvious; that all this flow can be reduced to a circulation of images is far-fetched.

This is even more the case if we add the extent to which marketers increasingly and reflexively exploit precisely this broad sweep of interconnections, treating the life of their goods as 'cultural' in an almost anthropological sense. For example Moor (2007: 46–7) correctly treats the idea of design audit or brand audit as deeply significant (and we could usefully extend this as an academic tool for researching models and their looks): rather than asking about the impact of the images they produce, it is common marketing practice to try to catalogue the total social presence of the brand, to register every context and process in which it plays a part, every practice in which it is mobilized. The idea of a design or brand audit is to document the total heterogeneous assemblage that is the brand, without starting from presumptions about images versus materialities or production versus consumption. Wissinger gives us a snapshot of how to do this for the model as brand which we simply have to extend ever further into the social landscape to see where and how the model's look appears.

In the design audit, brand managers recognize the idea of brands as distributed objects, looking at every social site as potentially contributing to the construction of this object: 'any site where a brand appears is a potentially communicative medium' (46) to the extent that brand managers must attend to 'the entire environment of visual and material culture that should be coordinated in order to render it more coherently communicative' (47). As is now widely recognized in cultural theory, this instrumentalism cannot be regarded as (just) simple exploitation or domination, in that the social field with which brand consultancies engage is a space of complex, heterogeneous and unpredictable processes. The emergence over the past few decades of cool hunters and viral marketing, the employment of commercial ethnographers and semioticians, all testify to a recognition that brands as objects exist in a cultural space with a logic that evades narrowly economic or production-based knowledges. The relationship between production and consumption is construed less as achieved domination than an ever-fallible attempt to ride a shape-shifting tiger as profitably as possible. And in the process, the relationship between production and consumption becomes ever more complex. One example of this is obvious: there are numerous feedback loops, including the increasing *production* of feedback loops by producers themselves. Several authors (Arvidsson 2006, 2005; Lury 2009; Ritzer and Jurgenson 2010; Zwick et al. 2008) place great emphasis on ways in which 'prosumers' are increasingly drawn into production through specific market research mechanisms (focus groups, test marketing, etc.) and through enlisting consumer labour as part of the production process (prosumption). That is to say, the fluid interconnections between production and consumption are increasingly institutionalized and exploited as part of the very construction of brands. In the case of the model, we certainly need to look at the ways in which knowledge of the consumer is (both tacitly and formally) integrated into the production process.

From 'Impacts' to 'Attachments' and 'Qualifications'

If there are multiple and practical connections between producers and consumers that can be traced, then we need to be looking at many kinds of 'impacts and influences', moving in many directions, and not decidable in the abstract: we are faced with inescapably empirical and contingent questions that demand a more ethnographic response. The question of the social impact of modelling might be rephrased as, how are consumers of modelling (e.g. young women) involved in the complex assemblages that we gloss as 'brands' or 'looks'? And the answer is obviously not going to be simple or singular. If we only think about the impact of modelling in terms of circulating representations, then we have very limited and specific ways of thinking about the work these representations do when they enter into the social world (above all, the metaphors of reading and of textuality), and this generally resolves into a story about the ways in which subjectivities are constituted in and through ideological systems of meaning or wider cultural structures.

This reduction of the wide and heterogeneous apparatus that constructs brands across broad social fronts to an encounter of subjectivities with texts seems pretty implausible. We could simply refer again to Moor's brand or design audit: consider all the *kinds* of situations in which we encounter a 'look' in everyday life, and all the *kinds* or modalities of practice through which we might deal with it: where, when, how, through what mechanisms and in connection to what other entities are brands or looks *present* to us and what practices arise? The stereotypical young woman as potential victim of size zero imagery is not simply engaging with specific represented bodies in reiterated texts; she is engaging with body values through everyday dress practices; social networks and peer relationships and competition; regulatory structures (e.g. school or workplace dress codes, formal and informal); leisure spaces, practices and regulations; complementary commodities and aesthetic forms (e.g. the relationship between music cultures and fashion); domestic and familial dynamics;

retail structures; aesthetic genres such as modelling competitions and reality TV formats; and on and on and on. The list is *in principle* incomplete: it cannot be specified in the abstract but only in empirical cases. What is important is not providing an alternative theorization but rather a different methodology: thinking about models through the notion of the brand as assemblage suggests other ways of analysing encounters with looks and with valorized bodies.

Above all, the analysis outlined here points us away from asking about the impact of an object and points towards the ways in which people are involved in the assemblages that actually make up the objectivity of social objects. One way in which this has been pursued is through the notion of 'attachment', which has generally served as a way to think in very practical terms about the ways in which people and objects become embroiled with each other. Put more directly: what are the precise mechanisms through which young women might attach themselves to a look that valorizes skinny, white bodies? This question is itself to be understood as part of a wider question about the process of 'qualification': ANT-influenced theorists have asked, how do things (and people) get their properties, or qualities? Qualities are neither inherent in things nor socially constructed (ascribed by subjects): the whole focus on networks and assemblages has been an effort to avoid this choice—subjects and objects only have properties at all by virtue of the relations and connections through which they can act.

A model's look is clearly not a set of qualities intrinsic to her, nor is it a set of qualities arbitrarily projected onto her as a sign; rather, we can and should catalogue the determinate processes unfolding over time through which the look comes to be understood and performed (temporarily) in a particular way. As Harvey et al. (2004) argue, qualities are understood as the outcome of a collective process rather than individual valuations or intrinsic properties. Drawing on Cochoy, Callon et al. (2005) describe the complexity of the customer interactions with products that take place in the context of 'a socio-cognitive arrangement that situates the different products in relation to one another' (36), for example on the supermarket shelf where products are arranged in relation to one another. Here a legion of different mediators seek to qualify the product, to identify and test its properties. This testing and qualification does not end at the point of purchase; indeed, whether a customer chooses one or another orange juice on a supermarket shelf comes down to complex arrangements within the domestic and private arena of the home/family where customers continue to evaluate and test products. For Lury, 'the brand comprises a sequence or series of loops that *entangle* the customer' (Lury 2004: 7), and these processes are ultimately fed back to producers who attempt to keep customers. As we have already noted, there is clear evidence that firms are increasingly integrating consumer testing and qualifying into corporate calculation, constructing ever more rationalized feedback mechanisms to attach goods and consumers through specific qualities. The brand itself can be seen as a way of organizing this process, providing a kind of container within which these myriad qualifications might be rendered manageable and organized over time. Through looping, consumers are brought into 'the performativity of the brand' through such things as customer profiling techniques and, in turn, this enables 'the introduction of qualitative possibilities into the abstract objectivity of the brand' so that 'more qualities or attributes' are assigned to the brand. There is, Lury notes, no instantaneous relay between brands and customers; temporal delays are managed by brands so that they remain reliable and consistent, while also managing shifts in customer tastes and preferences over time. The brand, is, therefore, a device for managing and coordinating the market.

There are at least two major implications of the idea of attachment: Firstly, it directs us to the precise mechanisms through which different actors come to perceive different qualities in goods and, in doing so, we should understand their desires or revulsions for things through the same mechanisms: we are attached or detached to this or that brand/image/model through socio-cognitive processes that, in part are determined by technical apparatuses—packaging, imagery, advertising, and a host of other newer media, like Twitter—and are situated within complex and diverse practices on the part of actors. Secondly, attachment is an intrinsically active process (which is not to value it as good or bad)—to be attached to something is to be connected with it in material as well as affective senses (again these cannot be separated out). That is to say, the notion of attachment that has come from ANT directs us away from the investigation of desires and affects, and from presumptions about the power of meaning or the deep structures of subjectivity, and suggests we start instead from the very mundane techniques and practices through which people might be attached to things. An early formulation of this line of thought is very applicable here: Gomart and Hennion (1999) look at the production of two kinds of passion—for recreational drugs and for music—as events that emerge from specific arrangements. Rather than reducing these emotionally charged attachments to the actions of either objects or humans, Gomart and Hennion ask 'what occurs?', that is what languages, procedures and devices ('dispositifs') have been effected which result in attachments? Different kinds of experiences, different modes of action and being, different senses of agency are imagined and enacted, are institutionalized and then emerge from specific social arrangements (see also DeNora 2002).

Thus, to understand how models might be said to 'influence' or 'affect' someone, such as a teenage girl, we do not need recourse to deep psychological investments and psychic processes, nor descriptions of metaphysical-like 'power' operating in mysterious ways on her body/mind. In place of effects or power which are epistemologically impossible to verify we are required to provide detailed descriptions of attachments; we are directed to follow the many diverse ways in which particular models and looks are incorporated into her daily life. Through these various devices and practices we can trace the connections and entanglements; the many investments in, and forms of attachment to, particular models and imagery.

Emergence, Performativity and Macro-Structures

The practices around modelling (including consumers' engagement with it) are sites of real labour, and with indeterminate outcomes: we cannot know what the 'social

impacts' of modelling are without actual empirical investigation because their qualities arise from a contingent distribution of heterogeneous elements. That is to say,
there is a clear assumption of 'emergence' in this kind of analysis. As Lury (2004:
51) acknowledges in her analysis of the various actors and agents in the brand process (marketers, designers, consumers): 'While all these accounts are a necessary
part of describing the brand, they are not sufficient even when added together. They
privilege purposive actions, and do not acknowledge the significance of the self-
organizing elements of the brand as a complex, indeterminate and open object.'

By the same token, simply interpreting texts for their ideological structure or
treating them as examples of 'capitalism' or 'patriarchy' will not tell us how modelling enters into the actual moulding of specifically gendered people or the valorization of particular aesthetics and bodies. Model 'looks', and consumer engagements
with them, are not merely instances or examples of deeper macro-logics; they are
real mediations with emergent properties.

On the other hand, macro notions such as 'ideology' or 'culture' or 'gender' need
to play a different role in accounts of models as brands: the actors involved themselves generally use macro notions like brands, looks, gender, consumption and so
on. The idea of models as brands points us to the performative character of such
macro claims: rather than treat them as true or false, we need to consider what effects such claims have. A simple example: bookers are constantly trying to identify 'the next look'. That is to say, they claim to discover a property out there in
the world, rather than to construct it by their own actions (see for example Mears
2011). The look is evoked by actors as an objective macro structure: the significant
issue is not the realist one (whether the claim is true nor false) but rather that such
claims are constitutive of the very situation being researched: models, bookers and
clients could not rationally pursue their projects without organizing concepts such
as fashion, looks and indeed 'culture' that provide an anchor and objectivity to a
multitude of mundane practices and technologies. The idea of the model as brand
foregrounds this performativity: cultural structures are not explanatory concepts but
rather claims made by actors that can be empirically investigated for the roles they
play in reproducing fashion looks. As a result we can look at the competing and col-
lusive characterisations of culture and significance that are invoked by social actors,
and see their role in constructing the model as brand and its circulation within wider
networks and mediations.

Conclusion

The intention of this chapter—despite its somewhat theoretical approach—has been
to consider a return to basics. Many researchers into modelling, creative industries
and cultural processes in general have followed a very long arc over many years.
In highly schematic form, we began with a critical-political impulse, very largely

inspired by second wave feminism, to treat images *seriously* both as sites of struggle and oppression and as symptomatic of wider structures of value and power. From the 1960s to the 1990s, this focus on representation enabled scholars and activists to confront and make visible central questions of gender, race, subjectivity, the reproduction of power relations and so on. This analytical path pushed the fixation of the critical gaze on representation to its extremes, notably in developments such as postmodernism, poststructuralism and the various cultural turns. Frustrated by the limits of this focus, some researchers in the past couple of decades have shown new attention to materiality and to social practices. For the present authors at least, this counter-tradition is identified with new economic sociologies such as Callon's (Callon et al. 2005), with material culture studies (Miller 1997, 2005) and with theories of practice (Warde 2005). While these have all been inspirational in focusing attention on the specific and unique mechanisms through which values are produced, circulated and exchanged—and without making a priori distinctions between things and signs—they have all raised doubts as to whether they could address the critical and political questions from which we started.

The present chapter has taken up just a few aspects of this return to basics: the kinds of approaches that have helped in producing cogent empirical accounts of fashion modelling as industry and career can also, we have argued, be extended to address the consumption of modelling. Indeed, by regarding the object produced through modelling—'the look'—as if it were a brand—a complex and unfolding event strung across disparate agents, relationships and situations—we are able to reconnect production and consumption through networks that include diverse practices, objects and images; we are able to consider the practices that construct the qualities of objects and people's attachments to these qualities (rather than trying to identify the impacts of images); and we are able to engage with the performative role of notions like culture, gender and representation in the practices of making and consuming models' looks. The consequence of this conceptualization, we hope, is to expand the reach of both research and politics beyond the model as image to the entire social field of the model as look and as brand.

Part I

–3–

From Artist's Model to the 'Natural Girl': Containing Sexuality in Early-Twentieth-Century Modelling

Elspeth H. Brown

Introduction

This chapter will sketch out some of the meanings of the term *model* in the first decades of the twentieth century, with a focus on the development of the modelling profession in the United States in the years surrounding the First World War. Most contemporary observers understand the model, a person who is paid to appear with a commodity as part of the sales effort, to be a fashion model. While this is certainly often the case, this chapter will distinguish four different (although often overlapping) types of modelling in the early-twentieth-century USA: the artist's model; the cloak (wholesale) model; the couturier model/showgirl; and the photographic model. Modelling is a form of labour where the models and other cultural brokers transform subjective aspects of modern selfhood—gesture, appearance, presence—into immaterial commodities, adding surplus value to manufactured goods that are then purchased by wholesale buyers or retail consumers. As a historian, my inclination is to situate these questions in the period in which the profession first emerged—in the first decades of the twentieth century. The modelling profession emerged around the time that merchandisers and psychologists began to sell not the product itself, but the benefit that the product offered: elegance, romance, sexual appeal. As one commercial photographer bluntly noted of the model's labour in 1930: 'she sells the stuff by making it desirable' (Kennedy 1930: 61).

Models sell commodities by using their bodies to produce commercialized affect in relationship to specific goods: glamour, elegance, cool. The vehicle through which these elusive promises are made is the model's performance of a new form of sexuality, one specific to the emerging mass culture industries of the early twentieth century. The four types of modelling discussed in this chapter all played a central role in producing a commercialized zone of public discourse that linked gender, class and racial meanings to commodity forms, and where sexuality became inextricably linked to the marketing and sale of goods. These forms of modelling, though distinct from one other in their cultural meanings, often overlapped in practice as specific models crossed from one type of modelling to another in the everyday effort to make ends meet: cloak models might migrate to couture; fashion models doubled as photographic models for not only clothing, but also consumer goods. The public understanding of the four versions of modelling sketched out here, from artist's model to photographic model, however, suggests a larger story about the efforts of cultural brokers to both draw upon, yet contain, the implicitly explosive sexuality of women on public display.

As cultural brokers, such as department store managers, couturiers or modelling agents, developed the field of modelling in the early twentieth century, they distanced the work of the model from the problematic sexualities suggested by nineteenth-century public women, particularly prostitutes. Building upon the sanitized, Anglo-Saxon glamour of the World War I-era Ziegfeld showgirl, whose history is densely interwoven with both couturier modelling and the charity fashion show, John Robert Powers developed a new vocabulary of female attractiveness based upon what he called 'naturalness' (to distinguish himself from Ziegfeld's 'glamour') that also channelled and contained the model's sexual appeal in a manner familiar to twentieth-century culture industries organized around the commodified display of the female body. The merchandizing of feminine sexual appeal was also a racial project as well, as definitions of female beauty articulated on the stage and the catwalk reflected and constructed a definition of 'American' beauty that was both white and Anglo-Saxon. The containment of the white female model's sexuality in John Robert Powers's interwar agency implicitly established black women models as the sexualized, racialized 'other' through which white female models' otherwise explosive sexual appeal was sanitized and cleaned up for new consumer audiences. This sanitized version of (white) female sexuality, so central to modern consumer culture, has a history densely interwoven with the modelling industry: pleasurable to view, yet curiously nonerotic, this manufactured an appeal that calls out to the viewer, yet remains nonetheless inaccessible.

In his work on the Victorian barmaid, the historian Peter Bailey very usefully suggests a name for the oddly passionless version of modern glamour: *parasexuality*. The term combines two otherwise discrete meanings, both of which rely on distance. First, there is the prefix meaning of 'almost', or 'beside'—as in paralegal, or paramedic. Also, however, one finds the definition of *para* as prevention against, as a prophylactic—as in parachute. The term suggests 'sexuality that is deployed but contained, carefully channeled rather than fully discharged'; as Bailey (2002) argues, it's the sexuality of 'everything but'. In historical terms, this is the sexuality of the pin-up, the beefcake, the chorus girl—and the model, I would argue. Like these modern types, the model inhabits a zone of enhanced public visibility; she (and eventually he) is available to the scrutinizing gaze, while eluding its implied dénouement. The implied sexuality of the model, the film star or the pin-up is contained, as Bailey has discussed in relationship to the barmaid, through distance. Material or representational obstacles between the bearer of parasexuality and the audience, such as the catwalk or the magazine page, work to protect the magical property that bears a close relationship to glamour; at the same time, the distance heightens the desire for the elusive object—close yet so far. The complex dance between corporeal display, public visibility and the *cordon sanitaire* of the runway, the stage or the printed page constitutes a type of managed sexuality that has proved central to the accelerated circulation of commodities in advanced capitalist societies.

This production of managed sexuality has been the model's chief contribution to the mass merchandizing of goods since the first third of the twentieth century. All of the female models discussed in this chapter—artist's models, cloak models, couture models and photographic models—produced and performed varying versions of corporeal display that were, however, historically overdetermined by dominant understandings concerning the meaning of unattached women displaying their bodies, in public, in commercialized settings. At the beginning stages of this process of rendering female corporeal display safe for the commodification of goods within a landscape of an emerging mass consumer culture in the early twentieth century, the model was indisputably seen as a sexually problematic figure, kinswoman to the prostitute, the actress and the bohemian (implicitly French) artist's model. At the later stages of this shift from public woman to girl next door, however, by the Second World War era, the model had been recast as a glamorous, yet nonthreatening, icon of modern beauty: her sexuality had been tamed, channelled and packaged as a key ingredient of commercial marketing.

The Artist's Model

Up until the first decade of the twentieth century, merchants or dressmakers displayed clothing either on inanimate store fixtures, often made of wax, which the French called *mannequins*. The Americans used the term *manikin* as well (spelled in a myriad of ways), but throughout the nineteenth century the term referred to a model of human anatomy, such as those used in nineteenth-century natural history demonstrations. Up until the First World War, with the exception of the artist's model, the term *model*, in both English and French, referred not to the human being, but to the commodity—the dress, coat or corset being sold. As in the early-twentieth-century term *typewriter*, which once referred to the woman who operated the machine, the new term slips between a description of the object and the person, as new aspects of human behavior and subjectivity become organized through the market. By around 1908 or so, the terms formerly used to describe the object—the model—migrated to the person, and trade accounts of department store merchandising, and the general press, began referencing 'living models', which had become simply 'models' by the late second decade of the twentieth century.

Before the 1920s, the term *model*—when referencing a woman—connoted a number of related social types, all of which implied a form of sexuality at odds with Victorian mores. The figure most closely identified with the term in the period before the First World War was the artist's model. Although I won't discuss this figure at length in this chapter, let me summarize that the term *artist's model* connoted a woman (rarely if ever a man) who was part of the demi-monde—a woman of perhaps bohemian leanings who would be willing to undress for money, and perhaps do more. Models were working-class women who began assuming the modelling stand in artists' Parisian ateliers in the 1860s; while artists and models did not necessarily do the nude posing to suggest immodesty nor an erotic prelude, popular discourse constructed the artist's model as an immodest working-class woman whose chastity was easily compromised (Waller 2006; Dawkins 2002). A sympathetic portrait of this type was immortalized in George Du Maurier's *Trilby* (1894), where the beautiful artist's model Trilby O'Farrell falls under the sinister spell of the musician Svengali. Another popular example was Pierette, the poor model for Pierrot, the 'hungry, discouraged artist' who is the hero of the much-performed pantomime *Le Reveillon de Pierrette*, which later served as a model for the plot for Lady Duff Gordon's 1917 fashion show/theatre piece *Fleurette's Dream in Peronne*.

As these brief examples suggest, the stock character of the 'artist's model' was seen as primarily a French import, where the 'artist's model' had become a figure in the public imagination with the rise of mass media and panorama literature during the 1830s and 1840s (Waller 2006: xiv; Dawkins 2002). In the US context, some representations of the artist's model allowed popular cultural representations of the lightly clad female form to avoid obscenity charges, as the popularity of early films concerning a variety of models such as *The Substitute Model* (Hobart Bosworth, 1912), *The Model's Redemption* (1913) and *The Model's Adventure* (1915) suggest. As bohemian tastes migrated to the middle classes, the romanticized version of the artist's model fueled the 'living pictures' of the nineteenth century through Ben Ali Haggin's extraordinary popular patriotic spectacles for Ziegfeld Follies in the late second decade of the twentieth century. The middle-brow appreciation for the artist's model continued through the late 1920s, resulting in (for example) a series of images and text depicting 'artists and their models' in the US women's magazine *Redbook*.

The Wholesale (or Cloak) Models

Closely related to the artist's model in the public's understanding of her venality, the 'cloak model' demonstrated ready-to-wear clothing for wholesale buyers, and would then sometimes entertain the buyers after hours. Although the cloak model, or wholesale model, continued as a profession after the First World War, it was the introduction of the cloak model to American audiences (often through literary and stage representation through, for example, a short story by O. Henry or Montague

Glass stage play) that paved the way for retail mannequins in the postwar years (Lowry 1920: 46). Out-of-town, male (often married) wholesale buyers would visit wholesale ready-to-wear manufacturers where the chief of the manufacturer's show-room would demonstrate the firm's clothing 'models' on the living model, one of several young women kept on staff to parade the clothing for the buyer's review. For example, in New York City in 1916, a wholesale maker of suits for larger women kept on staff sixteen models. In a typical day, the models appeared at the wholesale showroom at 8:30 a.m. to put on the clothing models available for sale; at 9:00 a.m., when the buyers arrived, the firm's models would 'parade' the clothing in a mass market adaptation of the couturier's fashion show, developed some years earlier in Europe, and introduced to the United States in 1908, as I discuss below. In between parades before prospective buyers, throughout the day the models would also help out the firm's sales efforts by folding advertising circulars or hanging completed clothing ('Selling "Stouts" in the Showroom' 1916: E8).

In the wholesale trade, the audience for the manikin parade was primarily the male buyers for a retail venue, such as a department store. Modelling became a key site for the elaboration of commercialized forms of heterosexual exchange that emerged with the rise of mass culture and urban forms of leisure in the early-twentieth-century United States. Although few sources discuss the informal sexual expectations concerning such commercial exchanges directly, there is some indica-tion that models were either expected, or chose, to socialize with the buyers outside the showroom. As one model wrote, despite arguing that it was a myth that models entertained buyers as part of their work, 'I'm not saying that I've never gone to din-ner or the theater with an out-of-town buyer, and I'm not even saying that, having gone with one of them, he hasn't tried to kiss me good night' ('An Almost Perfect Thirty-Four' 1923: 22). Some models anticipated these visits by the out-of-town buyers as a perfect opportunity for an all-expenses paid night on the town, as well as a chance to pick up a few 'gifts' of cosmetics or other consumer items. In an article ('An Almost Perfect Thirty-Four' 1923: 22) detailing her work as a retail and whole-sale dress model, 'Nellie' described two of her colleagues that, in her view, fit the 'conventional idea of models'. These women, though pretty in a conventional way, overdid their rouge and powder—both of which were just becoming acceptable for young women, but which retained their theatrical (and sexually available) connota-tions (for the history of cosmetics during this period, see Peiss 1998). 'Their sole ob-ject in life was to have a good time, and their pride was to graft as much as possible from the various young men of their acquaintance. They would spend hours boasting of how they had lured last night's swain into a drug store and held him up for a bottle of expensive perfume and a whole array of cosmetics.' 'Yet', Nellie continued, 'they were good girls who would have slapped the face of any youth who misinterpreted their motives' ('An Almost Perfect Thirty-Four' 1923: 150). The author of this *Satur-day Evening Post* article used the pseudonym of 'Nellie' to signify the 'about town' model, fictionalized in the 1906 popular Broadway production *Nellie, the Beautiful*

Cloak Model; from 1906 through the mid 1920s, the phrase 'Nellie the cloak model' was shorthand for working-class femininity on the make. As one observer noted (Kennedy 1930: 61) in 1930, the cloak model of this era was fundamentally also a sexual hostess for out-of-town buyers: 'it was generally conceded that their daytime work was supplanted by labour after office hours', to such an extent that 'outdoor evangelists included "cloak models" in their litany of brazen sinners'.

These models were fundamentally 'charity girls', working-class women participating in the commercialization of sexuality known as 'treating' in the years surrounding the First World War. As historians Kathy Peiss and Elizabeth Alice Clement have argued, working-class men and women developed the courtship practice as part of the growth of commercialized forms of leisure in early-twentieth-century cities (Peiss 1987, 1986: 110–13; Clement 2006: 45–75, 212–39). Working-class women who worked outside the home often, unlike the men in their family, turned over their entire pay packet to their mothers, as a contribution to the family economy. This dutiful practice, however, left them without the funds to participate in the emerging mass consumer culture, identified in 'Nellie's' anecdote as cosmetics, but also including movies, dance halls and other forms of commercial entertainment. Working-class women would often exchange sexual favours for a night on the town or the purchase of 'gifts'; as there was no exchange of money, no one (except vice reformers) saw the practice as related to prostitution. By the 1920s, this commodified set of expectations (the man pays; the woman 'puts out') became normalized, migrating to the middle-class practice still known as 'dating' (Peiss 1987, 1986: 110–13; Clement 2006: 45–75, 212–39). Because of this history, wholesale modelling retained an element of scandal for families shaped by middle-class, Victorian morals; as the fictional Nellie explained to her readers, when she told her parents she planned to become a dress model, 'a riot followed'. Nellie herself failed to see the pitfalls; from her perspective, seeking a living as a single girl in New York, she recognized the profession as 'the only occupation for unskilled workers that pays a decent wage' ('An Almost Perfect Thirty-Four' 1923: 150). Whereas reformers and anxious parents might see modelling as a 'hotbed of vice', to quote Nellie, or models as exemplars of a problematic 'woman adrift' in the urban landscape, by the early 1920s modelling represented the epitome of independence, femininity and glamour that a generation of new women identified with a postfeminist, postsuffrage female modernity and consumption (Meyerowitz 1991; Peiss 1998; Studlar 1996).

In the United States, the development of clothing modelling corresponded with the maturation of the department store and the women's ready-to-wear clothing industry. As a result, what had been primarily an intimate and exclusive practice of modelling unique gowns for high-end clients in closed showrooms migrated to free, public displays of ready-to-wear designs for a middle-class audience, who viewed models displaying the new fashions in the department store, charity fashion parade or Broadway show. Both sites for modelling clothing—the department store and the high-end couturier shop—bore a close relationship to the New York stage in terms of set design, costuming, choreography and performers (models). In the department stores, as Marlis Schweitzer (2009) and William Leach (1994) have shown, the growing importance of fashion pushed department store owners to theatrical strategies in merchandising goods. By the early twentieth century, the development of ready-to-wear clothing had catapulted the clothing trade to the third-largest industry in the USA, behind only steel and oil. The entire industry was largely derivative of French fashions before the First World War: US wholesalers and retailers sent buyers and other representatives to Paris, who copied the Parisian upper-class trade for the American mass market.

More than any other single development, it was the fashion show that introduced the model to American audiences. By the first decade of the twentieth century, US department stores were relying on the living model to sell clothing to not only wholesale buyers, but also to retail customers. The term *fashion show* migrated from the trade term used to describe the still-life display of goods and (nonhuman) manikins in the department store show window; after 1910, *fashion show* described the animated parade of living models who demonstrated clothing designs within the store itself ('The Easter Show' 1906: 101). Department store merchant Rodman Wanamaker prepared elaborate fashion shows for Wanamaker's Philadelphia store as early as the fall of 1908, when the 'fashion Fete de Paris' featured enormous picture frames trimmed in black velvet, with live models posed in the latest Paris gowns inside. Emerging from their frames, the models paraded down a walkway to the middle-class, retail audience, accompanied by soft organ music and the scripted commentary of the show's director, Mary Wall (Leach 1994: 102; Evans 2002: 283). Other stores soon followed suit: the trade publication *Dry Goods* declared 'the introduction of living models in the fall fashion show of Joseph Horne & Co., Pittsburg' a success in November 1910, and the first time a fashion show has been staged in that city (*Dry Goods* 1910: 33). Department stores hired young women to parade down ramps in department store theatres, often organized around themes such the 'Monte Carlo' or the Orientalist 'Garden of Allah'; in 1911, thousands were still coming to see the living models parade Paris gowns, millinery and wraps through an 'Italian Garden and Pathway through the Pergolas' installed within Gimbel's, one of New York's leading department stores. This show was so successful that it went through twenty variations in five years, with thousands of women pouring into the store daily to see the models parading up and down the theatre ramp in the newest styles ('The Gimbel Millinery Showing Is the Finest in the City', *New York Times*, 30 March 1911: 7; Leach 1993: 102; Schweitzer 2009). The success of these fashion shows led the National Retail Dry Goods Association to put together a list of suggestions for organizing similar events in 1913 ('Fashion Show as Trade Promoters' 1913: XX10; '12,000 at Trade Fair on the Opening Day' 1922: 25). During the war, the fashion show emerged as a favourite charity fundraising mechanism, further popularizing the spectacle for middle- and upper-class audiences (Evans 2002; Schweitzer 2009). By the early 1920s, the fashion show had become a standard feature of both wholesale manufacturers' events and department store retail selling methods.

Fashion spectacles such as those at Wanamaker's helped to render the work of the cloak model visible to young women, who besieged wholesale houses for modelling positions by the early 1920s. Celia Mohoney, who hired models for the clothing wholesalers clustered in New York's Seventh Avenue, told a reporter that she was besieged by applications in 1924, and suspected that the girls who wanted to be cloak models were outnumbered only by those who wanted to be movie stars. 'They picture themselves as strutting through gorgeous showrooms, bored but beautiful, overcoming buyers from Sedalia, Missouri and Ottumwa, Iowa, with awe and admiration. They want to be close to costly and alluring for a few hours a day, even though the evening finds them wearing again their own commonplace dresses' ('Yearn to Be Suit Models' 1924: XX2). A contemporary couture mannequin, however, expressed a more cynical view of the wholesale cloak model, and her position at the bottom of an emerging professional hierarchy. As Augusta, a blonde mannequin draped across a couture showroom's elevated chaise lounge, told a *New York Times* reporter in 1920, 'the best thing that can happen to that kind of model [i.e. the wholesale model] is to marry her buyer from Kansas City, where she can get fat at her leisure and wear ready-mades for life' (Lowry 1920).

The Couturier Model/Showgirl

A third type of model, in addition to the artist's model and the cloak model, was the high-end couturier model. These women, known during this period in both Europe and the United States as mannequins or manikins, demonstrated clothing for the society women who eschewed the emerging ready-to-wear industry in women's clothing and could afford to have their gowns custom-made. The couturier parade of mannequins, or fashion show, originated in the European couturier house and migrated to the United States in 1908. As Caroline Evans (2002: 273) and Nancy Troy (2003: 18–42) have argued, European designers began having young women walk around the premises wearing the house's designs as early as the 1840s; in 1858, the designer Charles Frederick Worth and his wife, chief mannequin Marie Vernet, imported the mannequin parade to their own *maison de couture*. In Paris, the annual opening of the horse races at Longchamp was marked by the 'grand parade of mannequins' where Paris dressmakers introduced the latest designs (in April); at some points, Parisian couturiers boycotted the annual showing, in order to prevent competitors from stealing their designs ('Paris Dressmakers Withhold Models' 1912: 3). French dressmakers also engaged mannequins to parade the gowns in the intimate drawing rooms of the couturier 'house', while American department stores, such as Adam, Meldrum, and Anderson, in Buffalo, New York, built elaborate 'French Display Rooms' as sites for the living display of Parisian fashions.

In January 1910, couturier modelling (as distinct from department store modelling) was introduced to American consumers when the Canadian-born, British clothing designer Lady Duff Gordon opened her first US 'house' on 36th Street in Manhattan under her British trade name, Lucile, Ltd ('Lady Duff Gordon' 1935: 17). Duff Gordon, often surrounded by a bevy of Pekinese and chows and draped in flowing chiffon veils, was a diva-esque icon of what we might now call the queer transatlantic fashion, theatre and design worlds (Mendes and de la Haye 2009; Greer 1952; Kaplan and Stowell 1995; Duff Gordon 1932; Etherington-Smith and Pilcher 1986; Schweitzer 2009). Duff Gordon brought her six living 'mannequins' to display her work in New York, and claimed in her autobiography to be the first couturier to introduce the mannequin parade to fashion merchandising (this was not true for Europe, but probably true for the United States) (Figure 3.1). Duff Gordon disguised the mannequins' working-class origins through a detailed training regimen, as well as by replacing their given names with exotic-sounding ones, such as Gamela or Dinarzade. The practice of one-name renaming echoes both that of the artist's model and the prostitute, whom fashion historian Caroline Evans (2001: 272) reminds us took a new, single name when entering a regulated brothel. The mannequin's job was to match the personality of the costume she was modelling, and to render it possible for the potential viewer to imagine herself in the same gown.

The First World War dramatically interrupted the couture pilgrimages made by elite American women to Paris each season, and so Parisian designers brought a

Figure 3.1 Duff Gordon brought her six living 'mannequins' to display her work in New York (this was not true for Europe, but probably true for the United States).
Source: Lady Lucile Duff Gordon (1932), *Discretions and Indiscretions*, p. 239. New York: Frederick A. Stokes.

show of clothing designed for the American market to New York for the first time in 1915. In this presentation, unique in that all the designers presented their work together, prefiguring the later 'Fashion Week', all the elements of the modern fashion show were in place: imported mannequins brought the 'inimitable walk that the Rue de la Paix made famous', in the words of a *New York Times* reporter; the gowns were presented with the aid of accompanying play; the designers bypassed representatives by presenting directly to buyers; and mannequins presented each costume on a raised platform extending through the rooms at the level of the chairs—the catwalk ('The Paris Fashion Show' 1915: X2).

Duff Gordon symbolizes the complex relationship between commerce, fashion, modelling and the theatre in the First World War era. While still in London, Duff Gordon staged elaborate fashion spectacles, installing a theatre in her Hanover Square showroom, complete with an illuminated stage and parading mannequins modelling suggestively named costumes, such as 'A Frenzied Hour' and 'Persuasive Delight'. The confusion over the term *model* continued through the second decade of the twentieth century, as dressmakers began naming their dresses after women's names, and the mannequins took new names that were hard to differentiate from those of the frocks themselves. Duff Gordon commissioned her sister, the novelist Elinor Glyn, to write texts for fashion events that were a combination of *tableaux vivant*, the stage play and the fashion show. In 1915, Duff Gordon took her talents, and her mannequins, to the Broadway stage when she was hired as the costume designer for Florence Ziegfeld; she designed costumes for the Ziegfeld Follies and other productions from 1915 through 1921.

Duff Gordon's couture mannequins became the first celebrity models when they were hired by Ziegfeld to perform on stage. Unlike chorus girls, the couture stage models did not sing or dance; their main role was to parade before the footlights wearing the latest gowns, whose designers were identified in the playbill. These stage models inaugurated the now-familiar combination of statuesque beauty, corporeal display, elaborate costume and sanitized sexuality known as the 'showgirl'. Lucile models who doubled as Ziegfeld showgirls during the late second decade of the twentieth century and early 1920s included the most famous of them all, Dolores; Dinarzade (Lillian Farley, also a favourite model for Edward Steichen); Mauresette (also spelled *Mauricette*), and Phyllis. 'Dolores' was a British-born dressmaker's model who moved from Lucile's New York couturier salon to the Broadway stage in June 1917, when she began performing in both the Ziegfeld Follies and the after-hours show the *Midnight Frolic*.[1] Born Kathleen Mary Rose, she was a tall (nearly 6-foot) working-class woman with a Cockney accent whom Duff Gordon renamed 'Dolores', while teaching her the confidence, poise and walking techniques central to Duff Gordon's mannequin parades (Figure 3.2). As the 'Empress of Fashion', for example wearing a Lucile gown entitled 'The Discourager of Hesitancy', she appeared with eleven other model-showgirls in a June 1917 Follies scene entitled 'The Episode of Chiffon'. Her job was to provide pure spectacle, to stop the show's

Figure 3.2 Dolores: born Kathleen Mary Rose (see Figure 3.1).
Source: Lady Lucile Duff Gordon (1932), *Discretions and Indiscretions*, p. 245. New York: Frederick A. Stokes.

forward narrative with a display of sartorial elegance and 'pulchritude'. The development of fashion on the Ziegfeld stage helped legitimize the productions as more than simply 'girlie shows' for the 'tired old businessmen'. By introducing fashion numbers as well as the kitsch of Ben Ali Haggin's *tableaux vivants*, Ziegfeld attracted a middle-class female audience whose presence legitimized the viewing of scantily clad female bodies as an instructive, rather than prurient, pastime.

Dolores's appearance on the Follies stage as a showgirl was also, at the same time, an appearance as a well-known model. Her work demonstrating couturier-designed gowns in Lucile's Fifth Avenue salon provided celebrity appeal for middle-class theatre audiences, who learned about Lucile's work, and her famous mannequins, through their stage performances. Dolores's success as the 'goddess of clothes' on both Fifth Avenue and Broadway made her a favourite choice to model high-end fashion apparel in contemporary magazines, such as *Vogue*, *Harper's Bazaar* and *Town and Country*. For example Condé Nast's staff fashion photographer at *Vogue*, Baron Adolph de Meyer, photographed her numerous times during this period (Brown 2009). In these fashion spreads, Dolores is identified prominently as the model, and her relationship with the Follies and Frolics emphasized along with her other public identity as a former Lucile mannequin. According to *Vanity Fair* in 1918, no other woman had been 'more widely posed or photographed than she' (1918: 48).

With the work of stage designer Joseph Urban and of choreographer Ned Wayburn, who like Lucile were hired by Ziegfeld in 1915, key aspects of the couture and department store mannequin parade became standard to Ziegfeld productions. The catwalk, for example appeared in 1915 when Joseph Urban introduced a transparent glass runway to the Midnight Frolics, the after-hours cabaret that unfolded on the roof of Ziegfeld's New Amsterdam Theater. The runway (or, catwalk) extended over the first two rows of tables and was illuminated with colored lights and air jets, allowing audience members to peer up at the performers through the glass runway. The chorus, attired in rather flimsy skirts, slowly filed along the glass catwalk, with the blowers 'lifting the skirts to dangerous heights', according to one reviewer (Glenn 2000: 163).

Choreographer Ned Wayburn recognized the model's dual appeal as an object of both erotic and commodity longing. Although most theatre historiography credits Ziegfeld with introducing the model-showgirl to the stage, Wayburn had included cloak models in his dance productions as early as 1906. The showgirl, Wayburn explained in 1906, was 'one of those cloak-model divinities that are svelte and stately, and wear Paris frocks, and are, oh, so haughty off the stage and on'. Wayburn, also known as the 'efficiency expert in girls', was famous for his precision work with varying teams of chorus girls borrowed from the Original English Pony Ballet (later, Tiller Girls) to produce what Siegfeld Kracauer memorably called the 'American distraction factories' of 'sexless bodies in bathing suits', among other costumes (Kracauer 1995). It was Wayburn who added the 'model' to the taxonomy of corporeal types of five categories, each with its own ideal measurements and slang moniker ranging from the shortest chorines, the Es, to the tallest, the A 'show girls', at 5 foot, 7 inches and taller (Cohen 1980: 139–40).

The best-known of Wayburn's dance numbers were choreographed for 'As', the model-showgirl. These numbers were organized through one of Wayburn's favourite movement motifs, directly related to the mannequin parade of the fashion show, and known as the processional. A simple processional might have four parts: a bit of dialogue or song introducing the theme (jewels, for example or expensive cars; during the First World War, patriotic themes such as the Allied nations); a song alluding to the beauty of the model-showgirls, about to enter the stage (well-known contemporary hits include Irving Berlin's 'A Pretty Girl Is Like a Melody'); the processional itself, which was fundamentally a slow-paced mannequin parade featuring the model-showgirls, usually involving a staircase upon which the A dancers (model-showgirls) maintained what were fundamentally fashion poses (Cohen 1980:154). So, for example on 15 July 1917 Dolores appeared for the first time in the Follies as a Rolls Royce automobile, one of six 'car girls' personifying aspects of the song 'The Motor Girls', performed by Mabel Berry. The job of the showgirl was fundamentally similar to that of the mannequin: to model the work of clothing designers, with the goal of stimulating both awe and desire, for both the clothes and the model wearing them. The job description was that of height, whiteness and the performance of a stately (and silent) femininity.

Wayburn's staging of the model processional borrowed directly from Duff Gordon's choreographing of the model's movements in the couture salon. In order to connote the elite elegance of the upper class that could afford such custom-made designs, Duff Gordon redesigned the mannequin's natural walk. Her goal was to have the models' movements suggest an aristocratic elegance designed to 'encourage a due humiliation in the rich bourgeoisie', producing an emotional, shame-laced prelude to purchasing (Duff Gordon 1932: 70). Duff Gordon made her mannequins walk up and down the showroom with books on their heads until they had acquired 'perfect poise of head and shoulders'. Duff Gordon's focus on the remaking of her mannequins concerned class passing. She sought 'incarnations of enchanting womanhood' whose poise and elegance would mimic that of their well-bred clients, sparking envy and acquisitiveness. Consequently, her models for movement were most likely the numerous treatises on deportment central to bourgeois self-discipline. These systems, such as the Delsarte system of physical culture or the later Mendensieck system, valorized the vertical, erect posture as both biomechanically superior to other poses, including (sometimes explicitly) the tilted pelvis of the post-First World War fashion model (Todd 1920; Georgen 1893).

The gestures and studied poses of the model-showgirl connoted the class and race-specific discourse of fine art appreciation. The model's poise and grace, the gowns themselves, as well as the Ben Ali Haggin *tableaux* that closed each performance, signified not only a middle-brow appropriation of high culture, but also the emotional cultivation deemed necessary for the appreciation of aesthetic forms. The discourse of 'civilization' in this period carried with it the often explicit assumption that those of Anglo-Saxon heritage represented the pinnacle of evolutionary development (Bederman 1995; Jacobson 1998, 2000; Ahmed 1994). The emotional sensitivity of the cultivated was part of this evolutionary heritage; while this sensitivity could sometimes become a burden (as in the case of neurasthenia), the capacity for deep (aesthetic) feeling was understood as an explicitly racial trait—of the Anglo-Saxon race, that is (Bederman 1995; Jacobson 1998, 2000; Ahmed 1994). Both Lady Duff Gordon, working with her mannequins, and Ned Wayburn, choreographing their movement on the Zeigfeld stage, sought to produce racialized discourse of grace, poise and elegance through the vehicle of their models' bodies and (e)motions. Through gesture, we can see the model-showgirls as performing a certain type of (racialized) affective labour, a form of which Wissinger (2007a,b; see also Ahmed 2004, 1994) has so brilliantly analysed in relationship to later forms of modelling. In this early case, models used their bodies to create emotional responses among their viewers: envy perhaps, in Duff Gordon's showroom; racial wonder, maybe, at the Ziegfeld Follies. Their affective labour was critical in the production and circulation of emotion central to the creation of audience. And this emotion was, in turn, central in the production of consumers, who made a beeline to Fifth Avenue department stores and couturier houses at curtain's close.

The popularization of the couturier model on the Broadway stage played a central role in shifting public perceptions of the model as a working-class 'charity girl' to an elite Anglo-Saxon beauty. This class-inflected migration from the wholesalers' workshops to the Broadway stage brought the figure of the model well into public view, while at the same time cordoning her off through distancing technologies such as the stage, the camera and the catwalk. Elaborated in tandem with an emerging film star system that depended upon the intertwining of femininity and celebrity, the model-showgirl in the late teens and twenties shaped an emerging construction of commercialized, public sexuality that distanced the model as a social type from her nineteenth-century history as a 'public woman'. But it was not until the business of advertising began depending upon photographic modelling that the model's sexuality became fully contained, managed and deployed as a central strategy in marketing goods.

The Photographic Model

All of the scholarship concerning modelling in this period focuses on the haute couture manikin and, to some extent, the stage; here, Lucile's model Dolores is the best-known example. But while Americans were attending Follies revues and department store fashion shows to see the newest trends, they were also encountering models in advertising photographs—often the same models, in fact. As numerous scholars have shown, the period before the First World War was the moment in the history of US advertising when it began to appeal to the consumers' subjective longings, rather than their reason; advertisers began to focus on the benefit a product offered (romance, or beauty) rather than the product itself (a bar of soap, for example) (Marchand 1986; Fox 1984). These new types of advertisements focused on creating an overall impression on the viewer, a more atmospheric approach that emphasized an emotional bond between the viewer and the advertising copy. The almost universally chosen route towards this emotional address was what the advertising profession called 'human interest': using human figures interacting with the product in a narrative tableau that spoke to implied (female) consumers' hopes, longings or anxieties. And although pen-and-ink illustration had long dominated American advertising, the prewar years saw the first successful incursion of photography into advertising, a trend that accelerated after the war. These new photographically based advertisements required models for their creation, yet there were—in the First World War era—no such professionals to be found.

The photographer who can be credited for creating the market for the final type of model I will be discussing in this chapter, the photographic model, was the New York City–based commercial photographer Lejaren A. Hiller (Brown 2000, 2005). Born in Milwaukee in 1880, Hiller moved to New York City in 1907, where he worked as a pen-and-ink illustrator for national periodicals such as *American Magazine* and *Harper's Bazaar*; by 1913, he had a $7,500-per-year contract with *Cosmopolitan* to provide photographically based illustrations for the magazine's fiction pieces. As Hiller continued to introduce pictorial technique into his fiction and feature illustrations, however, he also emerged as the leading photographic illustrator of national advertising campaigns, producing photographic advertisements for Corning, Steinway and General Electric, among other companies (Watkins 1959: 44–5). Hiller was the most accomplished commercial photographer in the United States in the First World War era, and it was his work, in both fiction and in advertising, which proved to art directors that photography had an important role in modern advertising.

In an era without a model industry, Hiller created his own proto-agency by hiring a full-time model scout, Jenkins Dolive, in 1918. The New York and photographic press reported that by 1918 Hiller had compiled a photographically based card index representing the faces and physical measurements of 2,000–3,000 working models. Each card featured two photographs, one frontal and one in profile, as well as height, age, weight and other pertinent details. Many of the models were known to movie and theatre-goers, while others were everyday New Yorkers whom Hiller decided represented ideal 'character types', subsequently convinced to pose. Eventually, in fact, Hiller stopped working with well-known figures (such as Marion Davies, whom he claimed to have introduced to his boss at *Cosmopolitan*, William Randolph Hearst) because, he argued, fiction and advertising required the subordination of the model's personality to the narrative, rather than using the narrative as a vehicle for the increasingly trademarked expression of the actress's stardom. Unlike the motion picture, where the audience expects the personality of a Mary Pickford to 'show through the part', Hiller argued, in print illustration the models 'must be a character in the story and nothing else' (Judson 1917: 10). The forward movement of the narrative, whether in fiction or advertising, was threatened by the star quality of the well-known actress. As a writer for *Printers' Ink Monthly* explained in 1922, 'the too-much-photographed face is unproductive of results' (Harrington 1922: 106). The models assembled for Hiller's studio included artists' models, working-class men and women seeking a little extra cash, occupational 'types' spotted in the city's streets and immigrant neighbourhoods, as well as a small group of middle-class women who modelled for the excitement and pleasure of 'being photographed with exceptional care in their best clothes'. While some models were contacted through the location scout, who would find the 'real east side tradesmen, real farmers' or other authentic 'types', others came to the studios through word of mouth ('Using the Camera to Illustrate Fiction' 1918: 13).

Hiller's photographic modelling archive indexed the physiognomic capital of an emerging mass culture industry. Unlike the nineteenth-century portrait, where the face's static features were intended to reveal, transparently, aspects of inner character, the models in Hiller's card index were valued precisely to the extent that their faces and expressions could shift to communicate new identities, new characters.

In the visual landscape of modern mass culture, the charm of 'personality' triumphed over immutable character, which in the context of commercial work would quickly limit a model's work prospects. A successful model was one who was able to appear in a variety of illustrations in different poses and situations while remaining, simply, a character in a story 'and nothing else'. As in the theatre, cosmetics helped 'make-up' these new characters, who inhabited the model's physiognomy as long as the photo shoot lasted. As Kathy Peiss (1990, 1998: 114) has discussed, the growing acceptance of make-up promised personal transformation, the ability to change the self through a shift in external appearance. Hiller took this transformation one step further, using models and make-up to communicate the transformative possibilities of consumption: ephemeral physiognomies sold the promise of authentic selfhood through the acquisition of goods.

It was Hiller's work photographing models for print advertisements that led to the founding of the first modelling agency in the United States. According to John Robert Powers's own account (1941), he and his wife, Alice Hathaway Burton, were both unemployed actors looking for work when Powers came across a newspaper ad for models, placed by a commercial photographer. When they arrived at the photographer's studio, the photographer (Hiller, I suspect, given Powers's head shot in Hiller's papers) asked Powers to round up an additional seven unemployed stage friends, as the advertisement required eight figures (Figure 3.3). This initial experience as

Figure 3.3   Powers as model. Powers is the model on the bottom left.
Source: Courtesy of the Research Center Collection, Lejaren A. Hiller Archive, Visual Studies Workshop, Rochester, New York.

a model led Mrs. Powers to suggest bringing together commercial photographers and the numerous underemployed theatre people of their acquaintance. They contacted 'everyone [they] knew', had their photographs taken, made up a catalogue of forty descriptions and measurements, and sent it to prospective clients in New York City, including commercial photographers, advertisers, department stores and artists (Powers 1941: 20–1). Powers, the founder of the first professional modelling agency in New York (in 1923), pointed out in 1941 that the shift to photography within advertising had created a demand for models, which his agency sought to fill (Powers 1941: 22–3; Leach 1994: 308).

By 1930, Powers had shifted the focus of his directory away from theatre towards advertising and fashion professionals. His clear purpose in directories from 1930 to 1932 is to place what are clearly 'models' in photographic print advertisements for consumer goods, including ready-to-wear clothing. No longer a 'casting directory', the 1930 book of black-and-white images included not only head shots and figure studies, but also the model's physical and clothing measurements underneath each image. By 1932, most of the photographs are credited to the period's leading commercial photographers, including Nickolas Muray, Underwood and Underwood (where Hiller was now vice president), Anton Breuhl, and Scandlin Photography, NYC. Commercial photographers in New York and Philadelphia took out full-page ads in the 1932 edition; an ad for Pagano photographers of 360 West 31st Street suggests that the implied reader (an art director, for example) let their firm choose the models for the shoot: 'One way to eliminate guesswork is to entrust us with the important work of selecting models for your photographs' (John Robert Powers Annual, vol. 8, no. 2, 1932, p. 16). The book's focus on advertising and fashion work is implicit in the catalogue's organization, which privileged both type of model (male, female, older, younger) and type of clothing (from lingerie to outerwear).[2]

Powers's market here was the growing advertising industry, which after prewar innovations such as Hiller's moved en masse to commercial photography as the industry's main medium, and which increasingly depended upon a sanitized female sexuality to sell goods. As Roland Marchand (1986) has argued, in the early 1920s, the photograph was still the exception in advertising art, with only 6 per cent of national ads in newspapers using photography as late as 1926. By the late 1920s, however, photography began a distinct rise in popularity, and surged after the Depression due to its relative cheapness in comparison to drawings or paintings (Marchand 1986: 149). Powers didn't advertise to high-end couturiers, as his focus was the culture industries of mass consumption, especially those that depended upon the photographic image. Powers eventually branded his agency through the standardization of American beauty trademarked as his 'long stemmed American beauties', and through the late 1920s and 1930s his main clients were advertisers and art directors seeking to sell a range of everyday household products to American housewives, from automobiles to toothpaste. As Powers knew, 'the use of photography [had] revolutionized the old methods of advertising'. And while the camera offered a clear view of the product, it also showcased the model: 'However great the care taken in posing them, however painstakingly lights were used, the camera revealed only what it saw. And the girl who was artificial, self-conscious, or who lacked poise, was mercilessly recorded on the negative' (Powers 1941: 23). As Powers continued, 'advertising, as everyone knows, is directed at women who do most of the nation's purchasing.' He needed a new type of female visage to be represented in these print advertisements: pretty, to be sure, but not 'artificial', stagey or vampish; models with whom potential American consumers would identify and emulate. 'My job', Powers wrote (1941: 27), 'was to find models with whom the women of the buying public would be willing to make that identification: models who possessed not only beauty, but breeding, intelligence, and naturalness.' He sought what he called 'the natural girl'.

Powers explicitly contrasted this 'natural girl' ideal with the reigning ideal of American Anglo-Saxon beauty, the Ziegfeld chorus and showgirl. Many of the women who answered ads for modelling were out-of-work chorus girls, whom Powers argued 'were unable to make themselves look like anything but chorus girls'—in other words, 'heavily artificial types [who] were not the models whose appearance the average woman wished to copy' (Powers 1941: 26). Powers's first models were also chorus girls out of a job; as he claimed, they looked the type as well: 'their make-up was extreme, their mannerisms exaggerated, they had a tendency to make themselves appear as glamorous as possible.' But as Powers recognized that this sort of vampish sexuality would fail to appeal to housewives, he 'cleaned up' the out-of-work chorus girl. Distancing himself from his show business predecessor, Powers claimed 'Zeigfeld's death was the death of the glamour girl. She has given way to the natural, well-bred, well-posed girl. . . . The Powers girl is now respectable. Popular' (Powers 1941: 24).

Powers constructed his brand of 'Powers Girls' through equally careful model selection and training, reflecting the class and race biases that the term *standardization* can gloss over. As Powers remarked, 'models are a commodity, a commercial product which must meet certain requirements' (Powers 1941: 45). Distancing his models from the profession's working-class origins in the artist's atelier and the wholesaler's showroom, Powers's models were white, middle-class graduates of Wellesley and Smith; Phi Beta Kappas and Junior Leaguers. His so-called long-stemmed American beauties were sincere, intelligent, well-bred and poised. Like Ziegfeld's model-showgirls, their cultivated whiteness also represented an 'admixture of strange and vital racial strains' which gave the American model a 'unique beauty', a 'keen intelligence for "presence"' that made American models the envy of Europe, according to one 1930 observer (Kennedy 1930).

Clearly, Powers's brand of American beauty varied from Ziegfeld's much less than he would acknowledge. Both Powers and Ziegfeld sought to produce a racialized version of American femininity that privileged an Anglo-Saxon beauty ideal whose cultivated, middle-class status was clearly signaled through gesture, presence, family history, and of course public relations. There were other similarities between Ziegfeld and Powers, however. Both impresarios of feminine pulchritude sought to distance their models from the industry's nineteenth-century roots, where both the artist and the cloak model were viewed as versions of 'public' women, close relatives of the prostitute. Both cultural brokers worked with the concept of distance to establish the proximity and protection afforded by a sanitized sexuality central to the commodi- fication of the female form under consumer capitalism. While Ziegfeld's stage and catwalk separated audience members from the model-showgirls, the magazine page separated viewers from the Powers Girls' chilly charm. In their distancing of the model from her more messy, morally questionable roots, Ziegfeld and Powers developed a new vocabulary for model beauty, one that privileged class and racial hierarchies to construct an emergent parasexuality predicated on commodification and containment.

Conclusion

As processes of industrialization and urbanization produced a mass consumer econ- omy in the early twentieth century, one that relied upon the elaboration of multiple strategies of enticement to grow domestic and international markets for consumer goods, modelling became integral to consumer capitalism. This chapter has sketched the historical roots of contemporary modelling in four variations of early-twentieth- century modelling types: the artist's model, the wholesale clothing or cloak model, the couture model/showgirl and the photographic model. Each type contributed ele- ments central to the development of the profession as it emerged in later years: a sug- gestion of immodest indifference to conventional sexual propriety; the co-production of modern forms of glamour and celebrity; a facility in the production of multiple physiognomies, gestures and looks in the service of commodified affect. A critical development of these early years of the profession, however, was the elaboration of a new form of public, commodified sexuality that straddled the putative divide between public and private. In the first two decades of the twentieth century, cultural brokers such as Duff Gordon, Dolores, Ziegfeld and Powers channelled the newly emerging sexual modernity of a new generation of women in public, containing it in the service of the commodity form.

'Giving Coloured Sisters a Superficial Equality': Re-Modelling African American Womanhood in Early Postwar America

Laila Haidarali[1]

Introduction

In 1948, Swedish newspaper *Dagens Nyheter* introduced to its readers Barbara Watson as it reported on the unusual American visitor on unusual business in Stockholm. Announcing 'Negress to Study Swedish Women's Clothes', the newspaper reported on an elegant African American entrepreneur, model agent and fashion editor who set out on a European tour in search of fashion that 'can be adapted to suit the coloured women of America' (*Dagens Nyheter* (a) 20 September 1948). But, Swedish readers quickly learned that Watson's fashion foray surpassed matters of mere style. Several newspapers covering the American's visit summarized in headlines: 'Coloured People a Newly Discovered Market' and 'Coloured People Should Have Their Own Styles' (*Dagens Nyheter* (a) 20 September 1948; *Svenska Dagbladet* 1 October 1948). Providing readers with a seemingly strange combination of fashion news, consumer market developments and race relations in postwar America, the Swedish press connected these disparate, and perhaps to its readers even unfamiliar aspects of US society near mid-century. Yet, as reporters explored Watson's role in training 'Negro Beauties . . . to be proud', they roundly connected fashion, consumer choice and evocations of equality that, throughout the postwar era, grew increasingly familiar to African Americans, either through their own efforts in the modelling industry, or from carefully crafted visual evidence in new consumer magazines. For the less familiar readership, Swedish newspaper reporters explained Watson's study of European clothing to 'be adapted to suit the coloured women of America' as strategy to 'bolster the coloured women's self-confidence . . . to be able to assert themselves with regards to the whites' (Watson quoted in *Svenska Dagbladet* 1 October 1948).

Two years earlier, this assertion of parity with white Americans through a self-assured display of appropriate clothing emerged in the opening of Brandford Models, the first African American modelling agency in the country, as depicted in Figure 4.1. Co-founded with commercial photographer, Edward Brandford, Watson

One of the first pictures of the original mod- | identification of the model. L to r: Cunning-
els was taken by Our World in Metropolitan | ham, Olden, Adaline Dolly, Vicki McKennon,
Museum in '46. Then as now, hat-box was the | Carole Drake, Dickerson, Jones, Eva Reeves.

Figure 4.1   Cunningham, Olden etc.
Source: John P. Davis Collection.

co-owned—and between 1951 and 1956, fully owned—the first enterprise to promote, book and manage African American models. Reporters from the Swedish press
learned of the agency's auxiliary, the Brandford Model and Charm School. In both
businesses, Watson and a talented team of African and white Americans facilitated
dressing models and the model-aspirant in modern, stylish clothes while training
them to 'make up skilfully, to move gracefully, to feel more sure of themselves'
(Watson quoted in *Vecko-Revyn* 15 October 1948). This confidence, Watson asserted,
not only enhanced the physical beauty of African American women, but also helped
ensure the successful and happy negotiation of their labouring, leisure and sexual
lives (*Vecko-Revyn* 15 October 1948). This rhetoric of stylized confidence assumed
particular importance for Watson who linked her work in crafting African American
women's beauty to larger concerns of African Americans' continuing second-class
citizenship in the postwar era.

By 1953, Brandford Models changed ownership and name to Barbara Watson
Models, although the nomenclature 'Brandford Girls' continued to be used for pioneering African American models. Barbara Watson, the new owner and former executive director of Brandford Models, epitomized the professional status of African
American women in the modelling industry. Watson's Jamaican-born parents encouraged academic and social excellence in their four children, who grew up on
120th Street, also known as Harlem's 'Millionaire Row'. Raised to exhibit good
manners, great thinking and purposeful social engagement, Watson envisioned her
work at Brandford Models as a contribution to race progress, an activism that, after

closing the agency in 1956, shaped her life's work as a diplomat. Watson's status as an educated, elegant, elite woman assisted in reinforcing the professional face of Brandford Models.[2] Journalistic accounts initially expressed some bemusement at Watson's vision of 'clothes and makeup as a means to solve the race problem in the United States' castigating it as 'what one may call an American point of view'. But, on further investigation of the 'dark-skinned' Watson's mission, journalists concluded that for African American women, this decidedly American pursuit surpassed mere vanity (*Svenska Dagbladet* 1 October 1948). Accompanied by Brandford model Sylvia Fitt, Figure 4.2 shows Barbara Watson on her 1948 European tour. News reports described Watson's work in fashion, beauty culture and model training as an innovative approach to race discrimination in the US. In a period of global postwar transitions and growing racial liberalism in the US, Swedish journalistic

Figure 4.2   Barbara Watson and model Sylvia Fitt. Barbara M. Watson Collection.
Source: Courtesy of Schomburg Center for Research in Black Culture, New York Public Library, Astor, Lenox and Tilden Foundations.

accounts framed Watson's attempt to 'give her coloured sisters a superficial equality' as resistance to white America (*Vecko-Revyn* 15 October 1948). While denouncing white America's 'degradation of the Negro race and their treatment as pariahs', the Swedish press simultaneously engaged in exoticizing Watson as a rare example of equality attained. So exceptional did Watson's deportment, dress and physical looks appear that it compelled journalistic conclusions on Watson as 'living proof that discretion and good taste have nothing to do with color of skin' (*Dagens Nyheter* (a) 20 September 1948). Despite her ambassadorship of African American women's 'superficial equality', Watson's physical appearance seemingly enraptured reporters who described the twenty-nine-year-old professional as a 'tall, dark, chocolate-coloured girl' who spoke in a 'soft, dark voice' and proved an 'exotic sight on a Stockholm Street' (*Stockholms Tidningen* 1 October 1948; *Vecko-Reyvn* 15 October 1948).

While the press in the relatively homogenous white country of Sweden welcomed and complimented Watson, their fascination with her as dark-complexioned and fashionably groomed inscribed anew the very images and cultural assumptions that positioned African American women as out of place in the modelling and fashion industry. Like other pioneers in the field of African American modelling, Watson had to contend with the delimiting view of African American women as colourful curiosities or beautiful dark oddities. Indeed, this exoticism—alongside other expressions of racialized difference that circumscribed African American women's relationship to prevailing notions of American womanhood—spurred Watson and others to contest exclusion in the US modelling industry, as well as establish businesses that catered to aspiring African American female models.

Watson's quest was not a solitary endeavour. The dual approach in constructing African American women's beauty as vital to socioeconomic success in post-Second World War America proved consistent with the efforts of others engaged in these early enterprises. As white, corporate America attempted to lure the postwar African American consumer, magazine editors, model agents and fashion advisers worked, often in tandem, to promote a direct challenge to the dominant, external perceptions of African American women's beauty as anomalous, picturesque or nonexistent. Framed in an integrationist, equality-based rhetoric, the reshaping of both the public and self-image of African American women played a crucial role in these postwar enterprises.

African American models, model agents and editors of consumer magazines strove to overturn the central tenets undergirding the US modelling industry. They did so by challenging the 'lily white standards' defining female beauty, as well as the widespread assumptions of dark-skinned people as 'exotic' other. By their very presence, African American models publicly demonstrated that 'the Negro woman . . . , too, has beauty which can be developed to breathtaking proportions' (Promotional Material, Barbara Watson Collection, no date). The model industry's early postwar rhetoric and representation of African American women's beauty challenged the colour line that segregated African American women from being considered beautiful.

At the same time, visual and written discourses on modelling assisted in expanding definitions of beauty as inclusive of personality, intellect, size, shape and complexion. In doing so, those involved in the fledgling African American modelling industry underscored the attainable, consumable nature of African American beauty and argued for inclusion and acceptance in the body politic.

For these reasons, the Swedish journalistic accounts are revelatory. They not only expose the transnational and domestic efforts of African Americans to re-model African American womanhood and combat African American women's treatment as outsiders; they also critique the perception of modelling and the quest for beauty as 'superficial'. Modelling, and the industry's dependence on cosmetics, clothing and physical appearance, seemed incongruent with challenging the material realities of African Americans at home: Jim Crowism, political exclusion, and social marginalization underwrote this group's second-class citizenship in the United States. Yet, by calling attention to the cultural figurations that reinforced views of African Americans as rural and backwards, and thus justifiably unprepared for the full rights of citizenship, challenges to gendered ideals of beauty exposed and attacked the undergirding logics that help sustain these very systems of exclusion. Pioneering models, model agents and early postwar consumer magazines challenged both the iconography and ideology that positioned African American women as neither women nor Americans. In addition, the history of African American modelling situates beauty culture businesses as viable economic avenues by linking beauty ideology to material realities. Such inquiry highlights how, with regard to equality within the realms of political rights, social inclusion and economic independence, the uneven distinction between the 'superficial' and the 'material' was simultaneously finite and fluid.

'Model' Work

As modelling created new work opportunities for African American women in the post-Second World War era, its role in reworking public raced identities emerged most clearly in the new visual discourse on African American womanhood. In the pages of postwar magazines like *Ebony*, *Our World*, and *Jet*, the glamourized female body publicly challenged derisive stereotyping of African American women as unattractive, rural and unkempt. Glossy photographs of beautifully coiffed, elegantly groomed African American women in chic, feminine, tailored clothes provided visual testament to this formula as simultaneously facilitating employment in white-collar jobs and enhancing social skills in integrated and segregated heterosocial spaces. Imagery of the glamorous feminized worker resisted the economic and social imaginings and realities of African Americans as rural, low-wage, service and servile workers. Most often, those images appeared through the static representation of women in advertising and film as mammies, maids and laundresses (Hill Collins 2000: 69–96; Bogle 2001). Certainly, models did not single-handedly create this counter-hegemonic visual discourse; however, their participation proved vital in the era's re-articulation of public raced identities that presented urban, chic and socially mobile African American women as ultimately 'equal' to their white counterparts—in no superficial manner. This assertion of gendered equality on racial lines reflected the broader changes in the postwar era's celebratory return to normalcy.

Changing labour roles for women during the Second World War and its immediate aftermath promoted serious realignment of raced and gendered socio-sexual roles. The wartime labour market facilitated the entry of women into jobs previously reserved for male workers. This labour was not experienced by all women in the same way: women's war work depended on a host of factors including class, race, ethnicity, region, age and marital status (Hartmann 1982; Berger Gluck 1987; Anderson 1996). By the war's end, many nonwhite and white working-class women continued to work—as they always had—but the majority of middle-class white women returned, though not always willingly, to the domestic front. The narrowing precepts of women's work and the rise of US middle-class identity emerged alongside a postwar anxiety that fuelled further entrenchment of traditional sexual attitudes and gender roles into US society and culture.

By the post-Second World War era, the nuclear family occupied centre stage and female sexuality faced containment within the family unit, although the reality was often more nuanced and complex. At this same time, mass consumerism and Cold War rhetoric sharply curtailed American womanhood into a formulaic expression of fulfillment through marriage, domestic motherhood and feminized heterosexuality (Tyler May 1999; Feldstein 2000; Meyerowitz 1994). While these gendered ideals also shaped middle-class understandings of African American womanhood, mass representations and raced gendered ideologies departed from the dominant model of white womanhood in several important ways. By the 1950s, this difference grew most apparent as representations of African American womanhood more readily merged heterosexual feminized identities and middle-class status as coterminous with respectable work outside the home (Meyerowitz 1993).

This representation reflected the material reality of women's wage earning as vital to African American middle-class status in the postwar years. Born largely from [relatively] higher incomes and greater job security, this middle class differed significantly from the old African American elite as more sizable and 'economically situated in the same income and occupational categories of the white middle class' (Wiese 2004: 124). African America's emerging and growing middle class comprised of women and men who worked in a number of professions, including entrepreneurs, whose initiation of small and sizable businesses focused on catering to African Americans, rather than continuing to service white needs, helped define the changing characteristics of the African American middle class (Landry, 1987). The postwar transitions of African Americans as middle class required the reworking of raced, classed identities. In this process, as gendered symbols of socially mobile African America, the representation of models assumed great importance. The exquisite clothes, dazzling smiles and professionally applied cosmetics of African American beauties announced a decidedly modern, material possibility for African Americans by casting them as equal participants in postwar America's mass consumer culture.

While class status and gender ideals structured postwar images of models, so too did the oppressive history of racism. The legacy of stereotyping African American women as desexualized Mammies, oversexualized Jezebels or grotesquely-formed Hottentots, combined with atrocious histories of sexual abuse, demanded careful construction of the public representation of women as models. Most often, models were presented as hard-working career women who, as trained professionals, never compromised moral standards despite their sexual attractiveness and glamorous life-styles. In addition, the visuals and media coverage on models invoked marriage as complementary rather than competitive with career while imparting visions of domesticity as devoid of rural, servile drudgery. By advancing the public identity of African American women as modern, urban and middle class, visual representations of beautiful models evoked the raced gendered female body as worker, wife and woman. This early postwar visual discourse disrupted the raced, classed and gendered meanings that equated beauty with whiteness, womanhood with middle-class lifestyle and African American womanhood with sexualized depravity.

By framing racial progress through socioeconomic mobility and freedom from sexual debasement, images of models helped construct the postwar vision of African American identity as economically ascendant, decidedly urban and dazzlingly beautiful (Haidarali 2005). Simultaneously challenging racist stereotyping and reaffirming conservative gender roles, this early postwar vision was both subversive in its claim to African American women's beauty and narrow in its definition of womanhood as it positioned feminized beauty, middle-class consumerism and heterosexual attractiveness as a strategic ideal for 'race' advancement. The photographic images of beautiful women consuming in middle-class fashion reflected an optimistic, integrationist belief that full civil rights would follow African America's wartime participation and patriotism on the home front. African American consumerism seemingly fulfilled the criterion of national identity, even if that participation was limited to marked purchasing of the nation's most newly recognized consumers.

A New Era for the 'Negro Market'

Modelling, as a profession opened to African American women, derived in large part from the recognition of African American consumers as an important demographic in the postwar economy. David J. Sullivan, one of the most vocal proponents to urge white corporate recognition of the 'Negro Market' quickly became the expert analyst on these American consumers. Sullivan, himself African American, underscored this group's untapped consumer potential in the rising median incomes among urban 'Negroe[s] and other races' from \$489 in 1939 to \$1,448 in 1947. This new prosperity was relative to the rise of median incomes among urban whites that, in the same years, rose from $1,325 to $2,999 (Sullivan 1945: 106)[3]; despite the continued gap between the economic realities of African and white American, the growing spending power of African Americans marked a relative advance. Like other Americans, their consumption resonated far beyond the mere purchase of goods. As Lizbeth Cohen demonstrates, the postwar era witnessed the intensifying correlation between values of 'freedom, democracy, and equality' with 'the process of mass consumption'. As the Cold War progressed, the connection between abstract values with consumer practices framed mass consumption as civic responsibility in the democratic nation or the 'consumers' republic' (Cohen 2003). White corporate attention to African American consumers demonstrated African American access, entitlement to and participation in, the political economy of America during the postwar years (Weems 1998; Chambers 2008).

As many—though not all—businesses and advertising agencies turned their attention to the untapped consumer base, market analysts like Sullivan (1943) provided guidelines for soliciting the 'Negro' dollar. Sullivan's prescriptions for luring the new consumer base warned businesses 'Don't Do This—If You Want to Sell Your Products to Negroes!' (1943: 48, 50). In addition to admonishing, 'pictures and terminology offensive to Negro dignity', Sullivan underscored how denigrating characterizations of 'exaggerated Negro characters, with flat noses, thick lips, kinky hair, and owl eyes' not only repelled consumers, but also did not 'exist any more as a matter of cold fact' (Sullivan 1943: 48). It is noteworthy that Sullivan qualified his rejection of racist stereotyping as archaic, rather than distorted historical mythology. Here, Sullivan seemed most concerned with convincing white businesses, and the advertising agencies who facilitated their success, that the 'Negro . . . spelled with a capital "N"' was a savvy urban consumer with growing expenditures on brand name items, personal care consumer products and clothing (Sullivan 1943: 50). For some white market analysts, Sullivan's recording of African American purchasing brand name and pricey personal grooming items proved the backwardness of African Americans as unsophisticated consumers (Walker 2007: 92). Yet, though jeered as uninformed, and perhaps even unnecessary consumption, this purchase of grooming products underscores a longer history of good grooming and respectable presentation as time-honoured tenets for African American social, political and economic progress.

As Evelyn Brooks Higginbotham explains, the 'politics of respectability', that particularly targeted late-nineteenth- and early-twentieth-century African American women, highlighted good grooming and demure self-presentation as a strategy to overturn the long history of oversexualizing and desexualizing African American womanhood (Higginbotham 1993). For migrating women fleeing oppressive social, political and economic conditions in the rural South, the importance of dress, deportment and good grooming assumed new weight in their transition—and success—in urban centres of the North and Midwest (Carby 1992; Hine 1989; Gaines 1996; Shaw 1996). Although some scholars including Victoria Wolcott (2001) have traced respectability's decline between the 1910s and 1930s, these prescriptions did not disappear. Rather, by the postwar period, the growing consumerist ethos reworked earlier understandings of respectable self-presentation as a mode for advancement by merging 'right' purchase of lifestyle public identity into a particularly classed, raced and gendered ideal.

Indeed, in her search for European fashion, Watson underscored the problematic of the US fashion industry. While the overproduction of 'bright-coloured frills and furbelows' annoyed Watson, the marketing of garish wear to African American women, and the reinforcement of their unequal status as they made poor consumer choices, infuriated her further. Watson (*Vecko-Revyn* 15 October 1948) disdainfully concluded, 'every vulgar, fussy garment produced by the American clothing industry comes to rest on these girls . . . because this kind of junk is all there is to be bought in the stores in the Negro districts' (*Vecko-Revyn* 15 October 1948).

For Watson, the fussiness of women's wear marketed and accessible to African American women intersected with additional concerns. Following a long tradition of African American respectability, Watson focused on steering women away 'from the loud color element in Negroes clothes'. This late-nineteenth-century prescription met a modern, urban twist as Watson steered women away from 'imitating the whites' color scheme' as ill suited to African American women (*Vecko-Revyn* 15 October 1948). In her attempt to give her sisters a 'superficial equality', Watson underscored the troubling view of African American women as rural, uncultivated and inordinately mired in bad taste. Reworking the older notions of respectability and reflecting the growing consumerist ethos in postwar America, Watson championed proper dress and grooming as strategy to represent urban women as modern, well-groomed and stylishly dressed. In the early postwar era, model agents like Watson connected their extensive searches for fashion as appropriate markers of freedom, material possibility and modern, urban status, to re-fashion African American womanhood.

Stepping up in Freedom Clothes

When, in 1946, Brandford Models launched its opening at the Hotel Astor in New York City, the *New York Age* celebrated its debut as 'another step up' and quoted African American actor Canada Lee's lauding the event 'an historic moment in our lives' (*New York Age*, 31 July 1946). Established by Edward Brandford, an African-descended, Jamaican-born commercial photographer, and businesswoman Barbara Watson, the agency dedicated to the promotion of African American models marked not only a milestone for African Americans, but also symbolized 'a new era in the advertising field'. At the Hotel Astor, reporters dubbed the fashions modelled as 'freedom clothes' and described the models as '20 sparkling girls who looked as though they had been wafted out of a dream' (*New York Age*, 31 July 1946). This commentary on young African American women parading in slacks, bathing suits and dinner gowns captured the unique quality of the moment as dream-like. As the spectacle of African American women 'dressed for freedom' intimated African

American social and economic mobility, and announced the public identities of women as urbanized, feminized and middle class, the visual discourse of models was framed in the larger context of freedom which, in 1946, translated mostly into physical freedom from the bonds of slavery.

Dream effects aside, the 'faery-footed youngsters' were not to be dismissed as brainless beauties or directionless divas. For example twenty-year-old NYU student, Edna Besson, who modelled a bathing suit, 'lives with her family' and found her first modelling job 'far more acceptable than the part-time clerical work she had been doing'. Brandford accentuated the respectable goals of these pioneering models who shared similar stories as 'students, artists and writers [who] have been dreaming for years of a project like this, where national advertisers can get copy befitting the Negro trade' (*New York Age*, 31 July 1946).

Prior to the opening of Brandford Models, very few African American women found representation in white agencies; when such inclusion occurred, fair complexions and ambiguous markers of racial identity facilitated entry. Often credited as the first African American model, Ophelia DeVore exemplifies the early integration of nonwhite women into white modelling agencies. Of African, Native American and European ancestry, DeVore left South Carolina for New York to pursue a modelling career. In 1937, at the age of sixteen, DeVore found success when she 'photographed [as] White', and clients 'selected [her photograph] on that basis . . . never question[ing] what [she] was' (DeVore as quoted in Summers 1998: 25–6). Despite her own achievement, DeVore quickly recognized the rejection and disparagement of African American people in print media and abandoned modelling to direct her energies at 'sell[ing] the idea of Black models to the advertising agencies' (Summers 1998: 26). In 1946, DeVore's Grace Del Marco modelling agency debuted in Queens, New York, quickly following the Manhattan establishment of Brandford Models. In the nation's fashion capital and in African America's most populous city home, other modelling agencies quickly emerged. During the late 1940s and into the early 1950s, Sepia Arts Modeling Agency, Bailey Modeling Agency and Gwyn-Lo Modeling Agency competed to attain Brandford's local and national success (Summers 1998; Haidarali 2005, 2007; McAndrew 2010).

Models and modelling agencies also participated in the Cold War production of African American culture by creating pin-ups for soldiers of their 'race'. In a 1952 press release, at the height of the Korean War, African American marines expressed their gratitude to Brandford Models for obliging their 'plea' to the agency to 'secure some pictures . . . to decorate our nearly erected Recreation Hall'. The request was made by Sergeant Watson at Camp Lejeune, North Carolina, who lamented that while 'pin-ups of white women' were 'at his disposal', the marines of his unit wanted 'some of our own girls too, God bless 'em all'. The appeal of both race pride and patriotic duty worked. Watson admitted that while the request was somewhat unusual, the 'girls rallied readily to the cause' and were 'thrilled' to assist the men in this manner (Barbara Watson Collection, Press Release, 15 May 1952). Figure 4.3 shows Watson

Figure 4.3 Barbara Watson, seated with models, 1951. Barbara M. Watson Collection.
Source: Courtesy of Schomburg Center for Research in Black Culture, New York Public Library, Astor, Lenox and Tilden Foundations.

and her models looking over the photographs taken for a cause that emphasized feminine, sexualized display as both patriotic duty and 'race' pride (Haidarali 2007).

Brandford Models obtained its broadest support and exposure from the new African American consumer magazines that also arose in the early postwar era. In November 1945, *Ebony*, a Chicago-based publication magazine first appeared providing space for the representation, celebration and consumption of middle-class lifestyles acquired through mass consumerism. In its first nine years of publication, *Ebony* thrived on depicting 'the positive, everyday achievements' that captured the 'happier side of Negro life' (*Ebony*, November 1945: 1). Directed at an increasingly urban African American audience and attracting international subscribers from the Caribbean, Africa and Europe, *Ebony* provided dazzling visual testament of an ascendant African American middle class when the majority remained mired in second-class social, economic and political citizenship. By 1954, *Ebony* reached a circulation of 500,000, becoming the most widely circulated and successful photographic magazine geared at an African American readership. In April 1946, *Our World*, a New York–based monthly first appeared and also depicted middle-class African America through photographic display. By 1948, *Our World*'s monthly circulation of 50,000 boded well for the magazine's future, but severe financial difficulties led to its demise nine years later. In 1954, *Ebony*'s sales also plummeted due to the changing political atmosphere, and sharpened criticism that its formulaic optimism failed to capture the ongoing and increasingly militant struggle for civil rights. By engaging a sombre and political focus, the magazine survived and remains today one of the most widely circulated African American popular magazines.

Despite the research highlighting the growing 'Negro Market' and the optimism of pioneering modelling agencies, African American models did not readily secure jobs to advertise consumer products in the new media markets. 'Through research and comparison', *Ebony*'s founder and editor, John H. Johnson (*Ebony*, November 1985: 52), slowly convinced some white corporations that 'an ad with a Black model would bring greater results than an ad with a White model'. Johnson's argument convinced some advertisers, resulting in 'duplicate advertising', which substituted African American models for white ones while maintaining the planning and layout of advertisements (Johnson 1989). For white corporations, duplicate advertising garnered new revenue. For African Americans, the effect, though less profitable, proved far more profound. Seemingly flouting postwar *de jure* and *de facto* segregation—if only in visual discourse—duplicate advertising demonstrated that, by occupying the same social spaces and purchasing the same goods, 'Negroes are like other Americans. Essentially we are all Americans first' (Johnson quoted in 'The Personal Equation' 1952).

In mass consumer magazines like *Ebony*, this testament to American status appeared through glossy photographs and celebratory written texts that fêted individual effort as triumphing over oppressive socioeconomic conditions. Issue after issue provided coverage of African American celebrities, including singer and actress Lena Horne, crooner Nat King Cole and dancer Katherine Dunham, alongside less well-known, but still noteworthy sportspersons, entrepreneurs, doctors, beauty salon owners, chorus girls and models. In 1946, *Ebony*'s coverage of Lena Horne, one of the most popular entertainers of the time, highlighted the star's glamorous daily life. *Ebony* enticed readers to not only share 'A Day in Hollywood with Lena Horne', but to also 'Meet the Real Lena Horne'. Photographs captured Horne's collecting of fan mail, lunching with music executives and posing in a 'bouffant gown' for Metro Goldwyn Mayer's 'noted portrait photographer' with pride in her rare achievements. Yet, *Ebony* also underscored Horne's rigorous work schedule by reporting on her early mornings, late nights and frustration with 'whites who expect her to be a Topsy' (*Ebony*, November 1947: 9; *Ebony*, March 1946). Indeed, Horne's elegant, calm sophistication, matched with her extraordinary talent, departed far from the stereotypical view of 'Topsy'—the young girl character in the 1852 pro-abolition novel,

Uncle Tom's Cabin. As the 'blackest of the race', Topsy's 'woolly hair . . . braided in sundry little tails . . . stuck out in every direction' and her 'filthy, ragged garment, made of bagging' elicited sympathy from its white readers in that era, but later developed into a pernicious stereotype of African American girls and women (Stowe 1852; 1966: 258). As African Americans increasingly critiqued and rejected racist stereotyping in America's postwar popular media, Horne's refusal to accept Topsy-like roles facilitated African American visions of their 'own', who, despite ongoing battles in Jim Crow America, managed to garner a modicum of success (Bogle 2001).

Although mainly attracting an African American readership at home, and an African-diasporic one abroad, international readings of *Ebony* further highlight the publication's role in recasting the image of African Americans as a 'raced' people. As one journalist for the Swedish *Dagens Nyheter*, who in 1948 at the time of Watson's visit had 'coincidentally' been perusing the African American publication, wrote:

> When one sees young, smart, intelligent, sometimes very rich people who in other respects live happy lives, one cannot help realizing how idiotic are the obstacles we try to put in their way. It is not only poor servants who are badly off—it is a whole people. (*Dagens Nyheter* (b), 2 October 1948)

Judged by this response, *Ebony* succeeded in demonstrating that African Americans were capable of middle-class lifestyles, savvy consumerism and the ability to prosper despite extraordinary political, economic and social exclusion; these images rejected racialized ideas of difference that justified discriminatory practices and policies. Yet, *Ebony*'s exposés challenged systemic discrimination no further; rather it reaffirmed the US democratic promise of capitalistic success through hard work while projecting an integrationist discourse of racial progress. Most clearly, *Ebony* defined middle-class status through mass consumerism of lifestyle, leisure and look as exemplified by celebrities and professional models who displayed this status as particularly accessible to African American women through hard work and proper consumption of feminized beauty products.

The ABCs of Modelling

> When the nation's top advertisers . . . switch[ed] to Negro models to plug their products, thousands of glamour-struck teenagers and campus beauties flooded the ad agencies with cheesecake photos . . . in most cases, the pictures were returned with the stock rejection letter . . . the more determined girls faced themselves with the serious question: 'What more do I need to become a model?'. (*Jet*, 23 April 1953: 38–9)

In 1953, *Jet*, a small, pocket-sized magazine, and another popular John H. Johnson publication, broached the question 'What Makes a Good Model?'. According to the mass consumer magazine, this matter seemed to haunt 'no less than 10,000 Negro girls [who] will try to become models this year', although 'less than one percent will succeed' (*Jet*, 23 April 1953: 42). Yet, as *Ebony* magazine reported in an article touting the 'Paris Model,' 'a girl trying to crack the model field must have the prerequisites as well as a willingness to work for a low income' (*Ebony*, Feb. 1950: 51). As *Ebony* celebrated the industry's growing inclusion of African American models in America's postwar era, it nonetheless categorized modelling as 'one of the world's most glamorous, and perishable, professions' (*Ebony*, September 1954: 100). Along with *Jet* and *Ebony*, *Our World* also addressed the serious career question 'What Makes a Model?' for the 'thousands [who] flock to big cities in search of modeling careers' yet, 'only few make the grade' (*Our World*, October 1953).

Writers for these magazines elicited answers from the business women and men who worked in the industry as well as from the models they employed, booked and represented to instruct readers on the 'ABC's of modeling'. At the same time, they noted women's tenuous position in the industry questioning, 'Can Negro Models Make the Bigtime?'(*Our World*, October 1953; *Ebony*, September 1954: 100). The model's portfolio, pictured in Figure 4.4, played a crucial role in displaying, booking and marketing the model's suitability for advertisers' needs.

Figure 4.4   Brandford model Barbara Sampson's portfolio. Barbara M. Watson Collection.
Source: Courtesy of Schomburg Center for Research in Black Culture, New York Public Library, Astor, Lenox and Tilden Foundations.

The success of African American models during the industry's early years appears defined by the model's embodiment of feminized characteristics that were both raced and classed. Colour or complexion, the mainstay visual marker of 'race' during America's early postwar era, played a critical role in regulating the success of working models. Colourism or intraracial colour discrimination that, among some African American communities, historically privileged light-skinned complexions is often assumed to be replicated in early mass media imaging of African Americans by African Americans. Yet, as I have demonstrated elsewhere, brown complexions assumed new privilege in postwar representations of African American models. Brown, a middling and mediating complexion, encompassed a vast variety of shades and facilitated the rise of the 'Brownskin' model as best exemplar of feminized, urban middle-class womanhood. While brownness lent itself to immediate visual connection of the model as nonwhite, it also celebrated narrow definitions of womanhood as neither *too* dark, nor *too* light-skinned. Respectively, these complexions potentially disrupted traditional aesthetic standards of feminized beauty or diminished the identification of the model as African American. As this industry's effort necessitated the immediate identification of the models it employed as African American, or at least, 'raced' women, the Brownskin model proved desirable in iconographic depictions of African American women's 'superficial equality' (Haidarali 2005, 2007).

In determining the basic criteria for modelling, all sources concluded that 'raving beauty' was not the essential characteristic to assure a model's success. Beauty itself remained difficult to define as mass-market magazines continually searched for 'The Perfect Negro Beauty'. Magazine articles often drew on the opinions of African American men—photographers, illustrators and celebrities—to help define female beauty, reinforcing that gendered views of womanhood were largely defined in terms of heterosexual attractiveness as envisioned by the other sex. One article drew on the 'expert' opinions of African American cartoon artist E. Simms Campbell (*Jet*, 13 March 1952: 32) whose 'sketch[ing] of hundreds of comely women' qualified his selection of nine African American celebrity women to draw a composite image of the 'perfect Negro beauty'. In his assessment of these nine women, Campbell selected the best features of each to compose his portraiture of the 'perfect Negro beauty'; it was an impossible collection of 'autumnal brown complexion', 'immense, lumi[nous]' eyes, a 'refined' nose, 'full-bodied . . ., yet not overly sensuous lips', a twenty-three-inch waistline, and, unsurprisingly, a 'full bosom' (*Jet*, 13 March 1952: 32–8). Despite this idealized portraiture, *Ebony* reassured the 'housewife or stenographer' that 'beauty does not always come wrapped up in a big-name package' or need necessarily embody Campbell's ideal. Yet idealized notions of female beauty persisted; *Ebony* reported the rejoicing of top photographers on the 'happy day when a naturally beautiful and photogenic woman walks into the studio' (*Ebony*, June 1951: 57). While this celebration at the rare pleasure of women's 'natural beauty' potentially limited beauty as an attainable ideal for all women, modelling-related industries offset this problematic by crafting ongoing coverage of self-improvement for ordinary women.

While 'natural beauties' were a photographer's dream, 'plain girls' frequently made desirable models. *Jet* described this seeming paradox as 'one of the many inconsistencies in the profession with which a model must contend' (*Jet*, 23 April 1953: 40). The paradoxical role of the plain girl in an industry devoted to beauty presented lucrative opportunities for companies to demonstrate transformation into 'glamour girls'. Along with other matters, consumer magazines like *Our World* advised women on the appropriate 'Color Combinations for Brownskins', for making up the varying 'brown' complexions of African American women (*Our World*, April 1949). To enhance and entice the other sex, while bolstering a woman's confidence, 'plain girls . . . [were] transformed through the magic of make-up' (*Jet*, 23 April 1953: 40). While cosmetics were certainly not new to the period, nor new to the urban African American consumer, the plain girl postwar visual discourse highlighted colour or complexion as an essential consideration in the making-up of African Americans (Peiss, 1998). The postwar consumer-based ethos of right consumption and right use commingled with race-proud declarations of beauty as attainable ideal (Figure 4.5).

One such 'plain girl' was neither plain nor a model, but a 'typical college girl' chosen to demonstrate that 'Negro girls are beautiful too'. *Ebony* selected Barbara Gonzales, the first African American graduate from New York's Sarah Lawrence

Figure 4.5 Two young black models check their make-up.
Source: Courtesy Eve Arnold, Magnum Photos.

College, to prove—through a 'picture test'—that 'Negro pulchritude ranks high despite U.S. lily white standards'. Described as 'naturally beautiful', Gonzales underwent a 'rigorous glamorizing process' to transform her into 'the ideal subject for the camera' (*Ebony*, July 1946: 19). Though she passed 'with flying colors', *Ebony* reported Gonzales's reluctance to 'use makeup in quantity' as the chief difficulty on preparing her for the camera. The college student who 'use[d] lipstick sparingly, rouge hardly at all' finally 'cooperated quietly' in 'put[ting] makeup on those pretty little lips' as this cosmetic was 'considered indispensable to a successful glamour operation' (*Ebony*, July 1946: 13). This 'plain girl' transformation did not involve a plain girl at all, as Gonzales's 'exceptional mind' and 'physical beauty' made her a woman of 'rare attractiveness' whose resistance to cosmetic use rendered her 'plain'. *Ebony* demonstrated that through proper lighting, make-up and dress, the photographic shoot produced a 'sexually-attractive, tastefully-cosmetized young lady whose curves and features are calculated to quicken the pulse and heighten the desire of a normal male'. Lauding heterosexual attractiveness and reinforcing women's object-status, *Ebony* suggested that despite Gonzales's academic achievement and physical beauty, only glamorous clothing, make-up and professional photography could transform the 'typical college girl' into a glamour girl equal to any white model (*Ebony*, July 1946: 19). While magazine stories of plain girl transformations offered both instruction and testimony to the accessibility of beauty for the average-looking woman, these stories privileged glamorized female beauty as both icon and ideal.

In addition to stories and pictures of plain girls like Barbara Gonzales achieving the model look through right cosmetic use, professional models in fashion shows and pictorial layouts provided primary testament to this possibility of transformation. This therapeutic and transformative power endowed to consumption of commercial goods, including make-up, reflected the more general consumerist ethos transmitted to American society as a whole (Lears 1983; Leach 1994). Through these displays, African American women learned how to accentuate their looks through consumer products and feminized adornment of their bodies. This so-called beauty guidance, first available through the founding of modelling agencies, formed one of the cornerstones on the mission to impart 'superficial equality'. At the opening of Brandford Models, Mary Louis Yabro, Brandford's white fashion stylist classified 'beauty guidance' as one of the model agency's significant roles as 'the Negro woman has had her own problems in makeup and in clothes which have been disregarded' (*New York Age*, 31 July 1946). While defining glamour, beauty and self-transformation through right cosmetic use and appropriate fashion, photographs of African American models provided abundant testimony to the growing ideals of womanhood as defined through feminized, consumable beauty. Professional make-up artists and hairdressers worked to beautify professional models, as depicted in Figure 4.6.

In the postwar era, women's sexual appeal also assumed a consumable quality. As 'bigger incomes help boost glamour', *Jet* questioned 'Are Negro Women Getting Sexier?' and in doing so, connected growing disposable incomes with the ability to consume and groom women's heterosexual display. Although debating the real

Figure 4.6 Models in preparation for a cover shot, with hairdresser James Landeros.
Source: John P. Davis Collection.

effects of glamour on emotional and sexual happiness, *Jet* celebrated 'America's new prosperity' as finally permitting African American women to 'acquir[e] the opportunity to be glamorous'. No longer limited to models and celebrities, *Jet* found that ordinary 'Negro women throughout the U.S.' embraced the 'chance to be physically more appealing than ever before' as one mode of enhancing socio-sexual status (*Jet*, 31 January 1952: 28–31).

While visage and the ability to enhance one's facial features appeared crucial in discussions of the criteria for modelling, the body itself proved equally important to the model's success. The 'sleek, glamorous "model form"', emerging from 'proper dimensions' of identical bust and hip measurements and slender waistlines, was the epitomized standard for postwar models. According to Sylvia Fitt, one of New York's top African American models, sound nutrition, good grooming and regular exercise assisted in the maintenance of her 'near perfect 34–24–35 measurements' (*Jet*, 23 April 1953: 40). Model and Charm Schools, such as Watson's, provided instruction in graceful, physical fitness, as depicted in Figure 4.7. Despite the popularity for 'angular shapes' in the New York modelling industry and the reinforcement of slender bodies in 'high fashion magazines like *Vogue* and *Harper's Bazaar*', *Jet* noted that model agents and model school directors were noticing a growing demand for models who exceeded these ideal measurements (*Jet*, 26 June 1952: 34–5). Barbara Watson and Ophelia DeVore both commented on the growing request for 'tall girls with wider hips and bigger bosoms', hopeful that 'in a few years, maybe our girls can start eating substantial meals again' (*Jet*, 23 April 1952: 34). Apparent to both women were the unrealistic and damaging demands of the modelling industry, yet proportions of acceptable female models—like other variables in the models' physical appearance—varied according to venue and audience. For example fuller female figures won favour as models for illustrators who, according to at least one account, seemed less concerned than photographers in capturing a 'willowy and lithe' figure (*Our World*, October 1953: 39).

Demand for less lithe female bodily proportions reflected the postwar celebration of the voluptuous female form that emerged unapologetically in unabashedly sexual photographs that proliferated in the pages of early postwar magazines. Noting that

Figure 4.7 The most energetic of Brandford's original models is petite dancer Billie Allen. *Source*: John P. Davis Collection.

the 'brownskinned model found her place in the multi-million dollar, glamorized leg industry' that displayed much more than the female leg, *Jet* celebrated the artistic merit of the sexualized imaging of women commonly characterized as 'cheesecake'. According to *Jet*, 'cheesecake' was 'always artistically pure—never vulgar' (*Jet*, 10 July 1952: 32). Cheesecake's visual discourse of bikini-clad women in suggestive—though not pornographic—poses reinforced the object-status of feminized, sexualized womanhood as both the provocateur and object of desire. In her analysis of sexualized 'girlie pictures' including borderline erotica and pin-up imagery, Joanne Meyerowitz argues that 'the rise of popular erotic images was one component of the broader transformation toward a modern sexuality that assigned heightened value to nonprocreative sexuality'. Flirty and frivolous, these images assisted in the movement of 'women's bodies from the margins of obscenity to the center of mainstream culture' (Meyerowitz, 1996: 9–10). Indeed, cheesecake imagery typified many of *Ebony*'s pre-1954 covers and pictorial discourses on postwar womanhood and in doing so, drew ambivalent responses from readers. While some praised the displays as evidence of 'racial advancement', others admonished the 'immoral' display as vulgar and inappropriate (Meyerowitz 1996).

While facial beauty and physical proportions factored into a model's success, so too did height, often viewed as a model's premium. According to Barbara Watson, models averaged between 5 feet 6 inches to 5 feet 10 inches, although 'models as short as 5 feet 4 inches were sometimes used by illustrators who drew, rather than photographed them'. Shorter models also found work 'posing for hats, jewelry, and so forth'. Watson explained the essential element of height as necessary to 'complement the line of clothes . . . [while] a shorter girl has a stubby effect in photography and cannot display clothes to the best advantage' (Barbara Watson, Lecture, Barbara Watson Collection). Although shorter women faced clear disadvantage in the modelling industry, taller women also endured the problematic of being too tall.

Some women who endured 'difficulty in placing themselves' turned to the Glamazon Model Agency that catered to the particular challenges facing exceptionally-tall women. White owner Sandy Edmonson opened the agency and modelling school to African American and white women, as well as to 'the only Samoan model in the United States'. Edmonson permitted entry to women 5 feet 7 inches or taller. Glamazon's tallest model stood at a statuesque 6 foot 2½ inches. As *Our World* reported, tall women, prior to the opening of Glamazons, resorted to less reputable work as 'strip-tease dancing, night club host[essing] and chorus work' due to the limited demand for tall women in modelling (*Our World*, November 1954: 71). Despite Edmonson's assistance in training and booking women, calls for 'Negro Glamazons' mostly came from 'artists for calendars, coloring, illustrations or for proportions' as the market for fashion modelling failed to embrace too-tall models. Like others in the industry, and hopeful for the longevity of her business, Edmonson remained optimistic of changing ideals of women's beauty. Yet, *Our World*'s caption: 'Glamazons: Beauty by the Ton', reinforced the anomalous appearance of these women. The photographic display that accompanied the text departed from typical images of bathing-suit-clad beauties. Posing in martial arts stances and defensive holds, Glamazon models provided visual evidence of women in untraditional and, by feminized standards of womanhood, aggressive ways. Similar to standards of beauty, shape and size, height, when assessed as criteria for modelling, reflected conservative aesthetic and social ideals of the feminized female body, while also sometimes playfully distorting their fixed boundaries (*Our World*, November 1954).

Can Negro Models Make the Bigtime?

By the late 1940s, professional models achieved varying degrees of success in print media magazines like *Ebony* and *Our World*. Primary amongst the problems facing these pioneering models was limited demand for African American models during the late 1940s and early 1950s. Modelling proved a precarious and competitive occupation for African American women, the majority of whom worked only part time in the industry; this was also true for the few men who joined the ranks.

As the *New York Post* reported 'All about the Negro Models' (1955), individual models offered testament to the challenges they faced. The *Post* spoke to Dolores Jackson, a twenty-five-year-old model who had been working for six years in the field through Brandford Models, who commented that despite once being a 'novelty in the field' and now having found greater acceptance, African American models still had far to go (for this and quotes following, cf. 1955: 30). Jackson observed that although African American models had 'the same influence over [their] audience as the white model has over hers . . . [they] just don't get the work'. While Jackson noted that success was possible, she complained 'you can go just so far and no more'. Jackson pinpointed the problem as continuing racist attitudes by providing an example of models, who, after being hired for 'showroom jobs on Seventh Avenue . . . lasted only a couple of days'. Although businesses proved willing to hire African American models, their customers—in this case Southern buyers—did not 'approve of Negro girls being displayed in the showroom'. Department stores, Jackson also noted, resisted employing African American models for fear of offending their clientele. Direct rejection on the basis of race was never given. As a model's appearance determined her market value, department stores exploited this rationale for not employing African American models; according to Jackson, 'They always say we're too tall, or too short or too fat or too skinny . . . but actually I'm sure it's because we're coloured' (*New York Post*, 16 June 1955: 30).

The lack of steady work translated into only part-time modelling for many who aspired to the field. While earning an hourly rate of pay ranging widely from $10.00 to $50.00 an hour with a median income of $25.00, African American models enjoyed parity with white models. The real obstacle to a steady income was the limited work that demanded even the 'busiest Negro photo models' retain their white-collar jobs as receptionists, typists and secretaries (*New York Post*, 16 June 1955: 4, 30; *Ebony*, September 1954: 101–6).

Despite these limitations, model agents Barbara Watson and Ophelia DeVore remained optimistic, believing 'the Negro model market will grow as the Negro consumer's market becomes more appreciated' (*New York Post*, 16 June 1955: 30). While both Watson and DeVore foresaw the day when modelling could allow women to live 'well on [their] earnings', and DeVore predicted 'it may well be possible in about three years', Watson went further in defining the problem as one rooted in societal attitudes that defined difference through racial identity and remained convinced that 'the Negro model will find her stature . . . when it is no longer necessary to identify her as a Negro model' (*New York Post*, 16 June 1955: 4). But that moment was not close at hand; throughout the late 1940s and early 1950s, the 'Negro model' found greatest acceptance within her own communities. Appearing in local fashion shows, community and church benefits, beauty contests and consumer magazines, 'Negro' models displayed gendered, racialized bodies that exemplified urban African American woman in glamorous, dazzling fashion. Among American audiences and communities, the raced, classed identity of the 'Negro model' emerged as a source of pride, and testament to social and economic progress.

African American models met the needs of community, advertisers and mass-market magazines by participating in fashion shows, beauty pageants, print advertising, wholesale showrooms and retail stores. The latter two venues were the most lucrative for models, as employment in such spaces often translated into steady incomes that permitted some financial security for pioneering postwar models; these spaces proved most resistant to hiring African American women. Among the few who succeeded in securing such employment was West Coast model Patricia Anderson who, as 'one of the first three Negro models hired to model clothes in an exclusive white dress shop in Beverly Hills', departed from the more common employment of African American models to display fashionable style to African American audiences (*Ebony*, September 1954: 104). This advance was even more anomalous, as African American models on the West Coast endured a more precarious living than their East Coast sisters. In New York, those lucky to secure these positions included Elaine Brooks who found work as a showroom fur model. Brooks recognized her unique position stating, 'As far as I know I'm the only Negro model on Seventh Av. in any kind of wholesale business'. Yet, ambiguous markers of racial identity or ignorance—or both—elicited questions of Brooks's identity: 'I'm treated well', Brooks stated, 'But most people want to know if I'm from Turkey or Peru, or some other exotic place. Some of them can't believe . . . a Negro girl can be a model. It isn't prejudice as much as a simple lack of thought' (*New York Post*, 16 June 1955: 30). Despite Brooks's softening of such questioning to lack of consideration, repeated inquiries of racialized national identity and the invocation of 'exotic' reinforced stereotyped and narrow views of African American identity, as well as female beauty, as unexpected and extraordinary.

This heightened 'exoticism' also emerged when advertisers, editors or businesses specifically requested African American models. For example when seeking models for a lingerie layout in the late 1940s, *Glamour* magazine sought 'coloured models' believing that 'classical features and coloring would best show off a new line of elegant boudoir attire' (*Ebony*, September 1954: 103). This specific request for African American models was premised on sexualized ideas of raced bodily display. At once troublesome in its exoticizing of the African American female body in overt sexual display, *Glamour*, a mainstream white magazine, found models of colour neither offensive nor upsetting to its predominantly white female readers.

While magazine layouts, wholesale and retail modelling and print advertisements remained common and coveted forms of model work, models regularly participated in community fashion shows organized by civic clubs, sororities, women's organizations and charm schools. As community events, fashion shows often ended with live music and dancing that completed the interactive and participatory nature of community fashion shows. Here, within the confines of the needs and approval of African American communities, models proudly paraded womanhood's beauty as well as increasingly class-based ideals of femininity, good grooming and sexual attractiveness. The majority of models displayed their fashionable bodies and superb smiles 'gratis in fashion revues because of the publicity they receive', while top models like Sylvia Fitt and Sara Lou Harris 'are forced to turn down invitations they receive because of lack of time and usually appear only in the top shows' (*Jet*, 13 April 1952: 42–4). Organizers, in return, often donated the proceeds of the show to 'worthwhile civic organizations and charity groups', further reinforcing modelling's early efforts to enhance race and social progress while gaining publicity and experience in runway modelling (*Jet*, 13 April 1952: 46).

Most often, women modelled their own clothes largely due to limited corporate sponsorship of these events. In doing so, models demonstrated their acquisition of stylish suits, evening gowns and creative millinery wear, providing further testament to savvy consumption and personal style. Radio commentary on a Harlem fashion show in 1950 captured this role of fashion shows to encourage and stoke women's desire to hone their own looks. In an introduction to the coverage of *Club Sudan*'s fashion show, the radio announcer stated:

> Sometimes visitors to America criticize the tendency for American fashions to follow a mass-production pattern. A waitress in a restaurant is very likely to wear the same dress as a bank president's wife—they may even buy their clothes at the same shop. . . . This is one of the challenging problems which democratic fashions create. But American women try to solve this using ingenuity in the choice of accessories and color combinations to give their costumes individuality. (*Women's World*, 8 June 1950)

No greater display of individual achievement through stylish display at fashion shows can be found in the postwar era than Dorothea Towles's fifteen-city tour in the early 1950s. After two years working as a house model for European and Parisian designers, including Christian Dior and Elsa Schiaparelli, Towles attained celebrity status at home largely through coverage in the African American press; *Ebony* and *Our World* proudly proclaimed the Texas-born 'Los Angeles girl' the 'most publicized Negro woman in Europe, with the exception of Josephine Baker' (*Our World*, August 1952: 42). Magazines reported how Towles 'brought six trunks of real showstoppers to this country for fashion shows', proving that 'a Negro model can "sell" a $15,000 gown in Europe' (*Our World*, August 1952: 44). Greater than the ability of the African American model to advertise such goods through model display, however, was the private ownership of a 'dazzling wardrobe' that established one as a 'pace-setter for others' (*Jet*, 6 December 1951: 40–1). As Towles clarified in a later interview with Barbara Summers, she invested her savings to purchase of 'a wardrobe [she] could never afford', and did so only through model discounts and 'go[ing] through and pick[ing] out the things that were in better condition and get[ting] them cleaned' (Summers 1998: 201). As Towles toured the nation parading her spectacular gowns and chic European wardrobe, audiences at fashion shows, ranging from those on college campuses to New York ballrooms, witnessed the display of the 'daring, bronze-blonde' beauty who testified to the possible success of African American models on the world stage. Like Watson in her attempt to refashion the style of African American women, Towles understood her role in helping 'American black women dres[s] differently and fee[l] good about themselves'. As a result of her extensive fifteen-city tour and instruction of women at sororities and colleges, Towles concluded that she 'saw [African American women] dressing more creatively, more internationally. They could say, if she could do it, I can too' (Summers 1998: 203).

Conclusion

By the mid 1950s, African American models, though attaining only limited success at home and achieving some recognition abroad, were roundly celebrated in communities and consumer magazines as the idealized epitome of urban womanhood. Models assisted in forging a public visual discourse of African Americans as capable of middle-class lifestyles, savvy consumerism and the ability to prosper despite extraordinary political, economic and social exclusion. By expanding narrow definitions of women's beauty, the early African American modelling industry publicly revealed the superficial bases of racialized ideas of difference. Simultaneously reinforcing narrow gendered dictates of women's beauty, these classed-based representations would, by the mid 1960s and early 1970s, meet militant challenge from black feminists. Yet, in the postwar nation where these distortions proved useful in justifying discriminatory practices and policies to those at home and abroad, the re-modelling of African American womanhood challenged the very 'superficial' nature of equality in post-Second World War America.

–5–

Fashion Modelling in Australia[1]

Margaret Maynard

What you're selling is your ability to sell clothes through a photograph. You must have respect for the garment you are modelling—in my opinion this garment is your tool to make money. (Del Hancock, model, *Flair* (Mar. 1965): 51)

Professional female fashion models and the aesthetics of attire are central to stimulation of consumer desire. In fashion photography, the persuasiveness of the image with its creative ambience offers a different kind of allure from clothes on catwalk models. The question is how did photographic modelling function in Australia where a nexus between couturiers, high society and numerous plush magazines did not exist quite as it did in say the US or France (Quick 1992: 46). During the first half of the twentieth century Australia's published images of female fashion models were part of complex and shifting sets of creative, technical and business activities, many of which had a local tenor.[2] These images, by no means entirely overshadowed by those in British, French and American fashion magazines of the time, were produced within particular and identifiable social and cultural circumstances. The latter included availability of technology, pay scales, specific ratios between catalogue and fashion magazine work, different kinds of clientele and retailing in Sydney and Melbourne, local climatic conditions, tastes and types of model, some of whom lacked the specialized experience of those trained overseas. It is difficult to point to a precise 'look' that characterizes Australian fashion images, but there is little doubt that isolation and a small population were key defining factors suffusing the spheres of fashion publishing, modelling and the related quality garment industry until the 1960s.

Importantly, underpinning the local fashion market was a pervasive, sometimes conflicting local rhetoric inflecting both published discussion of fashion models and descriptions of fashionable dressing (often making comparisons to the US or UK). This included definitions of ideal female attractiveness, etiquette, physique, professional attitudes to work, photogenic qualities, taste in clothing and so on. Prior to the 1950s, it focused chiefly on what constituted national characteristics in appearance, subsequently becoming more concerned with comparisons between local and international models and their attire. Fashion magazines, autobiographies of photographers and models, interviews with former models and stylists reveal the distinguishing circumstances that surrounded both the modelling profession and definitions of feminine attractiveness.[3]

Aspers, in his important text *Markets in Fashion* (2006), aptly demonstrates that the fashion photographic market is a complex cultural and commercial activity and that meanings in these two spheres will likely produce differences, even tensions, between aesthetic values and economic imperatives. He also brings to our notice surrounding modalities and networks of services that existed within this market, from that of the photographer, to the status of magazines, to clientele. Within this particular commercial activity, he notes variances between high-status fashion magazines and lower-status catalogues and mail-order publications. We can usefully compare all these points to the situation in Australia during the mid-twentieth century, the period with which we are presently concerned.

The model a fashion magazine editor chooses to use, or what a photographer deems aesthetically pleasing in a subject, including her repertoire of posing techniques, is something affected by relevant historical and geographical factors and culturally in flux. The 'look' of fashion constituting its desirability continually enters into immediate relationships with consumers, but needs to be read and understood as framed by multiple factors; the context through which it is mediated providing density of meaning. Thus, the Australian fashion photographic model, like any other, has been and is a 'part' player in a web of photographic practices and advertising particularities. This said, the co-dependent notion of the 'part' player does not negate the prominent role some mid-century local models took in the fashion 'shoot', their exceptional range of talents and/or those who went on to develop prominent business careers in fashion and the media outside modelling as such.

The chapter takes as a point of departure what Aspers (2006: 30) conceptualizes as 'a collective process' within the contemporary fashion image-making market, with its plethora of discrete categories, which are nevertheless interconnected. There are separate market categories for models, hairdressers, magazines, agents, make-up artists, photographers, camera technology and so on, linked into a business network of considerable density. This said, the clear categorization Aspers identifies between editor, fashion editor, art director, photographer and photographer's agent (2006: 43, 55, 57), was hardly evident at all, given the improvisatory tenor of much Australian fashion photography before mid-century, and in some cases even the following decade. Entwistle (2002) in her study of the male modelling industry also remarks on relations in the fashion photographic market and makes much of the unstable aesthetics of models' bodies. Her point is that within this prestigious marketplace, these networks of relations between model, agency, magazine and photographer identify and confer cultural value on one model above another (2002: 336). Importantly, she points to the fact that while modelling today reaches out to global markets, different cities have their own local economic requirements (2002: 324). It is possible to show that the markets Aspers identifies in connection with recent European fashion photography had their own local historic, geographic, aesthetic variances and specificities in Australia. In addition, if we consider the historical aspects of modelling, Entwistle's findings regarding the differentials of the global fashion modelling market are also applicable within Australia during the period discussed.

I explore what were the particularities of the comparable Antipodean fashion photographic market during the mid-twentieth century. After a brief account of the early history of modelling, the focus will be primarily on three defining factors: an extremely limited local fashion press; the state of fashion photography struggling to gain ground despite technological limitations (including lack of access to photographic film); and a small, but active postwar fashion industry. Up until mid-century some models, although able to find work in country towns or even larger centres like Brisbane and Adelaide,[4] gravitated to the major cities of Sydney and Melbourne. Each of the latter had its own characteristic social milieu, cultural priorities, climates and leisure activities, particular kinds of retail outlets and fashion requirements. Melbourne was a dignified city with a colder climate, and after the Second World War the centre of splendid high-end couture and quality retail goods. Sydney was a rather different city, fresh, fast-paced, its beachside weather warmer, with more relaxed fashions and leisure requirements, although certainly with its own elite social set. Interestingly, at the end of the 1940s, the range of opportunities for models was greater in Sydney and the pay better than Melbourne (*Glamour* (Feb. 1948): 38).

Modelling and Its Early History in Australia

In order to understand the historical nuances within the networked markets of photographic fashion modelling in Australia it is important to know something of the background to the developing profession of modelling from the early twentieth century. The practice of demonstrating fashions on beautiful young women had begun in exclusive European couture houses during the nineteenth century, spreading to a wider class of audience via shows in department stores and popular theatre (Breward 2003: 105–6). From the later nineteenth century in Australia, actresses both on and off the stage proved one of the most accessible sources of fashionable style for consumers to emulate. Published photographs of socialites too offered fashionable examples. These women occasionally went on to modelling and film careers, like Margaret Vyner, a socialite and advertising model in the 1930s, later chief model for Patou in Paris (*Queenslander*, 10 January 1935, p. 36), who also worked for Norman Hartnell. Anything comparable to French salon modelling emerged much later in Australia. For instance designer salons in Melbourne's Collins Street using models for elegant parades rapidly increased in number after the Second World War (Whitfield 2006: 110), along with the bustling expansion of the city's Flinders Lane, the heart of the rag trade.

Employed in dramatic fashion plays and presentations immediately after the First World War, perhaps a little earlier, parade models worked mostly for high-quality department stores. According to June Dally-Watkins, one of Australia's most success-ful model-cum-business woman, who arrived in Sydney from the country in 1944, practically no modelling was taking place except for mail-order catalogues (Dally-Watkins 2002: 35). This seems an exaggerated claim, for department stores in Sydney had a history of using models, and from the 1930s fashion parades shown on Cine-sound and Movietone newsreels made their display widely accessible. Stores selected models from working-class staff members with good deportment and flair (Reekie 1993: 146 and Maynard 1999: 198) and the Berlei Corset Company (founded in 1919), for instance used 'industrial' women employees as fashion models (*Berlei Re-view* (Sept. 1925): 8). Fashion and lingerie shows were extremely popular, and drew on music and dance to enhance the seductive attractiveness of garments and acces-sories. Yet mannequin work carried a stigma of disreputability until after the Second World War, not even offset by the establishment of agencies from the 1920s (Conor 2004: 109). Dorothy Woolley, one of Australia's earliest-known 'figure culture' spe-cialists, had an agency in the 1920s, supplying her own troupe of young women for staged fashion demonstrations in Sydney as well as Melbourne (Maynard 2001: 123).

Exclusive stores, like David Jones and Farmers, were major employers of high-end parade and photographic models (for catalogues) well into the 1960s but news-paper advertising was the major source of work for photographic models. David Mist recalls this as a 'funny system' where newspaper adverts for retail stores provided his bread-and-butter work compared to the UK.[5] Mannequin work, as opposed to photographic modelling, changed after the war. It became better paid and carried less of a social stigma as a 'slightly suspect profession' (*Flair* (Sept. 1959): 68). In an article for *Fashion*, Lilian Rudique notes 'People do not faint when their only daugh-ter announces that she got a job as a mannequin. Respectable friends of the family do not bang their doors in her face' (June 1949: 19). By the mid 1950s Sydney had deferred to Melbourne as the centre for high fashion modelling. At this period Mel-bourne shops and exclusive retail stores like Georges were setting themselves up as particular purveyors of French style, although, to an extent, similar shops in Sydney were doing the same. At the 'Paris End' of Melbourne's main avenue Collins Street, there existed a sophisticated cultural ambience, and a number of small, influential salons like Le Louvre were focusing on French couture and its copies (Leong 1997; Whitfield 2006). Some fashion photographers were located there too. Whitfield sees this fascination with French fashion as ironically providing a context in which merits of Australian design could be discussed, necessary, she argues, for the future of the local industry (Whitfield 2006: 113).

Fashion photographic modelling had a somewhat separate history from manne-quin work. It grew more sporadically and was considered for the most part a more prestigious activity until the 1950s, perhaps due to early links with photographic celebrity portraiture. Interestingly the term *catwalk* only came into general use then. According to an article in the late 1930s entitled 'Model Girls', top-quality fashion photographic models had to have a perfect figure and high cheekbones, as the camera was unforgiving and companies could not afford retouching. They had to be able to dramatize garments, could be haughty and even bored, playing down their personality in favour of the outfit. There was a subset of photographic models, namely those used for everyday commercial work in less prestigious publications. Pretty faces and details of garment were more important here. Models needed to smile, be responsive and had to bring their own clothes to the shoot (*Table Talk* (July 1939): 12). Conflicting information about the two kinds of model (mannequin or photographic) exists. In 1962 *Flair* fashion magazine says models in France were expected to be good at only one type of modelling, but in Australia they had to do a bit of everything and therefore it was more exacting, versatile work (*Flair* (Jan. 1962): 23). Some, like top model Diane Masters, had this capacity to do both kinds of work, and she was known as much for her flair in parading clothes as her photographs. Renowned top mannequin Maggie Tabberer had the same capability, being almost too beautiful for the catwalk (it was said), as the audience looked at her rather than the clothes (van Wyk 2006: 86).

No agencies for photographic models are known until a photographer and highly enterprising businessman, Russell Roberts, opened a large-scale commercial photographic, advertising and model agency in Sydney, 'Russell Roberts Ltd', late in 1931 (*Photography* 4, 40 (Dec. 1935): 10). His business used specialist photographers for different genres of photography (very unusual in Australia pre–Second World War). The company retained good-looking young women, men and children on their books, undertook talent spotting and offered some training facilities (National Gallery of Australia Library clippings). Roberts's firm launched significant models Margaret Vyner and Patricia Minchin, and was responsible for recruiting June Dally-Watkins. The illustrated *Australian Casting Directory* (Nov. 1936), a quarterly magazine issued to Sydney department stores, commercial photographers and advertising agents, also notes it could supply screen, mannequin and photographic models.

Fashion photographic models, according to Margaret McGurgan (formerly model Maggie Deas) worked hard but not as hard as mannequins. Finding consistent information on payment for models is very difficult. Like the UK or US, photographic models in Australia were paid by the hour during the late 1950s, although one of the country's best-known photographers, Laurence Le Guay, said mannequins were frequently hired by the week and paid far less than photographic models. According to him, busy photographic models could get 60–70 Australian pounds a week (*Flair* (Sept. 1959): 60). According to Ann Felton, top photographic model and Model of the Year in 1959, this is an overestimation, so evidence is quite conflicting.[6] Nevertheless, Felton and Le Guay both agree that a photographic model received about eight guineas (a guinea was one pound, one shilling) per day and minimal fee for a shoot of about an hour was two guineas. Using Felton as a guide, a model working for five full days could theoretically receive 40 guineas a week. More experienced models did not receive higher pay but got more work. Even so, remuneration in Australia was certainly not impressive compared to the US where salaries soared for models in the 1950s (Tolmach and Scherr 1984: 93). When Ann Felton moved to New York in 1960, she was paid US$50 an hour, the equivalent of approximately 23 Australian pounds. By 1962 this had risen to US$60 an hour, although top magazines like *Vogue* paid far less, relying on the privilege of working for them. A fair number of the 'flocks' of models who left for overseas during the 1950s and 1960s achieved real success. Australian Pauline Kiernan, who found New York pay unequalled, was voted model of the year by top American photographers (*Flair* (Jan. 1961): 48). Things did improve in Australia. Pay scales rose in the 1960s and the best models were earning more like A$200 a week. As Australia decimalized in 1966, this was about double the amount earned a little less than ten years before (*Sydney Morning Herald*, 9 February 1967, p. 6).

Specific training for photographic models came later than for mannequins, but even in 1936 Margaret Vyner had to be taught to walk properly when she took up a position for Patou in Paris (*Home* (1 Feb 1936): 28–9). Russell Roberts's agency offered some guidance but it seems the first professional course for photographic models was set up in Sydney by well-known model Maide Hann in 1947, supervised by Rob Hillier, a respected fashion photographer (advertisement *Fashion* (May 1947): n.p.). In Hillier's studio Hann taught modern poise and posing techniques, grooming, cosmetic detailing, hair styling and dress selection, something regarded then as lacking in Australian women. By defining and following a curriculum specifically for photographic models, these classes marked a new and growing sense that it was a worthwhile profession. From the later 1950s a girl who posed strictly for professional photographers was entitled to call herself a 'model girl' (*Flair* (Sept. 1959): 68).

A handful of remarkable Australian models went on to do far more than this kind of work, showing their strength, business acumen and determination.[7] Of particular interest in Australia was that modelling was not a dead-end job for these particularly canny models, many of whom made noteworthy careers for themselves in the wider industry. Maggie Tabberer, one of Australia's best-known models, began her career in Adelaide in 1957 and then went to Melbourne, working for several photographers including Helmut Newton. Mannequin of the Year in 1960 (*Flair* (Aug. 1961): 47), she moved on to a stellar career in retail and the media. She has hosted her own television programmes, established her own promotion and publicity company, staged fashion shows, had her own fashion label and been a fashion writer and editor for many newspapers and magazines (van Wyk 2006: 85). Diane Masters was a famed model but also a fashion sketcher. In 1960, she and Hall Ludlow, a top Melbourne designer, were sent by the Department of Trade to important fairs in London and Lausanne to assist in the presentation of Australian wool garments. Later she was sent to Singapore in charge of all the show arrangements, interviews and entertainments. In 1953 Masters and co-model Bambi Tuckwell set up the Bambi Tuckwell Fashion Studio and Model College in Collins Street, Melbourne, the enterprise running for a few years.[8] Athol Shmith, the photographer, taught classes in photographic modelling for them.

Janice Wakely is another who was far more than an outstanding model.[9] She left Sydney for the more sophisticated fashion scene in Melbourne, largely because of better pay and the considerable amount of work available for store catalogues as opposed to newspapers. Based there by mid 1955 she worked for photographers Helmut Newton, Athol Shmith, Henry Talbot, Bruno Benini, and fashion houses like Myer Emporium. Helmut Newton encouraged her to take photographs, offering her a job as assistant, and by 1959 she was taking candid photographs of photographers during modelling sessions, including one of Newton and another of Athol Shmith shooting model Georgia Gold. In 1964 she established, with co-model Helen Homewood, the Penthouse Model Agency and Photographic Studio in Flinders Lane, Melbourne, in the penthouse premises used previously by Talbot and Newton. At a time when there were almost no female fashion photographers, this was probably the first professional combination of its kind in Australia. The studio flourished until at least 1969. Homewood trained models and did make-up, and the studio worked for fashion houses, retail stores and designers, with Janice doing most of the photography. June Dally-Watkins was another remarkable model. She set up her own deportment school in 1950 and in the following year was founder of one of Australia's most significant model agencies in Sydney (Dally-Watkins 2002: 72). In 2008 she was still operating a modelling school in Sydney and a model management business in Brisbane. Many models were extremely astute, and their later career successes in the wider industry are notable features of cultural life in Australia over many years.

The Fashion Press in Australia: Rhetorical Conflicts

High-status fashion publishing was slow to develop in Australia. Magazines printed photographic plates sent from Paris but the local industry was certainly developmentally behind that of the UK and the US. As previously noted, models found most of their work was for newspapers and store catalogues. Although a number of women's magazines had existed before, Australia's first dedicated fashion magazine *Fashion* was only published in Sydney in 1947, running for a mere three years (compared to the much earlier American *Vogue* purchased in 1909 by Condé Nast and still on newsstands). *Flair* and *Vogue Australia* came later in the 1950s. Innovations in photographic film were also slow to arrive. Even in 1961 when David Mist, a London-trained fashion photographer, moved to Australia he found it difficult to get much in the way of colour film (Mist 2005: 55). Whilst fashion news from overseas correspondents was surprisingly up-to-date, and imported magazines available, the local fashion photographic profession was sluggish with fewer opportunities than in Europe. For this reason, Helmut Newton left Australia for good in 1961, the market apparently too bland, offering him little scope for his inventiveness. In 1977, according to Featherstone (2005: 116–17), Newton is reported as saying (perhaps with the gloss of hindsight) the environment was an ultraconservative one, models looked like 'anaemic clothes horses' not real people, and it was difficult to find women willing to be photographed in their underwear.

Sydney was the centre of what little fashion publishing existed prior to the 1950s, perhaps because of the example set by an extraordinary style magazine, the *Home*, first issued as a quarterly in 1920. Its circulation was limited in the 1930s to 6,000–7,500 copies compared to, say, the *Bulletin's Australian Woman's Mirror* from 1924, the latter similar to a newspaper in circulation and appearance (Underhill 1991: 200).[10] With its brilliant modern edge, black-and-white fashion photographs, coloured art covers and sketches, advertising savvy, with plenty to interest men as well as women, the *Home* had lively illustrated feature articles on a range of subjects. It was an outstanding exception to the run of other rather drab contemporary local publications. Directed at the socially well heeled, it recognized a wider middle-class readership might find its good taste educational but its articles on the theatre, art, interior design and its fashion advertising were clearly aimed at the upper sections of Sydney society. From the start the *Home* was a great deal more than a fashion magazine and its high-quality production, both paper, typefaces and proto-fashion editorials (discussed below), something of an anomaly at the time.

Aside from a number of modest women's magazines and the *Australian Women's Weekly* (which began in 1933, offering a degree of fashion coverage in a mix of illustrations and photography), there were only two dedicated fashion magazines even in the 1950s and 1960s (both published in Sydney), and a short-lived Melbourne publication, *Australian Fashion and Beauty* (1959/1960). In Sydney there was *Flair* magazine that commenced in 1956 and the independent *Vogue Australia* that started in Spring/Summer 1959, edited by expatriate Londoner Rosemary Cooper. *Vogue* at 3/6d a copy was a little more expensive than *Flair*.[11] A prior publication tied to *British Vogue* was *Vogue Supplement for Australia* published between Autumn/Winter 1955 and Autumn/Winter 1957, often referred to as a 'double number' until Autumn/Winter 1959. Till then there had been a 'sad history for fashion magazines' in Australia (*Flair* (Jan. 1963): 56). That there were so few at this time demonstrates that the consumer base for high fashion was too small to make such a publication viable. Yet by the end of the 1950s, it was estimated Sydney had 400–500 models of all ages working through agencies (*Flair* (Sept. 1959): 62), probably indicating that fashion models, except for a handful of outstanding ones, must have been working mostly for in-store shows, retail mail-order catalogues, newspapers and general magazines like the *Australian Women's Weekly*. This is an interesting insight into the circulation of fashion information mid-century, and may well be particular to Australia and other British dominions like New Zealand, as opposed to say the USA with a far larger population, and an earlier history of publishing quality fashion magazines.

Vogue Australia was a genteel magazine, little different from its British counterpart in format, content and aesthetics and still using some UK photographers for decades, its target consumer the affluent, mature woman. *Flair*, rather less sleek, was lively and gossipy, aimed at sixteen-to-twenty-five-year-olds and was more in tune with stylish dress for everyday. Despite using outstanding fashion photographers, its print quality was inferior to *Vogue Australia* and its tone more down to earth. It often ran competitions, detailed careers and personalities of models and offered insightful advice on what might make a good photographic model. Articles on 'model of the month' appeared between 1961 and 1964. Early fashion models tended to be anonymous, apart from society beauties who doubled as models, beauty contest winners and theatrical celebrities (who endorsed beauty and other products), but *Flair* and other general magazines mid-century began to promote professional models as household names through sustained journalistic coverage. *Flair* almost obsessively probed details of their daily lives, their favourite foods, their pets and ran regular accounts of their activities such as 'Commuter Model: Behind the Scenes', a day in the life of model Del Hancock (*Flair* (Dec. 1961): 54) or 'A Day with Our Cover Girl' (*Flair* (Nov. 1962): 30). This is an interesting precursor to the recent popularity of reality TV shows focused on the private lives of models in Australia (as elsewhere) (Safe 2008: 24).

Sydney remained for some time the centre of fashion publishing. It was the best place to get modelling work after the war, but seemed to lose its high-fashion edge. Despite the fact that the major fashion magazines were published in Sydney, the bulk of work there at this time was for newspaper advertising and store catalogues rather than fashion magazines. As much social life in this city was characterized by its relaxed outdoor environment, it is not surprising it was reflected in the style of images produced with emphasis on the seaside and informal activities. For instance a photographer like Ray Leighton, based in Sydney, came to be primarily identified with beach photography and related attire. This was one sign the city's client requirements were more casual and different from Melbourne's proclivities for couture, the latter being the city towards which top models like Janice Wakely and photographers like David Franklin subsequently gravitated. In the 1950s, Sydney had the relaxed, almost bohemian Rowe Street cultural precinct with clothes and coffee shops, and the exclusive family-owned David Jones department store but it did not have the cachet of Melbourne. Even so, a number of significant Melbourne photographers, like Henry Talbot and Helmut Newton, still fulfilled commissions for Sydney magazines. There were apparently no interstate shoots until well after the war when air transport expanded (Dally-Watkins 2002: 46). Interestingly, in 1947 the *Sydney Morning Herald* noted in its article 'Fashion Takes to the Air' that for the first time in Australia the Hythe Flying Boat *Coriolanus*, which left from Rose Bay, Sydney, had four models staging a parade on board with the theme 'Miss Tomorrow Spends a Weekend Away' (27 February 1947, p. 11).

The Australian publishing media before the mid 1940s had been embroiled in persistent discussions about what constituted female attractiveness, initially in relation to national characteristics. The identification of a national type of woman had emerged late in the nineteenth century, sometimes defined as the 'Australian Girl'. Businesses soon found it useful to use the terminology of types as an advertising tool. During the mid 1920s Berlei Corsetry claimed its products suited this national 'type' of woman, generously proportioned, with a robust healthy body, a preference for the outdoor life and sport, someone sophisticated yet unfettered by conventions, 'gloriously Greek', almost 'barbaric' (Maynard 2007: 150). These criteria formed part of photographic beauty competitions at the time. National contests, like the Miss Australia competition that commenced in 1926, and a host of local beauty contests run by newspapers in the 1920s, implied 'women were included in, or excluded from, national and modern identity by beauty or visual dereliction' (Conor 2004: 173). In the 1930s and 1940s appreciative views of Australian women, said to possess unique national characteristics, continued to be acknowledged. Fashion writer Muriel Segal in *Home* magazine explained that, for her, the Australian 'type' was not as insipid as the American, nor as hard or conservative as the English—'and very easy to look at it is' (1 March 1933: 46–7). We have our own individual type of woman, repeated Melbourne dress designer Mavis Ripper ten years later, and she should be wearing locally designed fashions (Ripper 1941: 32).

But after the Second World War, the belief in and appreciation of a so-called Australian type dissipated as urban differences in fashion firmed. For several decades after the Second World War, acknowledgement of the existence of an admirable 'Australian type' was to splinter. What emerges in the fashion press is public discussion embroiled more broadly in notions of women's appearances and comportment, often linked to the business of fashion industry modelling, sometimes ambivalent or contradictory in tenor. Within comparative textual accounts, discussion included conflicting views about where local fashions and models stood in relation to those of Europe or the USA. The rhetoric is less about pride in nation than promoting the limited local fashion market to the world. The mix of criticism and praise for the appearances of Australian women is part of a paradox that runs through other aspects of local history; a self-conscious sense of inadequacy, perhaps a characteristic of provincialism. It is possible to argue that these differing views reflected concern about where precisely Australia sat within the 'civilized' world, part of what Richard Nile (1994) suggests is the community of perpetual provisionality in Australia. He observes in his book *Australian Civilisation* that 'deep anxieties about unbelonging run pretty close to the bone of being Australian' (1994: 12, 21) and that this is indeed part of the versatile nature of nationalism in Australia. The expressed belief in some quarters that Australian women, including aspiring models, were not up to scratch, was part of a widespread mood of the period popularly called the 'cultural cringe', where Australia, what Thompson terms the 'land of non-culture' (1994: 185), looked fervently to Britain and Europe for endorsement.

But the suggestion that Australian fashion and standards of attractiveness simply deferred to Europe needs qualification. For a start, the Olympic Games held in Melbourne in 1956 were seen as an opportunity to showcase Australian products including fashions. The city buzzed, its classy stores like Georges themed around the event (Carew and Masters 2003: 39). During the 1950s there were vigorous attempts to promote wool both at international parades and locally. In 1959, the Australian Wool Bureau ran one fashion promotion in London where marketeers gave colours Australian names like Boomerang Brown (Healey 2005: 8–9). Yet Katie Somerville, curator of the 2003–2004 exhibition 'Swish. Fashionable Melbourne of the 1950s' (Ian Potter Gallery, National Gallery of Victoria), says the 1950s was an odd time in Australian society, with many feeling the country still had something to prove. There was timidity too. Australia wanted to be the equal of the world yet showed a self-effacing and humble side (Burns 2003).

Given this greater competition with overseas fashion centres, and the new consumerist ethic occurring quite rapidly after the Second World War, it is hardly surprising that this generated self-consciousness in the media about the appearances of Australian women. As trade opened up and overseas travel became more feasible (in 1947 Qantas Airlines inaugurated its new Constellation 749 connecting Australia with the UK), there was greater comparative awareness of the standards of overseas fashionable dressing and modelling. A series of French fashion shows staged from 1946 are an example of how the fashion scene shifted after hostilities ended. Newspapers, radio and newsreels accorded sensational red carpet status to the French models (with their special 'French femininity') who came out from Paris with these couture fashion shows sponsored by the *Australian Women's Weekly*. Organizer Mary Hordern recruited six French models (Mitchell 1994: 42), giving the impression she felt local ones would not carry off the French garments so successfully. The excessive publicity given the celebrity French models with their flair and special looks seemed to take the shine off local models. It also brought to light the issue of Australian taste, said to be for less extreme fashions than French couture. According to Anne Matheson, foreign correspondent for the *Women's Weekly*, Australian women, destined to wear either originals or copies of these imported clothes, lacked appropriate poise. They had 'bosoms like verandas' (Maynard 1995: 48). This is a scathing view and misrepresents the sheer elegance of much high-end dressing, especially in Melbourne.

On the one hand, commentary on Australian models praised their personalities, refreshing and unaffected appearances, their stamina and healthy appetites (*Flair* (Sept. 1959): 68). Local models were often claimed the equal or better than any on the international stage but some, according to Diane Masters (personal interview), were too 'beachy and blonde' thus not suitable for all overseas designers.[12] Sandra

Legge, a successful model overseas, is rapturously described as having perfect measurements, 'high cheekbones, a wide mouth that curves into a Mona Lisa smile and
pool-like hazel eyes slanting upward' (*Flair* (Olympic Issue 1956): 56). On the other
hand, photographers, like London-trained David Mist, were a little equivocal about
Australian models, noting 'in Europe a model looks a model 24 hours a day' but in
Sydney they are a little more casual (*Sydney Morning Herald*, 9 February 1967, p. 6).
Australia's well-known photographer Laurence Le Guay is reported in the *Herald*,
and elsewhere, as claiming beauty wasn't enough to bring success to Australians, but
only helped them over the first hurdle. He noted that their personalities were the feature that made up for looks and lack of training compared to some overseas models.
It would seem that it was for their personalities that London, New York and Paris
eagerly embraced Australians, not their sometimes frizzled over-permed hair (*Flair*
(Sept. 1959): 60, 62). Yet this is the reverse of Irving Penn's view in the 1950s, for
he apparently felt showing personality was what a model should not do (Quick 1992:
85), certainly not on the catwalk.

Other commentators were in despair at the lack of self-confidence and poor
grooming, as well as behavioural and style inadequacies of aspiring local models
(*Flair* (Olympic Issue 1956): 54). *Flair* ran frequent articles on the physical and
temperamental characteristics (personalities) that made the best models. Much like
earlier etiquette books, the magazine offered plain-speaking advice to address these
problems. Whereas Australians were noted for their versatile capabilities, they were
said to lack the confidence and quality of deportment of English, American and Eastern 'girls' (*Flair* (June 1960): 41). In 1956, one article pointed out how lax Australians were in grooming compared to their overseas counterparts. If you look at ten
women, it said, 'How many have wayward stocking seams, badly cared for hair,
chipped nail lacquer, uneven hemlines and unbrushed shoulders—We could go on
and on' (*Flair* (Olympic Issue 1956): 54). Australians have good figures, said the
magazine, but 'literally creep along like bloodhounds, with noses to the ground'
(*Flair* (June 1960): 41). The article praised Australian girls over Americans for their
tendency to choose garments to suit their own tastes (not slaves to fashion like the
Americans) and with a desire to attract the opposite sex, but claims they still made
blunders (*Flair* (June 1960): 64).

Articles such as these, which waver between praise and condemnation of Australian women, crisply encapsulate the sense in which local fashion writing was
anxiously striving to define what constituted ideal and attractive female corporality
and comportment (as epitomized by fashion models) as compared with Europe and
occasionally Asia. The writing emphasizes the somewhat immature quality of reporting in the fashion press in some instances. It also reinforces the fact that published
images and accompanying press coverage of female fashion and its models were part
of complex and shifting sets of opinions, and techniques of wearing, many of which
reinforced the local tenor in fashion and its markets.

Fashion Photography

The cultural history of commercial fashion photography emerged tentatively in Sydney and Melbourne about the time of the First World War, perhaps due to an increased feminization of readership (Palmer 2005: 99). This early history is 'the struggle between drawing and photography for dominance', with graphic fashion illustration remaining the more persistent genre (Palmer 2005: 90, 96) for some years. Half-tone fashion photos were often slotted into unrelated slabs of text in newsprint magazines and newspapers as one-offs, not as editorials. By the 1920s, proto editorials in periodicals like the *Home* emerge. These were sets of photos on one, or at the most two, pages, chiefly grouped around a common event, theme, activity, type of clothing or centred on a season such as spring.[13] Stylistically, images were conventional and picturesque, photographers being slow to adopt modernist ideas such as stark contrasts of light and shade, unusual angles and settings, something that became more common in the following decade.

Fashion photography began to gain ground in the 1930s and assisted in the status elevation of models. Russell Roberts' Studio seems to have pioneered colour photography for fashion, with its potential for presenting modern glamour in image making, an example by him in the *Home* in 1933 probably the first. But fashion photographic advertising in this medium was sporadic, although printing did improve. In 1948 a new colour negative film for studio work was introduced called Ektacolour, becoming popular after the war (*Contemporary Photography*, I/8: 44). Even so, the practical possibilities for printing true and fast colours in local laboratories were uncommon until the 1950s (McQueen 2004), though raised standards for this kind of photography were confirmed by Le Guay (*Australian Photography* 1957: 11). The fact that colour came late to fashion photography meant magazine sketches seemed more vividly appealing compared to the black and white of photographs, until the 1950s at least.

Fashion photography and fashion photographic modelling were professionalizing after the Second World War, both gaining strength from the other, though even in the late 1940s some considered the standard of specialist photography to be low. In an attempt to raise its quality, an editorial by Le Guay in *Contemporary Photography* points out the reason. In America a creative fashion photograph could command thousands of dollars, but in Australia fashion photographers received as little as 5 guineas an image (1949, 2/2: 12). The few existing fashion magazine outlets continued to use some overseas photographers, and low pay gave little or no incentive to the creativity of local fashion photographers. Le Guay notes in the same editorial that the high-priced spectacular photography in American magazines was not to be found in Australian advertising because agencies and clients preferred stock shots.

Le Guay added that clients often approached local photographers with a clipping from a *Vogue* or *Harper's* magazine, saying 'We want it like this but cheaper'.

Former models Maggie Deas and Janice Wakely confirm they posed themselves based on what they might see in the cut-out of a magazine. There were limitations in their repertoires. Deas claims mid-century Australian models used only six to seven standard poses yet some photographers like Shmith took a good deal of interest in directing posing positions. Diane Masters says that he arranged every detail of the shoot, playing music and conducting the whole thing like a photographic performance. If models were to smile, he asked them to hold their heads up and say the word 'sex'. June Dally-Watkins does admit in her autobiography that studio modelling was a rigid affair relying on clever lighting and interesting backgrounds rather than poses, with heavy tripods requiring models to remain in one spot (2002: 37). But a newspaper article in 1967 quotes Laurence Le Guay saying that with progress in camera technology, electronic lighting and fractional poses 'the old type of stiff model is OUT' (*Sydney Morning Herald*, 9 February 1967, p. 6), suggesting that some of the conventions of posing were driven by technical limitations. Animation was now acceptable.

Outside shoots were reportedly often improvisatory. According to Diane Masters, there were no stylists, only photographic assistants, if that. Yet retail company fashion co-ordinators are certainly recorded as working by the end of the 1950s (*Draper*, 10 June 1958, p. 6). From the 1920s, magazines like the *Home* had fashion editors but there was no dedicated art director. But by the late 1960s, photographic shoots were becoming closer to those of today with more adjunct staff. Advertising campaign managers like Joy Jobbins began to exert their influence mid-century as she shows in her breathless autobiography *Shoestring: A Memoir* (2006). The dominating stylist was a rarity but agencies were intrusive in suggesting models and conveying clients' ideas (Verstraeten 1966: 22). Even so, many models were 'spotted' by photographers, for a good model was the photographer's greatest asset.

Le Guay claimed it was better to have a good model than a good photographer (*Flair* (Sept. 1959): 59). Rapport between them was important (Verstraeten 1966: 22). Maggie Deas says models did not feel disempowered by the whole process, rather the reverse. They might work with little direction from photographers, although sketch artists occasionally drafted out clients' ideas. Models appear to have often been as much responsible for themselves in terms of pose and feel for the showing of clothes as the photographer, but the latter chose the site. A model must 'pool her ideas with the photographer', she will often suggest a pose of one of her attractive angles 'and ideas come thick and fast', but the photographer also calls encouragement 'chin up a little—tummy in—breathe up now—good' (*Photo Digest* (Nov. 1957): 30–1). They were also required to involve themselves in selecting some clothes and do their own hair and make-up as did overseas models. Deas says they did everything—shoes, gloves and jewelry. Maggie Tabberer and Dally-Watkins concur, the latter saying they provided all the clothing if it was a commercial advertisement (Dally-Watkins 2002: 40–1). Diane Masters confirms she had to supply stockings, various types of bra, girdles, spare accessories, false eyelashes and hairpieces. This is very different from contemporary fashion models who, according to Soley-Beltran, feel significant lack of control over their own bodies and subsumed by the clothes they are required to wear (2004: 314).

Sleek high-fashion images by the country's finest photographers often hide a background of improvisation, with demonstrable incongruities between the printed face of fashion, the almost aristocratic hauteur of some 1950s and early1960s models in *Vogue Australia*, and occasionally *Flair*, and behind-the-scene technical practices. Even in the 1960s, working procedures during shoots at *Flair* remained haphazard and were sometimes achieved on the run. The magazine operated on a low budget, often using staff members and friends as models.[14]

As much as photographers and indeed models were endeavouring to achieve and project their professionalism, magazine employees, including editors, were sometimes multiskilled, taking photographs or acting as make-up artists. The fashion photographer Marie Boam (nom de plume of Mary Williamson, *Flair*'s editor from 1962) did freelance fashion articles for the magazine under other names and took some photographs. The clear categorization today between editor, fashion editor, art director, photographer and photographer's agent, identified by Aspers (2006: 43, 55, 57), was hardly evident, if at all in some cases, until the 1960s. Even the description 'Australian fashion photography' is hard to characterize, as it sits in an ebb and flow of ideas and references, sometimes imported, or unhinged from signs of national character or anything one could call an Australian 'look' (Maynard 2009: 457–8).

Fashion Industry

The professionalizing of fashion photographic modelling (in terms of pay structures and dedicated training) after the Second World War coincided with photographers acquiring reputations built specifically on fashion, and a revitalizing and maturing fashion industry. By the late 1940s the Australian industry was also experiencing a growth spurt, accelerating in the coming decade. In the new postwar economic climate, manufacturers were keen to sell their attire on the international market and a confident new mood and international outreach appears, especially noticeable in advertising but also due to newfound commercial links being forged between Australia, Europe and the USA. In the early 1950s, UK textile and clothing manufacturers tried to establish a strong market in Australia, so there were certainly two-way influences strengthened by the first royal visit of the new queen in 1954. The British fashion and textile industry was aware that there were regional tastes in Australia. It told its exporters to expect that Australian preferences in design and fabrics were not the same across the continent partly due to climatic differences from centre to centre. It varies 'as much from Darwin to Tasmania as from the Scottish Hebrides to Mexico', claimed the *Ambassador*, the British export magazine for textiles and fashions (1952, 3: 93).

Mid-century, the local fashion scene was becoming more and more impressive claimed *Vogue*, who were happy to support some local products in its features (*Vogue Supplement for Australia* (Autumn/Winter) 1955: 45). Conversely Australian fashion manufacturers and premier designers were keen to make their mark overseas and a number of round-the-world advertising trips were undertaken expressly to showcase Australian-made fashion and set it into an international framework. In 1952 June Dally-Watkins took a one-woman fashion show of twenty garments to agencies in the USA and UK. With her was a wardrobe designed by Sydney's Frank Mitchell, part of her intention being to set up a lend-lease exchange scheme for Australian models to work in the USA, the UK and Hawaii (Dally-Watkins 2002: 92).

In *Flair*'s inaugural year, 1956, it maintained that for the first time in the history of the fashion trade in Australia, fashion exporting, not fashion importing, had become important (*Flair* (Winter 1956): 33). Three years later it boasts Australian women are developing their own fashion 'look', 'indigenous to Australia as the tweeds of England, and the "white collar" fashions of America, are to their respective countries' (*Flair* (Sept. 1959): 65). The magazine notes that Australia has its own outlook on fashion. In the article, dress manufacturer Simon Shineberg of Sharene Creations suggests 'Australian Girls' are buying clothes suited to their own personalities and not as drab or conformist as Americans (June 1960: 64). *Flair* gives prominence to local clothes and designers, but is also extremely mindful of international dressing. By the 1960s, models and their appearances, as well as the aesthetics of the fashion image, were caught up in something of a discursive conflict in this relationship to the international.

Conclusion

Throughout the first half of the century, the appearance of Australian fashion photographic models seems not dissimilar from many in images made overseas. Yet the perception of attractiveness in the looks of models, and the markets in which fashion photography operated, had subtle differences. Working practices, photographic apparatus, the role of the photographer, expectations placed on models, retailing circumstances, indeed the social context, were oftentimes specific to the geographical and social climate of the time. The whole practice of fashion photography was far more relaxed than in New York, for instance (Verstraeten 1966: 46). It is possible to argue that the country's geographic isolation, limited high-status local publications, compared to the UK and USA, and the slow start to professional fashion photography had a somewhat negative impact on photographic modelling as a profession. On the other hand, many models overcame what hurdles there were and went on to important careers, some overseas. This brings us back to Aspers's arguments about the complex, networked nature of the fashion photographic business and the co-existence of aesthetics and pragmatic factors within the market. Clearly we cannot understand the nature of modelling simply by admiring the 'looks' of a model, without close study of the surrounding, often changing modalities and networks of services that existed, from the photographer, to technical developments, agents, the status of fashion magazines and editors. It is rare if not impossible to find Australian particularities in fashion photographs at this time, other than the aesthetics of the photo shoot settings or the nationality of the photographer, but this does not discount the fact that in the local fashion business mid-century, networks of production and marketing elements were firmly linked to specific historical and socioeconomic circumstances of the period.

–6–

Performing Dreams: A Counter-History of Models as Glamour's Embodiment[1]

Patrícia Soley-Beltran

Introduction

The beauty standards embodied by fashion models hold widespread influence over the dreams of consumers all around the world. Currently, models' images and social personas are key to the social construction of glamour by performing a visual code in which normative gender, class and ethnic identity prescriptions are inscribed. In this chapter I discuss research revealing the construction of hegemonic beauty embodied by female models as symbolic containers of cultural values. In doing so, I will also explore professional models' personal experiences as a critical strategy to dispel glamour's magic allure.

My theoretical framework assumes a notion of the body as an artefact resulting from the performative reiteration of collectively defined identity norms cited and re-enacted by each individual subject (Butler 1990; Soley-Beltran 2009). The body is assumed to be a sign of personal and social identity, a key to understanding the links between individuals and hegemonic definitions of identity, that is between subjects and social institutions. Learning to control the appearance of one's body is the first lesson in symbolic embodiment to produce an acceptable identity and behaviour. Our notion of self has moved from one based on the role played within a community to one bounded by the surface of the body (Elias 2000). Subjects now feel responsible for developing their own identity and expressing it in their appearance. To serve this need, commodified identities are packaged as lifestyles (Featherstone 1988). As a consequence of the identification of the self with the body, the body works as a skeleton on which these lifestyles can be hung. As a consequence, models, initially used as mere clotheshorses, have increasingly become physical embodiments of ideal identities. They have come to represent our ideals of beauty and social perfection, while they mimic the cultural values that have produced them and exemplify the success that sanctions conformity.

The starting questions of this chapter are: how has models' glamour been constructed? What cultural values do they embody? To answer these questions, in the

first section of the chapter I will present a cultural history of modelling paying particular attention to the construction of models' public personas through the addition of
layers of meaning: class, ethnicity, nationality and so on. In doing so I will approach
the study of models' bodies as 'natural symbols' (Douglas 1970), a notion with a
long tradition in interdisciplinary gender studies (see, for instance Warner 1985).[2]
In the second section of the chapter I will compare key cultural tenets underpinning
the construction of models' *glamour*, with professional modelling experiences. I will
do so from the first-person perspective of several professional models, as revealed
in empirical data gathered from diverse sources: in-depth interviews conducted with
ex-models and model agents, models' published autobiographies and my own experience as professional model. The final section concludes that models' glamour
is an artefact achieved by means of the careful construction of their social personas
and visual representations. However, their iconic status as embodiments of beauty
standards and the success that allegedly rewards their obedience to identity norms
crumbles in the light of their personal testimonies.

From Wax-Dummies to Supermodels

> In dreams, a writing tablet signifies a woman, since it receives the imprint of all kinds
> of letters.
>
> Artemidorus (quoted in Warner 1985: 3)

As Gundle (2008: 391) has shown, 'the vast majority of figures of glamour have
been women'. Specifically, fashion models' glamour is connected to the consumption of goods and the mass commercialization of clothes through an increasing array
of media displays. While there is conflicting evidence, the history of fashion modelling arguably started in the mid-nineteenth century in Paris with Marie Vernet.
Although house models had occasionally been used to show clothes in the house
of Gagelin, Marie Vernet, a sales assistant married to dressmaker Charles Worth, is
considered the first known fashion model. Since 1852, when Madame Worth very
successfully sported her husband's crinolines amongst the Paris aristocracy, the use
of living models or *mannequins*, has increased.

At the beginning of the twentieth century Lady Duff Gordon, owner of the dress-
making establishment Lucile, Ltd. started to hire women of poor origins whom she
would groom to look like upper-class women. She transformed the showroom into
a little theatre and used background live music for the first time (for a review of the
history of fashion shows see Evans 2001). Some models became celebrities, such as
Sumurun or Dawn and Gloria, the stars of the Selfridges's fashion shows. In spite
of their fame, models were not received in polite society since mannequins were
considered menials. To make ends meet, most of them were 'looked after' by men
(Sumurun quoted in Keenan 1977: 113).

This started to change in 1924, when Jean Patou, in order to enhance his sales in America, carefully selected white US women to model his clothes, so his North American clients could identify more easily with his designs. Patou's selling strategy imbued models with a new significance: nationality. This new treatment elevated the status of modelling and contributed to make it into a socially acceptable profession. The opening of the first model agencies in the USA and London reinforced its acceptability and attracted socialites to the profession through modelling schools, which also aimed to teach debutantes social skills and beauty tricks (see Gross 1996 for a journalistic overview of modelling agencies).

Models' types were also evolving. Patou's American models were tall and slender but not all designers used 'statuesque' model girls. Cristobal Balenciaga showed his clothes on 'short, stocky women' (Lucile quoted in Steele 1985: 218) whose shapes were closer to the looks of his French couture clients. Models' looks relate to their immediate historical context, the target market and the designers' style. For instance in the period between the First and the Second World Wars models' looks evoked a goddess-like image by means of the clothes, scenarios and artwork in the classic Greco-Roman style that appealed to an aristocratic audience. In contrast, the period during the Second World War demanded a more ordinary and cheerful type of girl. In times of austerity, the 'accessibility' of the dresses and encouraging smiles were the qualities the model was asked to represent.

In 1947, after the Second World War, Christian Dior launched 'The New Look' in his Paris salon and set fashion back into extravagance and away from practicality. The use of high heels, metres of cloth in the skirts and so forth immediately identified Dior's style with wealth and caused problems for his clients and models. In March 1947, during a photographic session in a Montmartre market, Dior's clothes scandalized the crowd, most of whom were suffering poverty, and a group of women beat a model and tore her clothes off (Beevor and Cooper 1994). Nevertheless, Dior's 'New Look' went ahead and the distinction it aimed to mark demanded a new style of personality: a worldly-wise, sophisticated woman in her mid-thirties with a self-assured look. Soon, the twelve top models in New York looked like Dior's standard type: haughty eyebrows and glossy groomed hair. In 1954 Chanel presented her 'Total Look', a compound of innovative design and a relaxed attitude that evoked leisure, and that was clearly differentiated from Dior's style. Consequently, Chanel's clothes were modelled on a different type of woman. Chanel used herself and her family members as models. Her mannequins, often young aristocrats who modelled for prestige, were styled on the looks and attitudes of the designer when she was younger.

In the late 1950s, Dior caused another outrage when essaying a new modelling strategy: to hire a dark, petite and inexperienced model called Victoire. The rich Right Bank clientele of the house of Dior considered her 'little Left Bank look' (Dior quoted in Keenan 1977: 121) as an insult, but, when Dior used her again the following year, the audience were enthusiastic and called her 'the very spirit of youth'

(Dior quoted in Keenan 1977: 121). Victoire's body was Dior's attempt to symbolize the times: the rising importance of a new class of clients for the ready-to-wear (*Prêt-a-Porter*) industry. Thus, by using a model whose looks did not correspond to high society, Dior's strategy revealed an aspect of models' looks that had not been highlighted so far: social class.

As mass production of the ready-to-wear was based on standard sizes, it required models whose measures would fit the sample collection used for shows and photographed for magazines or catalogues. Thus, as made-to-measure clothes were replaced by mass-produced ones, conforming to ready-made patterns became an increasingly important requirement for models, hence continuing the process of the homogeneity of the ideal body type that, according to Stearns, was initiated in the period between wars (Stearns 2002: 181). Other relevant changes taking place in the 1960s concerned technical developments that made possible the reproduction of fashion photography in newsprints, which together with magazines, became ubiquitous shop windows that allowed women from outside society circles to know what was fashionable. The demand for photographic models increased and attitudes towards models radically changed: modelling begun to be equated with business; models and photographers became the new elite of *beautiful people* as well as the heroes of several celebrated films, such as Michelangelo Antonioni's *Blow-Up* (1966).

Different types of beauties were required to market ready-to-wear for the middle and popular classes. Hence, the classy, aloof and lady-like attitude of models, like Barbara Goalen, gave way to a more sexy, friendly and relaxed disposition, and 'girls who exaggerate the realness of themselves, not their haughty unrealness like the couture models do' were on demand (Mary Quant quoted in Keenan 1977: 127). Jean Shrimpton was one the most famous new 'natural' models of the 1960s and a middle-class ideal: 'I embodied ordinariness—which is, of course, a hugely marketable quality' (Shrimpton quoted in Craik 1994: 105). In 1966, Twiggy, the 'cockney kid' and the first model whose public persona was explicitly characterized by having popular origins, embodied an 'innocence and image of youth' (Twiggy quoted in Craik 1994: 84) but also, as Benn de Libero points out, 'cultural industry made Twiggy into a myth about the wonderfully transforming properties not of politics or social conscience, but of fashion and style' (Benn de Libero 1994: 46); a promise I will come back to in the next section.

However, the ordinary 'girl-next-door' look co-existed with more exotic styles embodied by women like Veruschka and Donyale Luna, the favourite models of *Vogue* and *Harper's Bazaar*, respectively. Both were eccentric types insofar as they did not belong to the middle classes: Veruschka was a very tall and unusual German aristocrat, and Donyale Luna was a black woman. Although black models were starting to be used in the 1960s, as model agent Marshall affirmed they featured only as 'exotic' types: 'there was no room for the average-looking girl. . . . If you were black you had to be beautiful and stunningly confident' (Marshall 1978: 114).

The economic depression of the 1970s brought a more sober fashion and tougher looks to accompany it: models' performances became closer to fifties' haughtiness and aloofness than to the sweeter style of the sixties. For the first time and, arguably, not by coincidence, during the economic recession, models' fees were incorporated into the advertising campaign of the product they were endorsing. Lauren Hutton, described by the famous agent Eileen Ford as the 'humane face' (Ford quoted in Hartman 1980: 77) because of her irregular features, became in 1973 the most highly paid model in history: $200,000 for twenty days of work a year. Thus, the 'humane face' sold millions of beauty treatments partly by symbolizing the guaranteed fulfilment of the material needs humans are bound by. Hutton was followed by Margaux Hemingway who famously got a $1-million contract to promote a new perfume in 1976. To be able to 'look like a million dollars' became paramount during economic recession. The trend accelerated in the 1980s and had its peak with the appearance of the supermodel phenomenon.

The required models' personalities and body types continued to reflect the social context. The late 1970s and early 1980s' economic buoyancy led to a demand for models who could display great 'energy' and sense of 'fun'. A variety of looks co-existed: from boyish, to 'pretty babies', to full-figured women. The increasing numbers of American customers for European fashion brought the 'Californian look' ('natural', tanned, healthy) into great demand in the male and female modelling market. At the end of the 1970s and early 1980s, some famous mannequins, such as Jerry Hall or Grace Jones, combined the catwalk work with an active and notorious nightlife in discos and nightclubs. The association between modelling and hedonist behaviour has continued to the point that models' 'partying' lifestyle is currently associated with their public persona and the products they endorse. Kate Moss's public persona, for instance is a prominent example of the 'rock chick' mirrored on the 'rock star' (Koda and Yohannan 2009: 207).

In the 1980s, fashion increasingly became a global business and advertising spread to attract larger markets. Once again, the appearance of the models' very high fees, the supermodel phenomenon, coincided with the worldwide recession at the end of the 1980s. Supermodels became 'famous consumption objects' (model Veronica Webb quoted in Elgort 1994, n.p.) whose extraordinary salaries became an inseparable part of their image. As Christy Turlington (in Koda and Yohannan 2009: 134) plainly put it, 'we make a ridiculous amount of money'. In 1994, the Corsa Vauxhall campaign 'The Supermodel' featuring five supermodels was presented as the most expensive campaign in the history of British advertising, because of their fees: 'it's actually part of the mythology that surrounds the Supermodels. . . . And it reflected superbly on us' (Stephenson-Wright responsible for the campaign, quoted in Jones 1993: 151–2). Indeed, supermodels were so expensive that they became a status sign among designers. Valentino placed a $25,000 full-page advertisement in the papers with a picture of three supermodels parading at his show to refute the rumour that he was not able to pay their wages (Blanchard 1995: 9). Supermodels' popularity increased so much that they became 'far more important than even the collections' (Jones 1993: 11). But why such hype?

In a moment of economic insecurity, the supermodels were reliable sales tools, 'a safe bet' (Mathews, fashion bookings editor at British *Vogue* quoted in Rudolph 1991: 6) and a marketing strategy since 'for an unknown company, you show the world that small as you are, you have the twenty thousand dollars (to hire a supermodel)' (model agent Galdi quoted in Gross 1996: 463). Moreover, supermodels were a proven commodity for they represented a 'global ideal' (Jones 1993: 164) of beauty, used by Western companies to target an international community: for instance Linda Evangelista and Christy Turlington sold Chanel in twenty-three countries; and Isabella Rossellini sold Lancôme all over the world. Obviously this global ideal entails uniformity of beauty standards since the preferred looks are those of the white population in the richest countries: 'despite a trend toward ethnic looks . . . in every country, blonde hair and blue eyes sell' (Chris Owen, director of British agency *Elite Premier*, quoted in Rudolph 1991: 64). The fact that the term *ethnic looks* is used to refer to all skin colours other than white effectively erases 'whiteness' as an ethnic look in itself, thus restating 'whiteness' as a characteristic of the hegemonic subject. The type of looks described by Owen still prevails amongst most current top models, such as Natalia Kurkova, Gisele Bündchen, Heidi Klum, Natalia Vodianova, Daria Werbowy, to mention only a few.

Supermodels, as a marketing strategy, involved a sort of visual neo-colonialism, insofar as in Europe and the USA, a model belonging to any ethnic background other than white does not get the same amount of advertising assignments or cosmetic contracts as white models, not even black supermodel Naomi Campbell (Hudson 1994: 8)—who has campaigned for the inclusion of a wider variety of ethnic backgrounds in modelling. While Naomi Sims was the cover of the *New York Times* supplement in 1967, it was not until 1974 that Beverly Johnson became the first black model to appear on the cover of the US *Vogue*. Most of the nonwhite models tend to be featured in one of only four roles: musician, athlete, celebrity or object of pity (Jones 1993: 14–5), or model 'exotic/ethnic' fashion—this still being particularly true of black models. Although this trend has started to change and a number of magazines are now addressing nonwhite female audiences, thus attempting to construct positive constructions of black and Hispanic women, as Helcké notes, 'positive constructions of black femininity are systematically subverted by the inescapable commercial ties that these profit-making ventures (fashion magazines) have' (Helcké 2003: 12). Therefore, most advertisements in such magazines continue to star white 'Caucasian' women. Exceptions to this rule, such as Liya Kebede for Estée Lauder or Inés Sastre for Lancôme, present a sort of 'acceptable ethnicity', since their features are a diluted version of the ethnic groups to whom they are appealing (blacks and hispanos).

The relationship between ethnicity and nationality—as mentioned earlier, one of the significant layers of meaning projected onto models—is a complex one (Soley-Beltran 2008). Following the tradition of women as vessels for ideology explored by

Warner (1985), some models have been chosen as the embodiment of the nation, for instance Inès de la Fressange, the face of Chanel in the 1980s, who modelled for the bust of Marianne—a maid symbolizing the values of the French State—in 1989, and in 2008 became the first model to be awarded the Chevalier de la Légion—France's Legion of Honour. Also in France, Carla Bruni, France's former First Lady, acts as an unofficial French fashion ambassador. The idea of female models as a 'national product', embodying a notion of 'the nation' associated with a particular ethnic group and moral qualities, is present in modelling agencies and constantly appears in fashion publications. Frisell Elburg's research (2008) confirms the association of nationality, ethnicity and moral virtues in her study of Swedish models who are expected to conform to 'Swedishness': a combination of ethnic stereotypes about Swedes as well as moral expectations concerning their 'naturalness', honesty, health and modesty. Another instance is presented by the Spanish edition of *Elle* in its January 2009 issue devoted to 'Spain as label'. In a discussion ranging from fashion design to athletes and fashion models, a fashion editorial explicitly refers to 'the new woman of pure race'[3] (2009: 153). In this editorial, white-skinned and dark-haired Spanish top model Eugenia Silva embodies the look of this stereotyped 'purity', thus signalling the ongoing presence of the old Francoist notion of a 'Spanish race'. Silva's 'pure look' is implicitly counter-posed to what the modelling industry refers to as 'ethnic beauty', namely, that belonging to a hardly visible nonwhite 'Other'. *Elle*'s discourse is particularly relevant in a country such as Spain, given its rapidly growing population of Latin American, North African and Sub-Saharan migrants, whose ethnic diversity becomes symbolically excluded from the Spanish 'national look' (Figure 6.1).

However, a superseding of the exoticizing of nonwhite models might, it is hoped, be underway as signalled by the so-called Black *Vogue* (Italy, July 2008) featuring exclusively black models, or the November 1998 issue of British *Vogue* hailing 'British Beauty' featuring Jourdan Dunn, a black model; the latter openly displaying the bond ethnicity/nationality with a more inclusive attitude. In the commercial domain, l'Oreal's campaign in France also attempted to capture 'diversity in beauty' by featuring models of North African origin, in spite of the controversy concerning the alteration of Beyoncé's skin colour in an ad for one of the company's star products.

The model as a 'celebrated commodity' (Bellafante 1995: 65) is a product of the mass marketing of fashion that started in the late 1970s and early 1980s. Designers' licenses brought moderately priced clothes to the market and increased the models' exposure to the public through street ads targeting a wider audience. The growth of media attention towards the fashion world fostered a second wave of interest in fashion on a scale comparable to that of the dailies in the late 1950s. 'Style conscious' international channels like CNN or MTV brought fashion 'into living rooms in Atlanta' where 'people don't even need to buy $5 fashion magazines anymore' (black top model and writer Veronica Webb quoted in Bellafante 1995: 65). As a consequence, modelling became a flourishing business and a cultural phenomenon of growing importance. Models have even become a referent for eroticism: since

Figure 6.1 The issue of nationality as conceived in modelling is closely linked to ethnic stereotypes, as this cover shows. Similarly, ARENA features an interview with German top model Heidi Klum in which she is described as follows: 'she's all that's right about Germany: tall, blonde and full of North-Rhine milk-fed goodness' (Emery 2007: 156). 'Made in Germany', Vogue (Germany, August 2007). *Source*: Courtesy of Condé Nast.

Cindy Crawford's shot for *Playboy* in 1988, not only do a number of prostitution ads describe sexual workers as 'models', they have even replaced the famous *Playboy* 'bunnies' (Spanish *Playboy* entitles its 2003 July issue 'The 99 Sexiest Models', a trend that has continued since).

By the early 1990s the supermodels' glamour, a new mix of approachable style and celebrity status, had definitely become part of pop culture, featuring not only in beauty products, fashion runway shows and print campaigns, but also in musical videos, TV, cinema, calendars and commercial ads for soft drinks. However, the 1990s economic crisis coincided with yet another change in beauty standards: the displacement of the 'natural healthy looks' and the arrival of the *moda povera* look, the *waif*, the *grunge* style and its *blasé* attitude. These new fashion trends demanded looks that eventually departed from supermodels' high glamour, although some aspects of it still lingered.

Most famously, Kate Moss's 'super-real' body made her into an icon of the anti-fashion statement that fashion was keen to espouse. She was the second model since Twiggy to incorporate her working-class background into her public persona. Despite stirring an outcry that the images she made with photographer and mentor, the late Corinne Day, resembled child pornography, Day claimed that 'Moss' minimal body epitomised the "honesty" naturalness, cleanliness, ingenuousness that the nineties are demanding after the "high artifice" of the eighties' (Day interviewed in *Tatler* 1993: 30). In the words of Phil Bicker, *The Face* art director at the time of her famous 1990 cover, Moss as photographed by Day 'represented something very real: the opposite, in fact, of all the unreal high glamour of fashion . . . she had . . . a freshness that matched the times' (Bicker quoted in O'Hagan 2010). The trend established by Day's documentary style spread, so one year later Spanish magazine *Telva* echoed: 'everything is now ingenuous and clean. . . . Girls, not women are the healthy aspect of the 1990s' (*Telva* 1994: 86, my translation). As a consequence of this new taste for younger looks, the age for starting a modelling career lowered and underaged models are now not uncommon.

As a backlash against supermodels, the early 1990s saw these trends developing in fashion modelling: using older models 'with more meaningful lives' (Irvine 1994: 11), models with 'unusual' features (*Elle* Sept 1993; Jeal 1994), or anonymous 'real people' (Dudgeon 1994: 15), that would accompany the move towards deconstructivist and minimalist design. Often, these 'more real' models were professional models or actors hired from agencies like 'Real People' in London. Calvin Klein, for instance claimed that 'what is real is beautiful' (Klein quoted in Irvine 1994: 11) since allegedly, perfect looks can be achieved through plastic surgery. Thus, since 'perfection' became homogenized 'it's no longer couture; it's middle-market look', as a consequence, 'the unevenness of individual beauty adds value' (Klein quoted in Irvine 1994: 12). The continuation of this trend, albeit with a different philosophy, can be traced to Dove's 'Campaign for Real Beauty'.

These trends partly functioned as strategies to avoid supermodels' fees and fame, which were said to be eclipsing the clothes. At the time, all the 'style gurus' agreed that the trend for real, 'ordinary' people was 'just a revolution in fashion's cycle of reversals' (Klein quoted in Irvine 1994: 12). Nowadays, apart from some renowned names, fees have gone down dramatically, careers are much shorter and *real people* is a term regularly used in models' agencies to refer to persons with no particularly striking features who are often employed in advertising and underpaid, but who have not at all displaced the use of slender and tall glamorous models. In spite of the growing importance of actresses and celebrities in the promotion of fashion, not only are some of the 1980s Supermodels still active, but also new 'celebrity supermodels' have followed them, such as recycled Kate Moss or Gisele Bündchen.

Although the public exposure of top models might now be lower than in the 1980s, the supermodel phenomena succeeded in raising models' prestige as a strategy to support the spread of women's fashion and beauty standards worldwide. Models as the new celebrities and the 'luxury boom' (Lipovetsky and Roux 2004) of the 1980s came together with an increase of the power of fashion as a normative authority, feeding other enterprises, such as the global music and entertainment business. In spite of the search for 'realism' pursued in the 1990s as a reaction against 1980s dream-like glamour—captured by the documentary style of photography named 'dirty realism'—models continue embodying the glow of acquisitive power, social success, desirability and media attention. Indeed, the extremely lucrative careers of supermodels like Moss or Bündchen make headlines all over the world, thus continuing to embody the high rewards of body work and body capital through the transformational myth encapsulated in glamour. There is no doubt that, as the luxury goods and beauty industry so proudly claim, models' glamour shines globally. But, what is making them glow so brightly?

Speaking Dolls

> I am an optical illusion.
>
> (Top model Clotilde quoted in Lakoff and Scherr 1984: 111)

The cultural history of models I traced above reveals the social construction of these professionals as cultural icons through the successive adding of meaningful layers, such as class, nationality, ethnic background, earning power and glamour. In this section, I will deal with other aspects of models' public personas, the social conditions of their production, as well as its public and personal perceptions of their work. In doing so, I will draw from a set of interviews that are part of an empirical research project concerning the social construction of beauty standards and their public perception. The project, funded by a Francesca Bonnemaison Research Grant for Equal Opportunities and Gender, carried out ten in-depth interviews with male and female fashion models, and one model agent in Spain in 2009 (Soley-Beltran 2010b). The interviews dealt with modelling performance and body self-perception, as experienced by models themselves, thus using oral history as a valuable source in fashion research, as forcefully argued by Lomas (2000). In the project and the present text I take what Colebrook terms a 'pragmatic' approach to the study of beauty, that is a nonjudgemental stance that is not interested in establishing the rightness of beauty standards for women, but rather in researching 'how is beauty defined, deployed, defended, subordinated, marketed or manipulated, and how do these tactics intersect with gender and value?' (Colebrook 2006: 132).

Since the 1920s flappers, glamour has been produced as an 'artificial' kind of beauty associated with fashion, modernity and consumerism (Gundle 2008: 160).

Accordingly, the fashion business presents identity as an artificial construct that we can partake of if, and only if, we accept the transformational myth the industry promotes. A manual for models declares: 'a girl could be striking once she had been taught skin care, make-up and deportment by experts at a good school, and once her hair had been shaped and she had acquired a *personality*' (Dixon and Dixon 1963: 34, emphasis added). Furthermore, 'the nameless girls whose careers endure for years are the chameleons who lose their own identities in whatever the fashion of the moment happens to be' (fashion editor quoted in Keenan 1977: 136). Hence, manuals recommend: 'You must be so adaptable that your own personality can be constantly modified, played down or even radically changed to fit the requirements of each photograph' (Dixon and Dixon 1963: 80). Similarly, a disposition to accommodate character to appearance is desirable: 'Naomi [Campbell] learnt that . . . clothes have their own personality, and . . . [that] a good model becomes the clothes she wears, adapting her own character to complement the garment' (Jones 1993: 56). The disciplined supermodel confirms: 'everything I put on feels different, it's like a different character' (Campbell quoted in Jones 1993: 56).

The ability to adapt their image as chameleons do confers models a longer shelf life and defers the feared 'burning out' moment when the glamour implodes and these professionals are discarded as old dolls. However, the ability to adapt does not only concern models. This 'chameleonic' adaptability is a cultural and social value in its own right, given that the rapidly changing economic conditions also demand subjects with the capacity to acquire new skills, spatial mobility and general malleability, to adapt to a highly volatile job market.

Slenderness is another key element of the beauty canon initially incarnated by the flapper figure, which became associated with leisure and dynamism. All through the twentieth century beauty became increasingly standardized, and a slim body is now an hegemonic canon in Western countries where it stands as a sign of glamour, understood as the transcendence of material necessities, self-control and youth. Fashion models have become a slenderness ideal type and are defined by manuals as the 'skeleton of beauty', 'almost literally a clothes-horse' (Dixon and Dixon 1963: 25, 80). In modelling, being slim helps to focus the viewers' attention on the garments and away from the models' bodies; often other strategies, such as uniformization of the models' looks through wigs or make-up, are used in order to focus attention on the clothes. For reasons of space and scope, I will not go into the important issue of models' ideal slenderness as one of the possible causes for the increase of eating disorders. For a classic reference see Bordo (1993).

Besides malleability and slenderness, the search for the 'look' promoted by fashion inspires the exhibition of private life which gets treated like theatre, a performance. Thus, 'glamour is always theatrical' (Gundle 2008: 389), since it requires visibility in order to catch audiences' attention and trigger the envy look that sustains consumers' desire. Clothing and make-up are marketed as products that fit in with the individual's state of mind and allow him or her to express it, thus promoting them to 'wear' their mood. Self-expression through body and body surface works as an incentive for showing off and consumption is also exemplified by models' performance: 'to me dressing is an emotional exercise. If I'm depressed, I wear sombre colours. If I am alone, I wear something bright. If I am comfortable with myself, I'll put on wool socks and Birkenstocks, leggings and sweater' (Veronica Webb cited in Elgort 1994). As Barthes notes, in fashion the multiplication of personalities in a single being is presented as an index of power (Barthes 1977: 256–7). Since clothes are equated with personalities, the possession of a variety of garments that reveal different characters is interpreted as a sign of wealth and personal strength (see Soley-Beltran 2004a: 318, for an example of a major fashion editorial illustrating this issue).

Maybe owing to the surface exhibition and multiplication of personalities promoted by fashion, young models often feel confused in relation to their own personality or find it difficult to identify with the character they are asked to embody. As a consequence, they often report feeling unreal and empty, 'this crazy business . . . it's all about surface. Nobody cared about the real Janice, about what I had going on inside. And then I wondered, *What if I look inside and find nothing?*' (Raymond 2002: 175, emphasis in the original). Indeed, models are trained to perform a look encapsulating a 'personality', that, as Veronica Webb (in Elgort 1994) remarks, might be far removed from their own self, since they often are a 'fourteen year-old . . . dressed up to look like a sophisticated creature. They're not always what meets the eye'. Former model and photographer Corinne Day (in O'Hagan 2010) expresses a possible reaction to the building up of 'looks': 'it was something I just felt so deep inside, being a model and hating the way I was made up. The photographer always made me into someone I wasn't.' As a consequence, modelling 'unconsciously and subtly inspires insecurity', as model agent Carolina Cabanillas (*Francina*, Barcelona) observes. Swedish model Ossa Stensson confirms this point: 'I thought I was a hot chick until I started working as a model. Now I'm conscious of every part of my body, of things I had never been previously aware and that I will now be conscious of forever' (Ossa quoted in Soley-Beltran 2010b: 76).

The promise of success through body transformation and style, that fashion discourse symbolizes via models' chameleon-like character, and the public display of their lives as spectacle, is particularly visible in the discourse of economic and social improvement of young women who, reportedly, have risen from poor backgrounds to achieve fortune and fame through their modelling career. Concerning modelling as a professional option for women, two myths surface: the traditional myth of the model who marries into money or society, and the newer myth of the model as an autonomous self-possessed woman.

Concerning the first myth, a 'fairy story for grown ups' (Jones 1993: 11) full of commonplaces such as those presented in the 1950s Hollywood film *How to Marry a Millionaire*, it reiterates a notion of woman as an object whose beauty is instrumental for upward social mobility. Given that celebrity and economic success rewards conformity to normative identity patterns, models seem to establish the positive limits of such patterns, thus acting as the reverse of prostitutes who, in Juliano's analysis (Juliano 2002), symbolize its negative limits. Thus, it could be argued that, in opposition to prostitutes who are 'fallen' women, models are 'ascended' women. In certain professional circles, it is not uncommon to find young women who combine both jobs to make ends meet or to increase their earnings, as Sumurun herself declared (see above; also see Gross 1996: 417, 425).

Instances of models marrying into money are often given by the glossies, such as British actress Elizabeth Hurley in the UK, Spanish model Laura Ponte in Spain or Russian model Natalia Vodianova, who went 'from fruit seller to the world's best paid model' (*Lecturas* 2003: 90). The idea of models as 'rural Cinderellas' moving from rags to riches and charmingly embodying the 'image of the times' (Koda and Yohannan 2009: 191) supports the narrative of a 'rise from nothing' via *glamour*, understood as 'the illusion that individual lives could be enhanced and improved by ostensibly magical means' (Gundle 2008: 389, 388). However, in spite of this 'New Cinderellas' discourse presenting modelling as a fair chance of escaping poverty, in fact, only a very few young women actually manage to achieve economic stability working as models. Maybe some 'attain this idea they initially dreamt about: glamour, model life, travelling, living like a goddess, surrounded by fabulous people . . . [but] many of these [models] don't even manage till the end of the month, and they continue fighting for this ideal, they don't achieve anything and they continue, and continue, and continue . . . ' (model agent Carolina quoted in Soley-Beltran 2010b: 78).

With regard to the second myth, the model as an autonomous self-possessed woman in charge of her career, it is also a fiction devised by the fashion and modelling industries and reiterated by newspapers and popular literature. Allegedly, supermodels are to be admired for taking control of the commercial exploitation of their own sexuality, instead of leaving it to others (Jones 1993: 11; Rudolph 1991: 64); moreover, it is argued that self-management in the exploitation of sexuality is an achievement of feminism. Camille Paglia reiterates this myth by regarding supermodels as a very necessary 'icon and role model' since they have successfully achieved the goal of the nineties' women: 'to be sexual and career women at the same time' (Paglia quoted in Jones 1993: 11–12). In fact, very few models actually manage themselves, as agents and models declare:

> models have little control over their lives . . . it is about living by the look and advice of somebody else. . . . I'm managing you, everybody clearly understands that it is total control, you don't even visit your boyfriend without telling me. (Model agent Carolina quoted in Soley-Beltran 2010b: 70)

A model observed, 'I never felt in control as a model. I never knew what was going to happen to me next. And the girls who really lasted . . . never were the best models; they were just the ones who had these great business advisers telling them what to do' (Lisa Taylor quoted in Craik 1994: 82). There are, however, other ways of dealing with the job, such as those of Elle McPherson or Crawford, who sees herself as 'a president of a company who owns a product, Cindy Crawford, that everybody wants' (Crawford quoted in *The Fashion Book* 1998: 117).

In spite of the professional reality described above, in fashion discourse, beauty is associated with socioeconomic power and high self-esteem. Indeed, self-confidence is an emotion models constantly perform, although the aesthetical and emotional expression of social status and self-assurance has varied from Dolores who played 'Empress of Fashion, the Discourager of Hesitancy' in Ziegfeld Follies (Evans 2001: 283), to the 'polished *froideur*' that signified 'class' (*The Fashion Book* 1998: 54, referring to model Bettina), ending in the permanent euphoria of being 'three or four glasses of champagne high' (Moncur 1991: 2) or 'the great "fuck you" moment when you looked like you had it all' (Webb quoted in Perkins and Givhan 1998: n.p.). Yet the performance is undercut by models' perceptions of their bodies as alien to them:

> The profession inspires and suggests unconsciously and in a very subtle manner an abysmal insecurity . . . the laws of the market are what make these girls feel more and more insecure all of a sudden. (Model agent Carolina quoted in Soley-Beltran 2010b: 75)

Nevertheless, in the eyes of the public, to 'be' a model is tantamount to obtaining the 'official certificate' in beauty, certifying normative compliance and social acceptability. By embodying alleged physical perfection and permanent self-confidence, models' images and public personas make people believe in the utopian possibility of avoiding the discredit and abjection that menaces many women for not conforming to aesthetic and behavioural norms. The underlying notion is that self-confidence can be achieved through conformity to beauty standards, and that such conformity is rewarded with self-deserved assertiveness and a better social position. However, models are aware of the faked aura surrounding their job:

> the job is a little mythified . . . because a girl opens a magazine and sees everybody is perfect . . . one does not see reality . . . one is overcome by a feeling: 'oh, I will never be like these [girls]', but one should know that . . . there is a bit of a lie in all this . . . not a single picture is published without Photoshop. (Model Lavinia Birladeanu quoted in Soley-Beltran 2010b: 87)

The association of modelling with an ideal state is not only related to a high income thus alluring the disenfranchised, but also to the imagined possibility of living in a pleasant dream, an illusion promoted by designers: 'I don't even want to be a lady. I want to be a woman . . . the clothes are so beautiful. It's fantasy' (Isaac Mizrahi quoted in Perkins and Givhan 1998: n.p.). Similarly, Dior declared: 'The world is a cruel place, women must become their smile' (Dior quoted in Quick 1997: 71—my translation); and Ralph Lauren declares: 'I do not design clothes, I design dreams' (Lauren in *Marie Claire* 2003: 132). Therefore, what is being promoted is a fantastic idea of womanhood paired with the aspiration to an existence beyond restrictions. For this reason, it is affirmed that models' bodies 'transcend the limits of culture' (Versace 1997: 7) and fashion is celebrated as a postmodern phenomena, given that: 'when substance is dead, style lives on' (Fink 2000: n.p.). Hence, models' public personas can be interpreted as 'simulacra' (Baudrillard 1993), that is sophisticated artefacts performed and marketed by a team of professionals that become the reference for gender perfection and desirability as if they were 'real'.

The artificiality of beauty standards and models' public personas is articulated in a contrast between real/unreal beauty present in the modelling discourse. Such contrast is superseded by conceiving the body as an artefact constituted by the reiteration of collectively defined norms regulating identity. If we understand the body as the site of the interaction between the individual and the collective, we can account for the special erasure between the private and the public spheres that models experience. A number of them have a very acute perception of the gap between 'private' self-notion and the 'public' image that is demanded of them, as this model observed:

> I felt intimately involved in my job since my own emotions were reflected in my body and its movement when performing. In contrast, I felt strong limitations were being placed on the expression of my private self, since I had to adjust to the publicly established canons, which felt to me like a prison. It felt as if I was in a school for young ladies being trained to be the courtesan. (Cristina)

Often models feel alienated from their own image. The need to consider one's own body appearance as a professional 'instrument' forces models to undergo humiliation with 'professionalism' since their job involves being used 'as a piece of flesh' (top model and agent Wilhelmina quoted in Hartman 1980: 77). Interestingly, alienation is accompanied by models' awareness of the performative action their job has on their self-perception: 'to a certain extent, you become your own image' (Cristina); 'one gets reduced to an image. And for the profession, to a surface. One unavoidably becomes egocentric. One permanently looks at one's navel' (Fressange 2002: 115). Moreover, their sense of self is deeply affected: 'I always had the crazy idea of buying dresses thinking that I would feel better. As if feeling well in my body would come from the exterior and not from myself' (Fressange 2002: 117). As a consequence of having to be self-centred as a job requirement (Gross 1996: 6), models suffer from an acute sense of exposure and fragility: 'The more visible I become the more invisible I feel' (Moss quoted in Mackay 1995: 3). A similar experience is described by Polly Dorothy MacGowan, the fictional model starring in the film *Qui êtes-vous Polly Magoo?* (written and directed by William Klein, 1965; cited in Gross 1996: 37):

> Who am I? I'm Polly, Polly Magoo. But between us, I'm not sure how I can answer you. You ask who I am. Sometimes, I ask myself, too. They take my picture. Everyday, they take my picture, and that makes millions of times that they've taken my photo. And each time they take my picture, a little bit less of me is left. So what can I have left in the end? I ask you.

Seventies top model, Apollonia von Ravenstein, presents a testimony of the confusion endured by many young models:

> You are thrown into this arena, thinking people love you for who you are. There was some emotional disappointment and a lot of learning about human nature. I didn't really feel that people cared about what I was like. They had to love to be with me because I was a gorgeous young woman, and tall and beautiful, and a lot of fun. But I did feel an emptiness inside, and a certain sadness, because there was such untruth, it was such a fake. It is very overwhelming and terribly exciting, and it can be profoundly empty at the same time. I didn't understand people, I didn't understand what they were after, the promises they made. (Ravenstein quoted in Gross 1996: 287)

Indeed, models often feel different from the picture they portray: 'I felt bad inside my body and very rarely splendid' (Fressange 2002: 117, my translation); or 'It's hard to work on the catwalk . . . you are surrounded by the forty most beautiful women in the world. You see all your imperfections and none of theirs' (Cindy Crawford cited in Rudolph 1991: 66; for more examples from celebrity models see Soley-Beltran 1999). Moreover, agent Carolina Cabanillas, from *Francina and Volitif* (Barcelona), estimates that only 20 per cent of models gain security from their job, whereas the other 80 per cent become more insecure, given that it forces them to 'live by the gaze and the advice of others, it is like living in a prison, it debilitates them' (Carolina cited in Soley-Beltran 2010b: 71).

Becoming a commercialized commodity also affects models' self-perception and sense of dignity: 'in the end what matters is your turn-over and the money you are earning because, if one earns a load of dough, they [the agency] will bow at you' (Mireya Ruiz quoted in Soley-Beltran 2010b: 80); Gora's experience, in another interview, confirms: 'to me the hardest [part] was at the agency, if you had been working a lot for a period, you would arrive and they treated you as the queen, everybody would say hello and speak to you. If there was a period without work, they ignored you. This is what hurt the most' (Gora quoted in Soley-Beltran 2010b: 80). The objectification in modelling work is related to the production of glamour, as a quality of thrill and wealth, since models' public personas are surrounded by an aura of desirability, admiration and economic and social success.

Glamour works by presenting itself as inaccessible and magical, while, at the same time, it must be seen as attainable in order to fulfill its double task: fostering envy by creating an aura of desirability around a particular product, and promoting the consumption of the publicized item. As Berger showed (1972: 133–4), in advertising, the supposedly 'new' transformed state achieved by the consumption of the advertised products is presented as an enviable and fascinating situation. In order to support this belief, it is necessary to build up an aura surrounding those persons that have undergone this positive change, supposedly caused by a specific product or fashion garment. The allure is embodied by advertising subjects, models, as 'technical bodies' (Craik 1994) whose image is hired to visually represent glamour. As a consequence, the looks and public personas of models get surrounded by an apparently enviable aura. Hence, advertising promotes the 'look of envy' that fosters desire towards a product or a body standard by creating a sense of uneasiness and inappropriateness. Consuming the product would rarely erase this sense of unsuitability, in spite of this being precisely the promise embodied by models as examples of its transformational properties.

In my personal experience as a fashion model, far from giving me a feeling of empowerment, as was often assumed, the 'glamour' I embodied made me anxious, for I was aware of arousing a desire I knew I could not possibly fulfill. By contributing

Figure 6.2 As a model I performed a very happy, smiling person, to enact a series of characters that ranged from young women to middle-aged house-wives. This picture was taken at the end of my career. At the time I was simply unable to smile without bringing on facial muscular spasms. Model: Patrícia Soley-Beltran. Photographer: Emerico Mancuso. Body painting and styling: Carmen Benages. *Source*: Patrícia Soley-Beltran.

to the performance of the 'the looks of envy' that characterizes the construction of glamour (Berger 1972: 133; Gundle 2008), I felt I was exposing myself to others' frustration and accusations of leading them to dissatisfaction. As a consequence, I lived in fear of my own 'model' self and others' craving (Figure 6.2).

As we have seen, to embody an utopia has its downsides, such as being alienated from one's own image, being considered as unreal or intellectually handicapped, becoming the object of envy and so on. In fact, the image of models as 'independent' (Castle 1977: 84), or 'young self-possessed women' (O'Neill 1985: 101) crumbles as one learns about their complete dependence on their agents, their chronic insecurity concerning their physique, the health hazards caused by dieting, the amount of unrecognized emotional labour that goes into it (Mears and Finlay 2005), and the lack of confidence ex-models then go on to experience in their subsequent careers due to the assumption that they only get work because of their physical appearance (Foley 1989).

In order to keep a minimal sense of personal dignity, models develop strategies to distance themselves from their model persona in the shape of critical autobiographies (such as Moncur 1991; Fressange 2002), documentaries (as in former model Sara Ziff's 2008 documentary *Picture This*) or artwork (such as the work of artists Susanne Junker, Chris Mundy or Vera Lehndorf—whose artistic name as a model was Veruschka). Lehndorf's portraits explicitly aimed to work 'against my modelling career' (Lehndorf quoted in *The Fashion Book* 1998: 483) by painting her naked body mimicking several backgrounds (stones, the rusted walls of old factories) to the point of making it disappear, thus counteracting 'Veruschka, a fictitious character symbolising pure perfection'. As such, she became 'one of the most famous and well-paid models in international fashion' (Lehndorf and Hubertus Ilse 2006).

Conclusion

> *La beauté n'est que la promesse du bonheur.*
>
> (*De l'Amour*, Stendhal)

Considering beauty as a very powerful symbol and approaching the true *backstage* of fashion—not the one supposedly 'revealed' by the banal pictures of the wings of the catwalk, but that of the social *dispositifs* (apparatuses) that constitute female beauty standards—proves to be a fruitful exercise. As the cultural history of fashion modelling discloses, the social construction of models' images and public personas conveys symbolic meanings concerning class, nationality, ethnicity, social mobility, self-control, malleability, wealth, power, success and the alleged self-assurance that accompanies them.

The glamour surrounding models is produced as a pleasant dream linked to consumerism, narratives of economic and social improvement, and obedience to the cultural values defining and regulating the normative standards for acceptable identity.

Hence, their allure can be considered as an artefact allegedly produced by the transformational properties of body work and the products they endorse. In sum, models' public personas symbolize an ideal self and allegedly demonstrate the possibility and desirability of its attainment. They have become icons of beauty and social perfection exemplifying success as a reward for conformity.

The experiences of professional models, however, reveal that such performances have their drawbacks, such as lack of control over their professional careers; alienation from their own selves, bodies and emotions; personal insecurity; commodification and so on. Nevertheless, the discourse conveyed through models presents glamour as a relatively affordable quality, providing one obeys the prescribed bodily standards and makes the right consumption choices. Through its visual power, the industry of luxury goods spells its magic to create unattainable icons inspiring desires whose fulfilment is forever deferred.

Models are both performers and subjects of performativity: they are performers insofar as it is their professional duty to efficiently embody the collectively defined standards of visual identity; they are also subjects of performativity insofar as they are themselves constituted by their disciplined reiteration of these standards. As shown, models learn to exert a tight control over their bodies, facial expressions, appearance, public conduct and self-understanding in accordance with prescribed ideals, while their public personas are fashioned into sophisticated artefacts through the successive addition of layers of symbolic meanings.

The study of modelling discloses how an artificial construct, models' public personas, can become a reference for prestigious imitation and desirability as if they were attainable and real. As I have argued elsewhere (Soley-Beltran 1995, 1999), in ancient English the term *glamour* was etymologically related to the word *grammar*, since *glamour* was the aura that surrounded those who, by virtue of being literate, hold spelling power. In the age of visual communication, models are emblems of cultural values and their *glamour* is still related to the economic and social power allegedly achieved through the consumption of the advertised goods and lifestyles. When models break their silence, their testimonies 'dispel' glamour as a carefully crafted fiction.

Part II

–7–

The Figure of the Model and Reality TV[1]

Stephanie Sadre-Orafai

Introduction

For the first time in its more than fifty-year televised history, the Miss America pageant lost its network contract in 2004. Citing dwindling viewership, ABC withdrew sponsorship from the then eighty-four-year-old competition. Whereas in the 1990s the pageant boasted twenty-seven million viewers for the annual single episode, in 2004 it drew fewer than ten million, costing the network nearly $6 million for the rights to air it (de Moraes 2004). While the pageant eventually found a home that year on CMT, a cable country music channel, other shows with seemingly similar objectives of aesthetic evaluation flourished in network lineups. Cheaper to produce and occurring in a serial format over several weeks, shows like *America's Next Top Model* (UPN 2003), *Man Hunt: The Search for America's Most Gorgeous Male Model* (Bravo 2004) and *Sports Illustrated Swimsuit Model Search* (NBC 2004)[2] augmented the traditional beauty contest with an increasingly popular reality television format—the 'TV talent/job search' (Ouellette and Hay 2008)—and replaced the pageant stage with the backdrop of the fashion industry. Denaturalizing beauty, these shows emphasized the production practices that went into the creation and valorization of aesthetic performances and the multiplicity and nonexclusivity of a diversity of aesthetics related to niche markets (e.g. trends in male, swimsuit, commercial and/or editorial fashion modelling). Seemingly more in line with feminist and liberal multiculturalist critiques of the disjuncture between ascribed and achieved status and social justice through their deployment of what literary theorist Douglas Mao has phrased 'the labour theory of beauty' (2003), these shows both changed the terms by which contestants were judged and deemed beautiful and ostensibly made the process not only more transparent but also more accessible.

While neither interest in nor reality-based programming about models and the fashion industry is necessarily a new phenomenon, the rise of shows like *America's Next Top Model* at a time of waning visibility and name recognition of working models is notable. These shows signal the expanding definition of fashion commodities to include not only fetishized objects alienated from the processes of their production (e.g. a designer handbag or a fashion photograph) but also the lifestyles and labour of fashion producers themselves. Unlike shows that appeared on cable network television in the late 1980s and early 1990s, such as *House of Style* (MTV 1989) or Canadian-produced imports like *Fashion File* (1989) and *Fashion Television* (1985) syndicated on E! Entertainment Television, recent fashion reality shows do not rely on the popularity and celebrity of models for their appeal. Emphasizing instead the labour required to produce aesthetic images over and above their contemplation or aesthetic evaluation, they complicate the ways audiences encounter seemingly unquestioned assumptions about beauty. In the absence of supermodels or even famous named models, these shows fill the vacuum with new reality stars qua models. In so doing, they reframe the figure of the model. In fact, the rise of these shows marks a popular shift in interest from models as celebrity personalities to an interest in modelling as a quotidian and allegoric practice. Whereas previous programmes highlighted the glamour and exclusivity of modelling and fashion professions, recent shows underscore the broad applicability of fashion work, chronicling unknowns' attempts at these practices. These shows present an alternative way of reading models' bodies, performances and images as a kind of evidence, or index of particular forms of labour and desire, rather than solely as icons or representations, which provides new measures of effective (and affective) images.

In this chapter I explore how an emphasis on labour and a reframing of fashion images as evidence on these shows reinforces structural hierarchies and inequalities even as it appears to challenge them. Placing the proliferation of these kinds of shows within a broader framework of commercial multiculturalism and shifting trends in fashion industry production practices (e.g. the globalization, multiplication and fragmentation of design practices, the rise in prominence and importance of stylists and casting professionals and the expansion and professionalization of the modelling industry), I argue that recourse to seemingly neutral terms like *evidence* and *effort*, which are present both on these shows and in the modelling industry itself, not only mask discriminatory judgement processes, but also reinforce durable theories of visibility, personhood and authenticity. Following Ouellette and Hay's observation that the placement of 'TV talent/job search' reality shows in creative industries, like music, fashion and other performing arts, is purposeful and re-presents the demands of an increasingly flexible economy (2008: 131), I show how these programmes advance tenets of new forms of neoliberal labour (cf. Wissinger 2007; Entwistle and Wissinger 2006). That is by using idioms of desire and labour (both the internal work of self-awareness and the external work of becoming a medium through which this internal work and the work of others can be displayed) these shows place the burden of failure and success on individual contestants isolated from broader social dynamics and structural inequalities rather than as individuals enmeshed within them.

This chapter is part of a larger ethnographic project on model casting and development practices in the New York fashion industry in which I explore modelling and casting as metaphors for broader racialized practices of typification, evaluation and social interaction in the USA.[3] I argue that similar ideas about labour, desire and desert animate model industry practices, shaping and reinforcing how models are positioned vis-à-vis other industry actors, particularly in terms of how agency and creativity are differentially recognized and rewarded. Rather than use the ethnographic data as cases of 'actual' or 'real' model development meant to correct or corroborate the 'fake' mediated representations of development on these programmes, my goal instead is to show the broader cultural transformations and enduring structural inequalities and hierarchies by which both are guided. To this end, I focus on the figure of the model. In using the concept *figure*, I follow an eclectic trajectory of anthropologists (Carnegie 1996; Haraway 1997; Hartigan 2005; Linder 2007; Weismantel 2001) and literary theorists (Lowe 2006; Mao 2003) who have employed the term to demonstrate the mutually constitutive power of stories, images and stereotypes and the embodied and interactional effects these constructions have as they 'hover above everyday life, distorting actual relations between people and recasting them in their own strange image' (Weismantel 2001: xxvi). The figure of the model provides a unique vantage on both contemporary US society and the everyday practices and politics of the fashion industry. As these shows reshape the figure of the model and its meanings in contemporary society, it is critical that we understand how it happens. In the next section I trace the development of these shows, showing their reach across network and cable stations and countries around the world.

From Miss America to *America's Next Top Model*

America's Next Top Model (*ANTM*), one of the first and arguably the most successful version of the modelling 'TV talent/job search' format, first aired in the USA in 2003 on UPN, a subsidiary network of CBS Paramount. It was created by executive producers Tyra Banks, a well-known African American model, and Ken Mok, a reality television producer who had previously worked on *Making the Band* (ABC 2000), a similarly themed 'TV talent/job search' centering on composing and grooming the next 'boy band'. Initially producers used Banks's own modelling career trajectory as scaffolding for the show's structure and competition challenges and drew judges and industry sponsors from her personal contacts. While weekly episodes of the tenth season, which aired in the first half of 2008 on the CW network (the resulting network of the 2006 merger of UPN and Warner Brothers' WB network), averaged domestic viewership of around four million (Kissell 2008), the show captured numbers as high as 6.19 million in December 2006 for its eighth-season finale (Kissell 2006). In addition to being simultaneously broadcast and syndicated in more than 100 countries (Hirschberg 2008), *ANTM* is also a lucrative franchise with licensed national and regional versions in current, former or proposed production in more than twenty countries, including Sweden, Denmark and Ukraine (Guider 2005); Australia, Brazil, Britain, Canada, China, the Czech Republic, France, Germany, Holland,

Hungary, Norway, the Philippines, Russia, Thailand and Turkey (Schneider 2006); and most recently Finland, Croatia, Italy and the Caribbean (Lew 2008). Outside of officially sanctioned international franchises, similar concepts are produced around the world either as serials or one-time specials, including versions in Belgium, Nigeria, Ghana and Honduras. VH1, a Viacom-owned cable music television station, secured domestic syndication rights for the show in 2005 (Martin 2005), and alongside its sister station MTV, routinely screens *Top Model* marathons, including episodes of English-language franchises like *Britain's Next Top Model* and *Australia's Next Top Model* alongside its own original model- and fashion-centred reality programming.

In the five years following the debut of *ANTM*, the number of similarly themed model 'TV talent/job search' series exploded in the United States, ranging from niche market programmes catering to women over thirty-five as on *She's Got the Look* (TV Land 2008), to shows like *America's Most Smartest Model* (VH1 2007) that lampooned the format. Other shows more closely followed the *ANTM* formula, but added key innovations aimed at capturing a more realistic process, by including younger teenagers and foreign-based models like in *A Model Life* (TLC 2007) or pitting male and female models against one another and shooting in 'real time' to allow for audience votes to decide eliminations as in *Make Me a Supermodel* (Bravo 2008). These programmes appeared alongside other model-centric 'docusoaps', or reality-based narratives structured around key characters and their relationships rather than competitions (Ouellette and Murray 2004: 4). Set against the backdrop of modelling agencies in New York, Los Angeles and Miami, these shows followed the working and personal relationships of both models and agents as they negotiated the ups and downs of casting and development practices. Shows like *8th and Ocean* (MTV 2006) set at Irene Marie Models in Miami; *Runway Moms* (Discovery Health 2006) based at Expecting Models, an agency specializing in pregnant and nursing models, in New York; *The Janice Dickinson Modeling Agency* (Oxygen 2006) set at the same-titled agency conceived for the show in Los Angeles; *Models NYC* (MSNBC 2007) based at Q Model Management in New York; and *The Agency* (VH1 2007) set at Wilhelmina Models, also in New York, shared slots with other fashion-based reality competitions. Precipitated by *ANTM*, these shows similarly focused on aspiring fashion professionals, including designers, as on *The Cut* (CBS 2005) and *Project Runway* (Bravo 2004); hair stylists, as featured on *Shear Genius* (Bravo 2007); magazine editors, like *Miss Seventeen* (MTV 2005) and *Stylista* (CW 2008); photographers, like *The Shot* (VH1 2007); fashion stylists, like *My Model Looks Better Than Your Model* (BETJ 2006) and *Glam God* (VH1 2008); press agents, like *PoweR Girls* (MTV 2005); and a mix of industry jobs, as showcased on *The Fashionista Diaries* (SOAPNet 2007).

While many narrative and casting choices on the shows are produced for entertainment value and to appeal to mass audiences rather than a documentary imperative, there is nevertheless deep industry participation. It takes the form of both corporate sponsorship of prizes and challenges, which provide opportunities for cross-platform promotion and advertising while also lending legitimacy to the programmes, and judging and guest appearances by industry professionals. Wilhelmina has been one of the most visible agency sponsors, offering agency contracts on two separate programmes while also being profiled on its own reality series. As such, the line between practices depicted on the shows and in industry contexts is blurry at best. In addition to this kind of complicit participation, a less anticipated or more begrudgingly admitted point of overlap is that these shows also serve as an initial impression of the industry and its dynamics to a wide range of aspiring hopefuls, particularly new models. As the starting working age of new models has steadily declined, being now somewhere around fifteen for high fashion or editorial models, it is not surprising that these shows are an increasingly important reference point for them. For example, three of the five finalists of the 2007 V Magazine/Supreme Management 'V a Model' contest listed *America's Next Top Model* as their earliest fashion memory. Ranging in age from thirteen to nineteen, the youngest three who responded this way were between eight and eleven when the show debuted. Amanda Laine, the fifteen-year-old winner, went on to book a spot in the highly coveted Prada lineup the following show season, a feat a US-fashion reality television contestant has yet to achieve, let alone so quickly.

Indeed, so successful is the reality format that when the Miss America Pageant moved to its new cable home on The Learning Channel (TLC) in 2008, show producers augmented it with a four-part reality series broadcast a month leading up to the live pageant telecast. Called *Miss America: Reality Check*, the show's press release described it as a much-needed update to the pageant format, bringing 'all 52 beauty queens together to live under one roof to undo everything they have learned about pageant basics and determine if their smarts, attitudes and looks hold up in contemporary society' (Miss America 2007). In an effort to connect with younger viewers and make the show more interactive, producers added a voting hotline, allowing the audience to vote one contestant automatically to the final sixteen. Hosted by actor Michael Urie, best known for his role as the catty assistant on ABC's popular fashion-based comedy-drama series *Ugly Betty* (2006), *Miss America: Reality Check* explicitly parodied 'pageant girls'. In the first episode, contestants were shown videos of people who were asked what 'Miss America' meant to them. While the first few were positive, the tone of the comments quickly turned, with people saying that the pageant was 'corny' and 'not cool'. Some respondents went on to say that the contestants themselves were 'too staged' and 'not like real people', with one person pleading to see 'the real girl behind the façade'. While ostensibly the show was about making over each of the fifty-two contestants to be more 'stylish' and 'relatable', the show was also a rebranding strategy for the pageant, seeking to reposition the Miss America icon as the new 'it girl' that was both 'modern' and 'relatable'. Producers accomplished this through the use of 'fashion' and the reality television format.

For example the three advisory panel members for the reality show who judged contestants each week, ranking the top and bottom three, and ultimately deciding the three show winners who received a $10,000 scholarship and new wardrobe, included a celebrity photographer, stylist and magazine editor from *US Weekly*. From styling and design challenges to 'fashion' runway-walking lessons, the show both implicitly and explicitly defined itself against popular reality television programming, like *Project Runway*, *American Idol* (Fox 2002), *Dancing with the Stars* (CBS 2005) and *ANTM*. In one commercial leading up to the live telecast, the voiceover narrated, 'Before there were "singing idols," "top models," or "dancing stars," there was a competition to be the best at everything. "Miss America Live!" The original competition series' (Stun Creative 2008).

The retooled marketing worked. The initial live broadcast and two subsequent repeats during the premiere weekend of *Miss America Live* drew an estimated 19.2 million viewers, posting enormous gains over the previous two years in key demographics, like viewers aged eighteen to thirty-four, which grew by 90 per cent over 2007 numbers, and an overall drop in the median age of viewers to thirty-seven, which was down by seven years from 2007 and fourteen years from 2006 (Miss America 2008). Given the popularity of both reality television and fashion-centred programming, it is clear why producers turned to these tactics. However, as I will show in the following section, that these were successful instruments supports a more generalized theory of beauty as labour, which ultimately was able to rehabilitate not only the image of 'Miss America' but also the figure of the model.

Reality Television and the 'Labour Theory of Beauty'

While there are many antecedents to the current iteration of reality-based programmes dating back to the inception of television itself—from quiz shows and amateur talent searches to daytime talk shows and hidden camera programmes (Ouellette and Murray 2004: 3)—the growing popularity and economic sensibility of reality television programmes as prime-time US network and cable fare is a relatively recent phenomenon. Characterized as 'an unabashedly commercial genre united less by aesthetic rules or certainties than by the fusion of popular entertainment with a self-conscious claim to the discourse of the real' (2004: 2), reality television's tipping point in the USA came with the debut of *Survivor* in summer 2000. Borrowing the format from the UK series *Castaway*, the popularity of CBS's *Survivor* set in motion a reversal of international media flows and represented a shift in both television content and production practices. As Magder notes, 'Until summer 2000, shows like these fell into the "alternative programming" category, a hodgepodge of down-market entries [. . .] and cable shows targeting younger viewers' (2004: 137). Like the growth of reality-based programming in the late 1980s and early 1990s as a response to labour disputes, including the 1988 Writer's Guild strike as well as nine others, the dilution of advertising revenues across a growing number of distributors and the fragmentation of television audiences by the uptake in number and accessibility of both cable television channels and home video options (among other factors, see Raphael 2004), the rise of reality television at the turn of the millennium marked 'a new era of product placement and integration, merchandising, pay-per-view, and multiplatform content' (Magder 2004: 152), ushering in an increased pressure to develop formats rather than programmes that could be stripped of their cultural particulars and exported through franchises around the world (145).

Alongside the competition series, the makeover programme has proved to be one of the most popular contemporary reality formats. While the idea of personal transformation is not new, media studies scholars agree (see for example Banet-Weiser and Portwood-Stacer 2006; Heller 2007; Miller 2008) that its delivery in a reality television format adds several key dimensions that shape its message and potential reception, particularly its ambient and ubiquitous presence in people's homes and combination of education and entertainment (Ouellette and Hay 2008: 102). The category includes a range of programmes like those focused on personal style, home décor and professional development. Each shares a preoccupation with a kind of Cartesian dualism of interior and exterior, seeking to reconcile the two, positing a flawed exterior needing to be brought in line with an authentic internal. As Heller argues, 'today's televisual makeovers emphasize physical change and material/ service acquisitions as the paths to genuine expression of one's inner self and better nature' (2007: 2). This focus on processes of making things visible is well suited to television as a media format. As Ouellette and Hay note, 'Television's cultural conventions, including its use of close-ups and formulaic narratives, make it especially useful for demonstrating techniques of self-fashioning in the form of dramatic stories that incorporate moments of intimacy, disruption, and suspense' (2008: 101–2).

Also at work on these shows is what literary theorist Douglas Mao has termed 'the labour theory of beauty', or the use of labour to resolve feelings of injustice over how society rewards 'the beautiful'. Mao argues that in the late twentieth century US public discourse is 'marked by a convergence between [. . .] explicit condemnation of inequalities [and] [. . .] relentless broadcasting of the benefits that accrue to the physically beautiful and that may be withheld from the unlovely or plain' (2003: 191). Situating their concomitant rise alongside the growing importance of images, Mao shows the flexibility of meritocracy as an ideology to accommodate both, using 'labour as the currency of justice' (224). He notes, however, 'the idea that effort is rewarded mutates rapidly into the assumption that effort is *always* rewarded, and that one may praise the lovely and blame the ugly without invoking ascriptive norms' (2003: 218–19, emphasis in the original). Sensitive to the political implications of aesthetics (and vice versa), Mao argues that the labour theory of beauty's framing of aesthetic inequalities as personal faults 'may be the most inventive re-legitimation of social hierarchy to emerge in the United States in the twentieth century' (193).

Providing a philosophical history of the 'long-standing tension between claims of beauty and justice' (191) in the first half of his essay, Mao focuses in the second half on current practices that seek to triangulate beauty, labour and desert in contemporary US society, taking examples from the diet and exercise industry, celebrity culture and educational and legislative campaigns since the 1980s that promote the equal treatment of individuals regardless of appearance. He singles out the fashion model, particularly the supermodel, as 'a figure who tips the balance so strongly away from visible effort and toward simple beauty that she (or he) threatens to test the limits of public tolerance' (2003: 211). In other words, despite what he characterizes as 'ceaseless fashion industry proclamations about how hard models work' (211), they still appear undeserving because their financial and public rewards appear to stem more from inherent or inherited sources of value (their appearance) rather than their effort.

Published in 2003 and more in line with popular representations of models from the 'supermodel era' of the 1980s, Mao's essay is unable to take into account the reframing of both 'modelling' as labour and the figure of the model as a 'triumphant everywoman/man' broadcast on shows like *ANTM*, which debuted in the same year. Indeed, shows like *ANTM* instantiate Mao's larger argument by foregrounding effort—an effort that should always be rewarded—at the expense of 'simple beauty', absolving the fashion industry of its elitism and superficiality.

However, it is more than a focus on the labour and effort modelling requires that is being demonstrated on these shows; it is also the didactic relationship between experts and novices. This enactment of a socializing process helps resolve the tension among beauty, effort and desert Mao identifies. That is it is model development, not modelling labour in and of itself, that ultimately recuperates the figure of the model, providing similar themes of self-realization, affirmation and transformation as seen on other forms of makeover television. The emphasis on transformation as a learned and socialized set of practices demonstrates the importance of effort and desire in the model development process. Indeed, as Ouellette and Hay write,

> The televised talent/job search is a form of makeover TV to the extent that experts, teachers, and judges seek to transform raw human potential into coveted opportunities for self-fulfillment through realization and expression of talent. (2008: 127)

While talent or physical beauty may be inherited and unlearnable, makeover shows and model-focused reality series underscore the work required to make these differences meaningful. Even on docusoaps set at modelling agencies, the development process vis-à-vis the model–agent relationship is a common theme. This theme not only legitimizes and makes visible the labour of the model, but also the labour of other industry players, particularly modelling agents and their proxies in the form of experts and panel judges.

In the next section I explore representations of the development process on *ANTM* and how they affect the reframing of the figure of the model. I am particularly interested in examining judging panels and challenge lessons, two features shared across the majority of fashion reality-television programmes, to see how development goals and issues are discussed. In my analysis I want to consider both the purposeful framing and casting choices producers make as well as the structural constraints the format engenders.

Framing, Casting and Structuring Labour
and Desire on Model Reality Television

Shows like *ANTM* struggle with maintaining a balance between projecting the expected glamour and stereotypical over-the-top-ness of the fashion industry with triumphant, up-by-the-bootstraps narratives of self-transformation. Producers also confront the problem of representing an elite cultural industry with not only high barriers to entry, but an internal logic that centres on the scarcity and inherent value of talent and physical beauty (as evidenced by the scale of international scouting networks, cf. Wissinger forthcoming) as a meritocracy. Accomplished in part through the genre's formal features of fusing entertainment with education, as discussed in the previous section, producers also achieve the resolution of this seemingly contradictory logic through specific framing and casting choices. Downplaying the importance of industry politics and dynamics (e.g. the influence of 'starmakers' like Prada casting director Russell Marsh or fashion photographer Steven Meisel; see also, Entwistle 2002; Trebay 2005) and relaxing prevailing industry preferences for age, look, body shape and size, as well as race and ethnicity, producers present a stint on the show as offering direct access to the industry. Failure to succeed then is only attributable to the contestant herself, since all other meaningful impediments have been removed.

Also, as discussed in the previous section, the show's format reframes beauty as a kind of labour that is independent of or can exceed physical limitations. It is presented as equally accessible to all and dependent only on acquiring a set of learnable skills, which must then be demonstrated in proper ways. Importantly, these skills and their demonstrations are only partially physical, depending instead on the calibration of inner psychological and affective states and making them visible on the surface of, or rather *through*, the body. Echoing other makeover programmes' emphasis on mediating inner and outer states, these shows highlight the instability of outward appearances and their vulnerability to inner changes. Indeed, as Wissinger rightly notes, modelling must primarily be considered a form of affective labour insofar as it focused on the 'capacity to constantly change appearance and personality' (2007: 235). This insight, taken to a much further extreme on these programmes, diminishes or overcomes the importance of physical appearances in a seemingly paradoxical way that holds outer appearances accountable or only meaningful in relationship to inner actions vis-à-vis affective labour.

Producers' casting choices aid this kind of framing. They often deliberately go against type and showcase contestants whose biographies challenge expectations of typical models. This practice is partly a structural feature of reality shows, which rely as much on the interpersonal drama of clashing and extreme personalities to make interesting and watchable television as they do on the seemingly 'objective' talent requirements, and partly a way of engaging the audience to imagine modelling as an attainable aspiration.

For example even from the first season of *ANTM*, producers routinely select models with strong religious convictions and then present a nude shoot early in the competition, as a way of challenging them to overcome their own personal beliefs through 'professionalism'. In other instances, they have selected and highlighted models with disabilities or diseases that would seem to be obvious impediments to working as a model, such as Mercedes in season two who had lower energy levels because of lupus; Amanda in season three, whose retinus pigmentosa qualified her as legally blind; or most recently, in season nine, Heather whose Asperger's Syndrome, a high-functioning form of autism, made it difficult for her to understand the affective subtexts of social interactions. Following this theme, in season thirteen show producers selected an entire cast that fell below the industry's height threshold, with no contestant taller than five feet and seven inches. In addition to these purposeful casting choices, there are also legal casting constraints, like the participation waivers that require contestants to be at least eighteen years old, which also contribute to the loosening of industry conventions of typical models such as age. Responding to criticism regarding the show's poor track record of actually producing successful 'top models', Banks told the *New York Times Magazine:*

> Of course I know what a supermodel looks like . . . but I also know that a show filled with 13 girls that have the right look and no personality is not going to be relatable or watched. I'm more interested in fighting for the racial mix of the cast . . . When I'm casting a dark-skinned black girl on 'Top Model,' I'm sending a message to the little girl watching at home that she is beautiful. (Hirschberg 2008: 45)

Vocal in media interviews and on the show that her casting choices are meant to contest industry standards and prejudices, particularly those regarding race and body size, Banks frames these challenges as deeply personal and based on her own struggles, but more important, her triumphs. Emphasizing perseverance, desire, sacrifice and hard work, Banks positions herself as a role model for contestants, diverting attention away from solutions aimed at changing the minds and tastes of industry image-makers and instead towards strategies for aspiring models to take responsibility for their own success *despite* industry prejudice. This type of framing was most dramatically presented during an episode in season four when two models, Rebecca and Tiffany, were eliminated from the competition at once but only Rebecca appeared upset while Tiffany seemed cavalier. Banks called them both back and admonished Tiffany for not taking the contest seriously. While Tiffany replied that she had 'been through stuff' and was 'sick of crying about stuff [she] couldn't change' and 'being disappointed', Banks became increasingly frustrated to the point of shouting at her:

> I have never in my life yelled at a girl like this. When my mother yells like this it is because she loves me. I was rooting for you. We were all rooting for you. How dare you! Learn something from this. When you go to bed at night, you lay there and you take responsibility for yourself, because nobody's going to take responsibility for you. You rollin' your eyes and acting like you've heard it all before. You've heard it all before? You don't know where the hell I come from. You have no idea what I've been through, but I'm not a victim. I grow from it and I learn. Take responsibility for yourself.

While Banks's success is the exception that proves the rule, her overreaction stems from her belief that her show provides aspiring models with an alternative, levelled playing field. In challenging industry standards but not holding the industry responsible, Banks puts the onus of transformation on the models themselves, requiring sincere desire and tenacity over and above mere physical beauty.

In addition to these framing and casting choices that emphasize desire over physical qualifications, the show's structure also contributes to the reconceptualization of the figure of the model through a labour theory of beauty. Each week contestants are coached to learn new skills from a rotating series of experts. These range from the technical, like posing, runway walking and dancing, to the more intangible, such as learning how to be charismatic. Each skill, however, is deeply rooted in learning how to display inner states through physical performances, and is tested through a series of three challenges: the first administered by the coach, the second in the form of the weekly photo shoot and the third in a challenge given by the judges. Models are primarily evaluated each week by the latter two during a panel critique and discussion by the judges. The judging panel is composed of four regular judges and a guest judge or judges from that week's challenge or photo shoot. Banks has been the only constant judge throughout the series, with the three other spots alternatively occupied over the first ten seasons by fashion model-cum-photographer Nigel Barker (cycles two through ten), runway walking coach J. Alexander (cycles five through ten), fashion stylist Nolé Marin (cycle three), fashion editors Beau Quillian (cycle one) and Eric Nicholson (cycle two) and fellow models Janice Dickinson (cycles one through four), Kimora Lee Simmons (cycle one), Twiggy (cycles five through nine) and Paulina Porizkova (cycle ten).

During these discussions models and their photographs are authorized as either successes or failures. Judges' comments include aesthetic evaluations of the models and photographs (e.g. the pose is beautiful or it's not, the neck looks long or it does not, the model is striking or she is not), but inferences about the psychological state of the models are also made through the photographs (such as 'you've lost the fire in your eyes' or 'it's a beautiful picture but you're holding back'). Held accountable for their own success or failure, the models' inability to perform is attributed either to their ineptitude as conductive mediums or improper psychological and affective dispositions.

Take for example these two critiques and proposed solutions offered to Nicole and Nik, contestants on season five, during the open judging panel. The photo shoot challenge consisted of posing seminude in a UK-style red telephone booth alone and then with the remaining six contestants. Both were praised for their photos, but still asked to do more:

Tyra: Here's your best phone booth shot.
Nigel: Wow. Very pretty.
Tyra: Sassy.
Nik: It looks fabulous, really good.
Tyra: I'll tell you, Nicole, going through your film, it frustrates me sometimes because I'm like, 'this girl is so gorgeous, she has so much,' but you're still not pushing through enough.
J.:   So whenever you think you're doing it, just do it extra.
Tyra: A little more.
Nicole: Okay.
Tyra: And here's your best shot. That's the first one wide that looks amazing.
Twiggy: Yeah.
J.:   Yes.
Twiggy: And you've got no clothes, so I love it.
Tyra: You have such confidence when you turn your head to the side. Face on, you're almost there.
Twiggy: Straight on you are beautiful!
Tyra: Right now you're just a model like this [looking to one side in profile] and you need to [turning to face her directly]
Nigel: Only you can do that. You have to believe in yourself.

A specific idea about the figure of the model is constructed through these mediated interactions. Comments like 'this girl is so gorgeous, she has so much, but you're still not pushing through enough' emphasize that physical appearances are only as valuable as the affective work behind them. Similarly the solution to Nik's inability to shoot from the front is to 'believe in herself'. These kinds of evaluations occur throughout the show and work to foreground that what is exceptional about each candidate is not her inherent beauty, which can go in and out of style, but rather her ability to become a medium for conveying and relaying affect (cf. Wissinger 2007). In this way the physical limitations of the body are subordinated to its somatic and psychic agency. The figure of the model is positioned as an ideal media form that transmits inner states outward. Subsequently, the inability to do this or to transmit the wrong states is cause for dismissal. Again, as Mao discusses in his formulation of the labour theory of beauty, this kind of framing calls attention to the body but only as evidence, not as an entity in and of itself. He writes,

> [W]e will likely go wrong if we adhere to the intuition that in emphasizing *mediation* (by labour), the labour theory of beauty must further weaken the belief that outside ex-presses inside. On the contrary, in a postaristocratic environment, as we have seen, effort will normally replace birth as the measure by which the self (qua subject of justice) is 'known' by others, and in so doing will tend to install itself at the heart of personhood. (Mao 2003: 224)

Illustrating this shift from birth to effort, in season fifteen, both Banks and the episode's challenge photographer, Francesco Carrozzini, reprimanded a contestant for failing to do the 'work' of beauty:

Francesco: You were not taking directions very well, especially on your body. I felt you were very nervous. The idea you gave me was that you were not trying hard enough because you are very beautiful and it looked like, 'I'm beautiful. I'm just going to show up in front of the camera.'

Tyra: My fear is that you are the noun and not the verb. So you were born a model, but you are not modeling.

Banks's distinction between being the 'noun and not the verb' is at the heart of the labour theory of beauty. More than just aesthetic labour, what is required is affective labour. Importantly, both Banks and Carrozzini frame the model's inability to take the necessary directions to make a pleasing picture not as a physical failure, but as a moral one. The criteria used for judging the contestants then are the desire to become a model, the simultaneous demonstration of versatility and authenticity and the ability to connect through photographic media, all of which are routinely framed as an affective or moral problem rather than physical. These principles are also evident during closed judging sessions, where the experts convene to discuss the individual merits of each contestant and the group's performance in general. In an acting-themed week during the fourth season, the judges evaluated the seven remaining models' Wonder-bra-sponsored photo shoot, attributing the failures and successes of the photographs directly to the models own personal internal struggles and not necessarily their lack or gain of technical skills. During their discussion, the judges praised Britney for her photograph's evidence of her increasing self-control, while they criticized Keenyah and Tiffany for their lack of mental commitment and focus during the session, which led to diagnoses of each model's desire to pursue a career in modelling:

Tyra: Britney.

Nigel: Britney's like a wild horse. She's finally beginning to tame herself and this picture's a perfect example. Sexy, yet not too hoochie.

Tyra: Keenyah.

Janice: She looks the same.

Boris: Yeah, I would love to see her personality come through a little more.

Nolé: I find her to be stiff, boring, like a freaky chicken.

Janice: She's not posing. There's no thought process whatsoever in this photograph.

. . .

Tyra: Tiffany.

Janice: Tiffany could be a couture model, but she just sucks with her attitude.

Tyra: I think she wants it but she's so intimidated by it, she'd rather say goodbye to it before it says goodbye to her.

Boris: I think she's got a lot to offer but I think she doesn't believe in herself yet.

Through their discussion, audiences are guided to see what modelling potential looks like and what proper forms of desire are. Like their photographs, models are expected to be both iconic and indexical. That is they must convey something larger than themselves—a type, an emotion, a mood—while also indexing something within themselves. What is reversed in this show, however, is the importance of indexicality. While Britney is rewarded for producing a 'sexy, yet not too hoochie' image, the judges credit it to her ability to 'tame herself', an inner transformation. This emphasis goes against popular understandings and circulations of fashion photographs as highly stylized iconic representations. Instead, programmes like *ANTM* demonstrate that these representations depend on evidentiary mediation between inner states and outward appearances, holding the photographic subject, rather than the viewer, responsible for inferences.

Conclusion

Model development, both as it is practised in everyday spaces of the fashion industry and as depicted on these shows, centres on the shifting relationship between internal and external transformation. Agents (and their televisual proxies) read models' bodies as reliable indicators or evidence of internal desires, motivations and effort during development even as they collabourate with models to cultivate an ideal of transmutability and flexibility. They routinely express limits to these transformations through idioms of personal desire, discipline, sincerity and inauthenticity. A labour theory of beauty reveals how this type of framing, while circumventing essentialist and ascribed notions of beauty and desert, collapses beauty with effort so that a failure to be beautiful is tantamount to a moral failure to do work. As Mao argues, this demonstrates how '*a rhetoric of effort can curtail discussion of the forms and meanings of equality'* (2003: 219, emphasis in original). This type of framing evacuates the broader social structure—both that of the fashion industry and society at large—through which fundamental inequalities are both created and reinforced. It is possible, however, to change the ways in which these are thought of as fundamental and insurmountable and to reform the practices that contribute to their sedimentation. What is needed are more critical analyses of not only how representations of beauty—both on television and in the industry itself—change but how the figure of the model itself is constructed and what ideological assumptions are smuggled in with it.

–8–

Made in Japan: Fashion Modelling in Tokyo

Ashley Mears

Introduction

On a warm night in the summer of 2006, I found myself in the backseat of a van in an alleyway in Tokyo's hip shopping district of Harajuku, seated with five fashion models from four countries. We are from Poland, Russia, Canada and the United States, and we are waiting our turn for a modelling audition, called a 'casting', at 9 o'clock at night.

It's been a long day, beginning at 10:30 this morning, and nine castings dispersed throughout the city later, none of use have yet had dinner. But we are in for a long wait, as Agnes,[1] a gregarious eighteen-year-old from Poland, announces, 'Girls, we gonna be here a long time!' Our van is one of seven other agency vans, each loaded with its own flock of *gaijin*—Japanese for foreigner—models. Dozens of models are everywhere: some standing in groups chatting, or sitting on the curb, smoking, reading or sleeping in their agency vans with their foreheads pressed against the windows. They are blonde, brunette, redhead, all tall and thin and young, and all Caucasian. For a bustling neighbourhood of Tokyo, noticeably absent in this scene are Japanese women.

After an hour, we are called to enter the building to meet the clients. Inside the white-walled casting studio, Taro, our representative who has driven us here, instructs the six of us to line up beneath bright studio lights facing a table, behind which eight Japanese people are sitting, two women and six men, some smoking, all wearing dark suits. The room is silent. Taro hands the clients our books—our portfolios of pictures—and as each client begins to flip the pages, Taro 'promotes' us individually, telling them each of our names, country of origin, age and a line or two of promotion. All of this takes place in Japanese, a language none of us speak.

The clients look from each of us to our pictures, to our manager Taro, and back to us. If they are interested in one of us, they may ask us to stay and try on a sample garment. If they are not interested, the client will hand the book back to Taro, say 'Thank you', and Taro will hand a set of car keys to the model, with his by now familiar phrase, 'Okay, please go back to van and wait.' One by one, we are told to go back to the van and wait. Back in the van, we talk about how many models there were at the casting, and Mac, a model from L.A., remarks, 'Well, whoever gets it should feel like a gold medalist.' Unlike, so she implies, the rest of us.

It is now 10 p.m., and as the van pulls off to take us home, Taro phones our modelling agency to give us our schedules for Monday. He calls out our names one by one and repeats the agents' directions: 'Ashley, please come to agency 11 o'clock. Vic, okay please go back to agency pick up job sheet, Mac please come to agency 11 o'clock.' Mac sighs and repeats her instructions; coming to the agency means another day of castings, and not a day of work. It means another day like today, a day of waiting to be judged.

Modelling in Tokyo: An Overview

On any given weekday in Tokyo, such casting scenes unfold for the approximately 150 girls[2] working as fashion models for the roughly fifteen modelling agencies that cater to Japanese advertisers seeking to brand their products with Caucasian faces and bodies. The *gaijin* models come from around the world on short-term contracts of typically four to eight weeks for guaranteed sums ranging from US$10,000 to US$50,000. Their images appear throughout the city—in magazines and catalogues wearing the latest fashions, on subway cars sipping new coffee drinks, on television commercials holding new cell phones and on billboards promoting everything from wedding dresses to the grand opening of the Omotesando shopping mall. The presence of Western models used to spur Japanese consumption begs two questions, the first one of broad scope concerning global flows of ethnic labour: What are so many Caucasian models doing in Tokyo? A second question follows concerning the particulars of doing display work in a highly competitive and uncertain market setting: what are the labour practices and strategies for working as a *gaijin* commodity?[3]

Based on autoethnographic analysis of the fashion modelling market in Tokyo, this chapter explores the relationship between the organization of an aesthetic market (Entwistle 2009) and models' labour practices. Models sell their 'look' to fashion clients, and their 'bookers', or agents, broker the trade. The term *look* may sound like a fixed set of physical attributes, but in fact looks are amenable outcomes of social processes, in which bookers and models jointly attempt to develop and package the kinds of personalities and appearances they predict clients will want. While existing research has documented the work involved in manufacturing looks in Western fashion markets (Entwistle 2009; Entwistle and Wissinger 2006; Mears 2008; Mears and Finlay 2005), this chapter examines the unique case of the Tokyo market in order to consider the kinds of work practices that emerge under conditions of extreme uncertainty in aesthetic production.

In the modelling markets of global fashion cities, looks are produced through a combination of commercial and artistic considerations. The Tokyo modelling industry, however, is unique among the major fashion 'capitals' for its orientation towards economic rewards and its relative lack of symbolic capital. Unlike New York, London or Paris, models come to Tokyo exclusively in pursuit of monetary gain, which typically comes at the expense of building their reputations and prestige. They are drawn to Tokyo by guaranteed contracts, which reward them with a lump sum payment at the end of their trip, regardless of their actual earnings (though in practice these payments come with considerable strings attached). Agencies in Tokyo have thus organized the market to maximize models' earnings and to minimize agency risks, in ways that make the Japanese modelling experience one of heightened objectification and passivity in comparison to markets in, for example London and New York.

Because the market structure in Tokyo limits their individual agency, models lack their usual repertoires of labour control such as emotional labour and networking (Entwistle and Wissinger 2006; Mears and Finlay 2005). Without ways to reduce uncertainty, models may try to attain self-respect by employing 'weapons of the weak'; that is forms of symbolic resistance undertaken by dominated classes in defiance of their oppressors (Scott 1985). In Tokyo, I witnessed models resisting their subordination with furtive expressions of contempt, frequently rooted in racial terms, for their Japanese employers and agents. If modelling is a site for sociologists to study labour and commodification under conditions of uncertainty (Entwistle and Wissinger 2006), then modelling in Tokyo pushes our understandings of labour strategies for coping with uncertainty in the aesthetic economy.

I begin by making the case for why modelling is important to study at this moment of expansion in the global aesthetic economy, and how I was able to study it. Next I explain the structure of the Tokyo modelling market, situating it within global fashion. I then analyse the work setting and uncertainty specific to the Tokyo market, and models' responses to working in it. I find that models experience information asymmetry, public rejection and heightened uncertainty—all exaggerated traits of modelling work more generally—such that Tokyo is a case of what I call 'extreme modelling', a condition of potentially alienated labour that models resist by drawing symbolic boundaries between themselves and their Japanese employers.

Theoretical Overview: Cultural Meanings and Aesthetic Marketplace

Before explaining what models are doing in Tokyo, it is first necessary to consider what it is that models do more generally. Fashion producers 'rent' a model's look for use in advertising and marketing media to promote the sale of fashion items. A look is code for a model's unique appearance that appeals to a particular client at a particular time and depending on the product being sold. Generally models share basic features of attractiveness, like facial symmetry, clear skin and particular height and size requirements (typically at least 5 foot 9 inches and size 0–6). Beyond these loose criteria, a model's bodily capital is sized up as a matter of personal tastes and evaluations of her physical beauty and personality (including how this translates into a photograph), all of which is described as her look (Mears and Finlay 2005).

Of course models do much more than promote the sale of fashion. The model look promotes and disseminates ideas about how women and men *should* look. In Tokyo, *gaijin* models represent a proscriptive mix of femininity and racial otherness.

The Cultural Meanings of Western Models in Japan

Cultural studies of Japanese fashion and beauty suggest that white models func-tion to unify Japanese identity in opposition to the Orient, a trope of Occidentalism that reverses Edward Said's concept of the western Orientalism (Carrier 1995). In Said's classic formulation, Orientalist discourses define the East as an exotic, infe-rior and monolithic 'Other' vis-à-vis the West. In an Occidentalist reading, however, models are benchmarks that let Japanese society know itself by what it is decidedly *not* (Kondo 1997). The appeal of *gaijin* models lies principally in their *not* being Japanese.

Indeed, foreign models are depicted in ways that comment upon, ease and contain anxieties over East and West (Creighton 1995; Darling-Wolf 2001; Goldstein-Gidoni 2001; Kondo 1997). *Gaijin* models are frequently shown posing nude or in under-wear, posed to appear exotic and sexy. They are often depicted as silly, harmless and incompetent in the ways of Japanese tradition, or in other scenes that would be inappropriate for Japanese women. In this interpretive reading, Caucasian bodies are rendered into curious and exciting things to look at, mere spectacles—*misemono*—that are no cause for anxiety (Creighton 1995, 1997; Goldstein-Gidoni 2001).

White models in Japan are also emblems of global racial hierarchies. Tapping into the cultural valuation of whiteness and Western bodies, advertisers can brand products with international sophistication through the use of *gaijin* imagery (Rosen-berger 1996). In reality, of course, national boundaries are not so fluid and global inequalities are deeply entrenched beyond the reach of most consumers' purchas-ing power. Yet for all of these cultural meanings, the *gaijin* look is fundamentally a cultural *product*; it is the outcome of an organized market, one that can be analysed sociologically.

The Aesthetic Economy of Fashion Modelling

Fashion modelling is structured like other markets in the growing cultural (Scott 2000) or 'aesthetic' economy (Entwistle 2009), and a model's look is a primary example of a cultural good. Such goods, including art, music and television, are imbued with high levels of aesthetic and semiotic content and their value is fluid, unpredictable and tied to networks of collaborative actors (Scott 2000). Similar to artists, musicians and publishers, fashion models work in a market characterized by intense uncertainty, inequality, the rapid turnover of fluctuating tastes and the combination of economic and artistic pursuits (Aspers 2005; Bourdieu 1993; Negus 1999; Thompson 2005). The people who work in markets like fashion face extremely high stakes of unpredictability, in which 'all hits are flukes' and 'nobody knows' what will be the next big thing (Bielby and Bielby 1994; Caves 2000; Hirsch 1972). Bookers never know which looks will be desired by clients, just as clients can never know which models will be most successful in selling their products.

Furthermore, like other labour markets in cultural production, modelling is structurally unstable, offering short-term freelance employment without benefits (Menger 1999). It is in sociological terms a 'bad job' because, like work in the secondary labour market, it is generally for low-to-average pay, requires low skills and no formal education requirements, and has no benefits (Kalleberg et al. 2000). The low entry criteria, combined with a cachet of being glamorous, result in overcrowding of the modelling market with a great deal of competition for relatively few job opportunities. Also called 'entrepreneurial labour', this workforce is 'risk-taking rather than risk-averse and willing to accept more flexibility in both jobs and careers' in exchange for flexible hours, association with 'coolness' and perceived glamour (Neff et al. 2005).

Models are different from other entrepreneurial labourers in the cultural economy because they are inextricably tied to the products they sell. To successfully sell their looks, models must manage both their bodily capital and their feelings, or emotional labour (Hochschild 1983; Mears and Finlay 2005). Scholars call this combination of physical and emotional work *aesthetic labour*, a term that emphasizes the body in discussions of work in the service economy as well as freelancers (Entwistle and Wissinger 2006; Witz et al. 2003). Aesthetic labour involves the simultaneous manufacture of an appropriate aesthetic surface and the imperative to 'project and produce' a particular 'self', in the form of 'personality'. As Entwistle and Wissinger argue, this poses new pressures for perpetual self-scrutiny and surveillance of the self.

No matter how degrading or demanding the workplace, sociologists argue (e.g. Hodson 2001), workers resist the alienating effects of labour by whatever means available, be it collectively or in small, individual acts of defiance. To counter the uncertainty, rejection and objectification of fashion modelling, models have been found to engage emotional labour in order to redefine their work as active performance, not passive appearance (Mears and Finlay 2005). They self-reflexively 'play the game' with a critical distance towards agents and clients (Mears 2008). And, like other freelancers in the creative industries, they take part in social networking in order to gain a reputation of employability (Currid 2007). Such strategies enable models to reclaim a sense of control over their volatile and precarious working conditions.

In the Tokyo market, however, such strategies are not available and models lose control, however limited it may be in Western fashion markets, of their 'commodification process'. Given the unique organization of the market, models cannot engage their routine strategies of resistance. There is, in other words, something *distinctly* alienating in the labour of being aesthetic when aesthetic labour is organized *entirely for* the worker. As workers in a foreign market, models are indeed rendered mere spectacle, to which they react with symbolic acts of resistance. By examining the unique case of modelling in the Tokyo market, this chapter extends the study of aesthetic labour and shows the limits of worker resistance under conditions of extreme uncertainty.

Analytical Autoethnography

During two summer vacations while I was a graduate student, I was invited to spend several weeks in Tokyo to work as a model. I had modelled in Atlanta while a college student, and more recently, had begun modelling in New York and London as a way to conduct graduate research on the aesthetic economy (see Mears 2011). This was not my first contact with the Asian modelling market; as an undergraduate, I first travelled to Osaka and Tokyo to model during my summer breaks, and after college, I spent six months modelling in Hong Kong. Upon entering graduate school in 2002, however, I 'retired' from the business, but soon found myself invited back for work in Asia by an agency I call Bon Model Management.[4]

As a model working within this structure, I experienced a unique set of emotional and physical labour challenges. That is the work in Tokyo *felt* different from modelling in New York and London. I use these personal encounters, which I recorded in a daily journal and have subsequently analysed through the autoethnographer's practice of self-reflection, to interrogate the relationship between the organization of aesthetic markets and the daily work experiences of being an aesthetic worker. My method of writing is best described as 'analytic autoethnography', for my use of self-observation, my participant status and inclusion of dialogue with coparticipants and my commitment to theoretical engagement (Anderson 2006).

Writing from my unique set of experiences privileges my vision of the modelling world, which is necessarily a limited field of vision. For one thing, I was older than most fashion models, by as much as ten years, and more educated than most, who were coming to work in Tokyo during their summer vacations from high school and even middle school. As such, my interpretation of the market is likely far more critical than most participants. Thus, while not a generalizable research report, this chapter offers a sociological analysis of the invisible backstage world of fashion modelling in Tokyo seen through the lens of an insider.

From the moment I arrived in Tokyo, I began the work of modelling, which includes attending castings immediately following the fourteen-hour flight from New York's JFK to Japan's Narita airport. I also lived in a shared model apartment each summer with one roommate, and I participated fully in model activities, which largely entails riding around for hours each day in a 'model van' en route to castings, driven by an agency representative known as the 'manager'. At Bon this position was held by Taro, a twenty-eight-year-old college dropout. I worked in nearly every type of modelling job in Tokyo: magazine shoots, catalogue shoots, catwalk shows, informal showroom work, a hair show and a television commercial.

Bon is situated among the higher ranks of model agencies in Tokyo; it represents models who work in high-end campaigns, catalogues and editorial pages in high-fashion magazines. Bon is a mid-sized agency that sits comfortably among its competitors of roughly fifteen international modelling agencies as a successful and well-reputed business since opening in the 1990s. Today it has a staff of ten employees: six bookers who work in the agency during the daytime, one office assistant and three managers, who are in charge of driving models to their castings and introducing them to clients. Every agency in Tokyo represents between ten and fifteen models at a given time. More models come largely during popular teenage travel seasons like the summer break or high-demand seasons like September. In 2006, there was a steady supply of fifteen women models working at Bon during the months of May through July, and about eight male models. The agency owned three agency vans; one van to usher male models to castings, and the other two primarily for women. Bon is located near several other modelling agencies in the heavily touristic Roppongi neighbourhood of Tokyo, and its models stay in agency-owned apartments located nearby.

The Labour of Being Aesthetic in the Tokyo Market

The modelling market in Tokyo is structurally different from those in other high-fashion capitals like New York and London. Because modelling in Tokyo is considered a money-making endeavour and not as prestigious or high-status as work in other fashion capitals in the global hierarchy, the work lacks symbolic rewards but offers economically lucrative contracts. The market is rife with stiff competition and high uncertainty, which Tokyo agencies try to negotiate by contractually holding models to strict standards of perfection. In addition to these structural constraints, *gaijin* models face limited means to communicate with their potential clients and bookers, and hence, they are unable to engage in networking or emotional labour, as they usually do to cope with the uncertainty and passivity of their work in Western fashion capitals. As a result, models resort to 'weapons of the weak', like racialized stereotypes and parodies of their bookers and clients.

Tokyo in the Global Fashion Field

Like other workers in cultural production industries, models build careers by strategically cultivating reputations of prestige which are convertible into financial rewards (Neff et al. 2005). Similar to the art field, the modelling market is stratified into two general categories of work, editorial and commercial, a division similar to the art world's split between avant-garde and commercially successful art (Bourdieu 1993; Entwistle 2009; Velthuis 2005). Editorial and commercial models work different jobs, have different types of looks, earn inversely related amounts of prestige and income, as Entwistle has also noted (2009). Editorial and commercial models also face different levels of risk and they appeal to different audiences, outlined in Figure 8.1 below (see Mears 2011).

Editorial jobs—such as magazine shoots and catwalk shows—are by far the least profitable on average, but also the most prestigious type of work that can potentially yield campaign contracts, the jackpot of fashion modelling. Commercial jobs—print advertising, catalogue shoots, television commercials and informal fittings and showroom work—pay the bills with consistently high earnings, it is considered a far less 'interesting' part of the industry than editorial work. For instance the day rate for an editorial shoot for *Vogue* magazine is just US$150, compared to US$2,500 minimum for a day of catalogue and US$250 for an hour of showroom. The magazine shoot is by far the most valuable work for its prestige and 'symbolic capital', despite its lower immediate economic capital (Bourdieu 1993). In the long run, the more prestigious form of capital may be converted into even more money than the immediately profitable catalogue job. Though commercial work will advance models' bank accounts in the short term, it will not advance their careers in the long run. This trade-off between economic and cultural capital is well known to producers in creative industries, from publishing (Thompson 2005), music (Negus 1999) and art

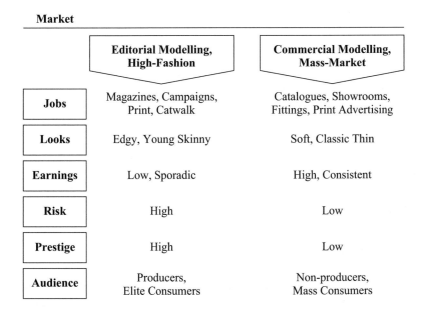

Figure 8.1 Editorial and commercial worlds in the fashion modelling economy.

(Velthuis 2005) to the field of fashion itself (Aspers 2005; Entwistle 2009), where status is not reducible to mere monetary terms.

A successful modelling career will strike a balance between low-earning but highly prestigious editorial jobs at the one end, and high-paying but low-prestige catalogue work and commercial advertising at the other. In key fashion capitals like New York, London and Paris, models work for both symbolic and economic capital, and together with their agents, they calculate the costs and benefits of forgoing one form of earnings over the other. Models come to Tokyo, however, in pursuit of pure profit at the expense of their symbolic value.

Tokyo is the only major fashion capital with a modelling market situated at the far end of the commercial sphere. Bookers from around the world send their models to Tokyo for largely economic ends; it is ostensibly a fail-safe market for models to 'cash out', often in the service of repaying debts that have accrued with their home base agencies, called 'mother agencies'. Year-round in Tokyo, with exceptions during August and December holidays, there is a constant demand for foreign models in both editorial and commercial work, with a large stock of Japanese fashion designers, product advertisers, magazine editors, runway casting directors and catalogue clients hiring *gaijin* models. Unlike magazines in Europe and North America, Japanese magazines pay models lucrative catalogue rates, starting between US$1,000 and US$3,000 a day. The trade-off to money comes with the loss of prestige, but of an acceptable sort since Tokyo is connected to the high-end global fashion circuit (Kawamura 2005). It is the most prestigious of money markets, with far better status and higher day rates than in neighbouring second-tier Asian markets like Taipei or Hong Kong. But unlike the fashion capitals of New York or London, Japanese 'tear sheets'—magazine pages—bestow less symbolic value and they are not ideal for use in model's portfolios elsewhere around the world.

In fact, during my fieldwork at a major modelling agency in New York, I sat beside a graphic designer at his computer in the Art Department as he carefully photoshopped Japanese Kanji characters out of a tear sheet. As he explained it, removing the Asian characters makes the image more acceptable for display in the model's portfolio. A magazine editorial with Asian script is not suitable to show to New York clients, because it carries the mark of lower prestige.

Not only is the Tokyo market symbolically positioned in the commercial sphere, it is reinforced as such by local agencies in Japan which are able to attract international star models by offering short-term contracts with guaranteed minimum payouts. Average contracts range between four to eight weeks for a gross amount of US$10,000 to US$50,000, and they can run higher or lower (and longer or shorter) depending on the model's status and her mother agency's negotiations. Gross contract amounts exclude taxes and agency commission, which takes 40 per cent of the model's earnings to yield her net earnings (though this fluctuates to a higher commission of about 50 per cent for models of Russian nationality due to Japan's tighter restrictions on Russian labour). These contracts are brokered by a handful of scouts, who tap into a global network of modelling agencies in exchange for a 'finder's fee' and, sometimes for a new model, an additional 5 per cent skimmed off her gross earnings.

The model's expenses are then deducted from her net earnings, and these can be quite costly. Sample expenses (in the mid-2000s) include a round-trip airplane ticket (from JFK New York, about US$1,000), accommodation in a model's apartment (roughly US$60 a night for a room in a two-bedroom apartment, or about US$40 to share a one-bedroom apartment), the cost of printing modelling cards (¥78,750, about US$755) and a weekly allowance of ¥20,000 (about US$190). The agency advances these expenses to the model, which she pays back from her net earnings at the end of her contract term. For example, in 2005, my six-week contract was in gross terms set at US$20,000, so my net guarantee was US$12,000 minus expenses. In real earnings, I made a net of US$15,580, but about US$5,400 paid in expenses, leaving me with just under US$10,000 in travellers' checks that summer. That yields an average rate of about US$230 per day. The following year I did considerably worse, going for eight weeks with a guarantee of US$15,000 net, and earning an actual net of US$16,229. After expenses, which totalled just under US$6,000, I left with about US$10,000 profit, roughly US$167 a day (see Table 8.1).

These sample contract figures are at the average-to-lower end of the spectrum of contracts. Among the models at Bon who spoke openly about their contracts, there was variation in both net payouts and length of working stay, as described in Table 8.2.

The promise of a guaranteed minimum payment acts as an insurance to the model's trip, certifying that her taking leave of the symbolically rich Western fashion circuit to 'cash out' in Japan will be well worth her time and effort. But in fashion modelling, as in all cultural production markets, there are no guarantees, and scouts and agents

Table 8.1 Sample Contract Terms, Expenses and Net Earnings ($)

Contract 2005	*Six Weeks*
Gross	20,000
Net	12,000
Actual Earnings	15,580
Expenses	5,400
Actual Net	9,900
Contract 2006	*Eight Weeks*
Gross	25,000
Net	15,000
Actual Earnings	16,229
Expenses	5,980
Actual Net	10,000

Table 8.2 Sample Contracts Guaranteed and Adjusted

Model	Length of Stay (weeks)	Guaranteed Net ($)	Adjusted Net* ($)
Dani	6	20,000	30,000
Nila	4	25,000	25,000
Carla	4	21,000	>21,000
Diane	6	15,000	12,000
Vic	4	22,000	12,000
Mac	8	17,500	20,000
Kate	5	10,000	6,000
Sasha	5	20,000	20,000

*before expenses

are quick to point out that guaranteed contracts demand the impossible: that agents somehow *know* a model will work, when in fact, *no one knows* if a model will work, and why—or why not. They know in general the physical attributes of models that tend to be successful, such as a range of acceptable heights (between 5 foot 7 inches and 5 foot 11 inches), skin tone (pale, not too many freckles and no tattoos) and age range (between fourteen and twenty-one, with some exceptions as in my case at age twenty-five). But within these bounds, there is considerable uncertainty. As the scout who arranged my trip explained, unexpected 'flops' are in fact quite likely:

> Absolutely, it happens. Even with girls that have been there before and done extremely well, you think it's a given, but then they get there and the clients have changed direction; they don't want that look anymore. They've used her too much already in the past. (Micah, scout, with ten years experience)

Similarly, the owner of Bon drew on a common trope of luck and timing when explaining to me why some of her models work superbly while others do not: 'It's just being the right look at the right time.'

If 'all hits are flukes' in creative industries, so too are all 'flops' left to chance. Therefore, Tokyo modelling agents are under the added pressure to guarantee minimum contract payouts. Without the guarantee, they would not attract international top models, which is important to build up their own stock of symbolic capital as a competitive, high-fashion agency. Yasuo, an agent at Bon, explained this to me when he discussed how Bon keeps its competitive edge among other agencies:

> Bon is a good agency now, we have good reputation. But, what makes a good agency name? The girls that come. The only way to get the big girl is to give big guarantee. You understand? So we have to pay each day for big girl to be here, it's a big risk if they don't work. We take big risk. (Yasuo, booker, with seven and a half years of experience)

As a risk-taker, Bon is not alone. Each of Tokyo's roughly fifteen modelling agencies are all competing in two tight contests. First, they must attract top international models by offering the most lucrative contracts. Second, their models must book enough high-paying modelling jobs to cover the costs of their contracts. Agencies have only a fixed time span, between four to eight weeks on average, during which they can turn a profit on their imported model. If the model does not work as well as was predicted, the agency takes a loss by paying her minimum contract guarantee regardless of whether she earned less. In the meantime, Bon may try to extract as much value from the model as possible by having her work for poorly regarded clients such as 'Shop Channel', Tokyo's equivalent of the Home Shopping Network. Shop Channel is usually reserved for models with the fewest job prospects because of its association with cheap commercialism, low pay (¥7,000 per hour, less than US$70), and undesirable working hours (between 5 and 7 a.m.). Bon is still unlikely to recoup all of its investment on a model even if she works daily for poorly paying jobs such as Shop Channel.

Managing Uncertainty: The Agency Contract

Because demand for any one model is fundamentally unknown, the odds of success are stacked against Tokyo agencies. To manage these risks, agencies like Bon have developed a number of strategies, most obviously in the form of strict contract stipulations aimed at taming the unpredictable market, the model's physical appearance and her behaviour.

To cope with the unpredictable market, Tokyo contracts contain a 'trial period' clause requiring that each model perform well in her first few weeks in order to validate her guarantee. The models must book a set number of jobs in a given period of time upon arrival, typically six jobs within the first twenty-one days, or for models deemed bigger risks because of their larger guarantees, the requirement may be seven jobs in the first two weeks. Should the model fall short of securing her required jobs in the trial period, the agency has the right to terminate the contract, or more likely, to renegotiate the minimum guarantee and perhaps also ask the model to stay longer in Tokyo to make up the difference.

Such was the case for Vic, a twenty-six-year-old American model of some international repute several years ago when she used to be a regular face in campaigns and magazine covers. At the height of her popularity two years ago, Vic came to Tokyo and worked every day, coming home after her first month-long trip to Tokyo with more than US$25,000 cash. But that was when she was still a familiar face on Parisian catwalks, a status that was, like fashion, fleeting. When I met the former star in 2006, she was keenly aware of how her top-model status had faded, and she felt the consequences. Vic fell short of passing her trial period, and her contract was renegotiated for a lower minimum. Her original contract of US$22,000 net for thirty days was in danger of termination, because she failed to secure seven jobs in her first two weeks (she secured just three). After several rounds of renegotiation and long-distance phone calls to her New York agency, she ended up with an offer of slightly less than US$20,000 for two and a half months. The difference, in effect, was a 60 per cent pay cut, from about US$700 a day to US$267 a day. Hence, the trial period enables Bon to cope with an unforeseen 'flop' like Vic by deflecting the risks of the market from the agency and onto the model.

To further reduce risk, an agency also exerts explicit control over its models' physical appearances. Roughly two weeks before a model leaves for Tokyo, her mother agency records and emails her body measurements to her Japanese bookers, including her height, weight, bust and hip size. Divergence by more than two centimetres is cause for contract termination. Further, the contract states that 'obvious changes in appearance', such as skin condition and hairstyle, including tans, tattoos and acne, may lead to a voided contract.

A final way the agency attempts to reduce risk is through the control of its models' behaviour. Models live in assigned apartments located in close proximity to the agency, and they are not encouraged to find their own accommodation. The contract may be terminated if the model does not comply with agency expectations or breaks agency rules, for instance for possessing or using illicit drugs, for 'behavior or performance which may damage the Agency's reputation', or for being repeatedly late. Models are not free to choose which castings or jobs they will attend, and models' days off are decided solely by their agencies. Failure to comply results in cancellation of the guarantee. From the agency's point of view, this is both fair and necessary for economic survival, because from the first day a model arrives in Tokyo, the agency is fronting the investment for her to be there, whether she is working or not.

The modelling market in Tokyo for *gaijin* models is separate from the market for local Japanese models, to the point that international models rarely see or interact with local models. Most agencies represent either Japanese or Caucasian models, and no agency represents black or African models. Hence modelling agencies in Tokyo reproduce the cultural value of Western beauty defined in Caucasian terms, with large eyes, a thin nose, tall and slender physique, and of course, white skin. Women with these traits in Tokyo come predominantly from Latin America, Eastern Europe, with European and North American women disproportionately underrepresented, an outcome of a global scouting industry that seeks Caucasian bodies from economically deprived countries.

Among the few agencies that represent both local and international models, local and *gaijin* models are kept separate; at only one casting during my research did I witness local and *gaijin* models being promoted side-by-side to the same client. This is most likely because clients seeking Caucasian models are not seeking Japanese ones. The reasons why are speculative. When I asked my booker Yasuo why there is a market for white models in Japan, he explained that Japanese models make much less money than foreigners because they are both more numerous in available supply and also less appropriate for certain forms of advertising: 'take lingerie, for Japanese to see Japanese model, it looks a little too like porn, too erotic, but if Japanese sees foreigner model, okay it is beautiful.' The girls' manager, Taro, used essentialist explanations of beauty to explain the prevalence of white models in Japanese fashion, which to him, is obvious:

> They look better than Japanese models. They have better figure, nice smile. . . . The client want to make a good image for their company, so that's why white models make more money.

Gaijin models, then, are doing many things in Tokyo. They are immigrant labourers doing the dirty aesthetic work—albeit of a glamorous sort—unfit for local women; they are also comic relief from formidable Western dominance, and all the while they are reaping the benefits of their white skin in the global racial hierarchy. Models, for their part, don't think or talk like this. Indeed the question, 'Why us, and why not Japanese women?' never came up during our many hours in the agency van, not because models don't acknowledge any difference between themselves and Japanese—they certainly do, often in antagonistic ways—but rather, like the rest of their working conditions in this foreign market, they neither understood nor questioned the organizational logics of their job.

Tokyo as Extreme Modelling

Research on the labour involved in fashion modelling has found that models are under intense physical scrutiny (Mears and Finlay 2005; Soley-Beltran 2004). Like athletes and strippers, models have a keen sense of their perceived physical flaws and are more likely to be unsatisfied with their bodies than women of similar age who do not work displaying their bodies (Brenner and Cunningham 1992). And like service workers, models must also do 'aesthetic labour', that is perform a desirable, cheery personality in addition to presenting an attractive physique (Entwistle and Wissinger 2006; Witz et al. 2003). Furthermore, as independent contractors for agencies, not as members of formal organizations, models do not perform aesthetic labour under the direction of supervisors or employers. They must learn to become attractive personas around the clock, and with little formal guidance of how to do so.

To counter these commodification processes, models stress the important role of personality, charm and wit in securing castings (Mears and Finlay 2005). They redefine their work as a skilful manipulation of emotions; they are actors in a game of emotional labour, not passive objects for mere visual display. Models also work to build strategic relationships within networks of potentially helpful actors and they emphasize networking skills as an important part of their success or failure. Through networking and emotional labour, models are able to 'not take it personally' when they face inevitable rejection. Like all workers, especially those in creative industries, models attempt to assert a sense of control and agency to an otherwise arbitrary and alienating hiring process. These two resistance strategies, emotional labour and networking, have limited uses for Western models in a market like Tokyo. Given this usual mix of high uncertainty and guaranteed contracts, the Tokyo market presents Western models with a unique set of challenges for day-to-day work that I describe below as extreme surveillance and objectification, and I document the resistance strategies models employ to counter each.

Extreme Surveillance.   Agencies seek to minimize their risks by controlling the appearance and performance of their models. They do this through the explicit surveillance of the model's body. When a new arrival first steps foot in the Tokyo agency, she is greeted and introduced to the staff, and then ushered into a small private room where her measurements and body weight are taken and recorded in her file, not unlike a visit to the doctor. This is partly a practical deed that must be accomplished to satisfy inquiring clients who may wish to know the model's waist, bust and hip measurements, and also more specifically, her inseam, hat size, hair length, ring sizes (all ten fingers) and precise shoe size. This is also the model's first test of satisfying the conditions of measurements stipulated in her contract. Should she be off the mark by a centimetre in the wrong direction, she will be politely asked to 'try' to lose weight, or possibly to gain weight should she be too slim. Explained Micah, the model scout:

> They measure the girls, as you know when they get there, and they have to be thin to fit the clothes. They're made tinier in Tokyo and they have to fit. So you know, you can be too skinny as well; you have to be in line. But they are the strictest because it's a two-month contract, and they're advancing money and have only a short time to make money for you and for themselves.

After the initial introduction to the tape measure, the agency may continue to monitor the model's body through further measuring, or threat of measuring, and explicit verbal requests. Often the agents explain this surveillance as the result of their clients' interests. For instance Shelley, an eighteen-year-old from Canada, was told by her booker that after a photo shoot, the clients 'called to complain' to Bon that her waist is 'too big'. She explained:

> They're like, 'You need to lose a few centimeters off your waist.' And that's okay, I mean, how hard is that, but when you're in Tokyo in the van it gets harder to keep busy or walk it off.

As a city, Tokyo is difficult for foreigners to navigate. The streets are not clearly marked and identifying the Japanese name of a building is an integral part of finding an address. Therefore, models are chaperoned to and from castings by an agency employee, their 'manager', who can chauffeur up to nine models at a time in one agency van, though this is an uncomfortably tight squeeze seating four girls in the back, four in the middle, and one up front. A long day may last twelve hours, from 10 a.m. to 10 p.m., fitting in about thirteen castings with pit-stops at convenient stores for food and snacks in between. This poses a dilemma for the models like Shelley hoping to lose weight either through exercise or healthy eating.

At other times in the van, models reported being verbally harassed by their bookers for being out of compliance with their measurements, as happened to nineteen-year-old Mac:

> I got yelled at today for my hips. She [booker] was like, 'You're a 92!' I was like, I'm sorry, I'm working on it, and she was like, 'But in your contract', and I said what about my contract?! It says I can't be out of line by 2 cm, which I'm not. I mean, I came to Tokyo thinking I was at 93, so I feel okay, and I'm trying. I could be ultra skinny, I could make myself sick, but I won't.

To minimize their risks, agents closely monitor models and allow them a slight margin of error before voiding contracts. While agents subject models to extreme surveillance, fashion clients in Tokyo subject them to extreme objectification.

Extreme Objectification. Much of the work of modelling in any city involves trying to *get* work through castings. In Tokyo this is a nonstop job in itself, and models are shuttled around the city to meet potential employers whether they feel up to the task or not. Of the sixty days I was on contract in Tokyo one summer in the mid-2000s, I attended casting calls for thirty-nine of those days (the remaining twenty-one days were filled with weekends, full-day photo shoots and an empty last week of downtime). I attended a total of 255 castings, and from these, I booked eleven jobs. Like the models with whom I spent my time, I could not figure out *why* one casting turned out to be more successful than another; we could, however, readily decipher the signs if a client is interested or not.

The casting takes a predictable form. It will last just a few minutes, though the wait may be up to an hour. Inside the casting studio or office, at the direction of our English-speaking manager, the models form a line-up in front of the clients, who are usually at least a pair of middle-aged or older Japanese men and women; sometimes the clients consist of a long panel of several clients seated like 'judges' behind a table. At some castings, models meet semiprivately at a table with the clients while the other models wait their turn. The manager hands the models' portfolios to the clients and 'promotes' each model with a few lines of praise, the English bits and pieces of which the models can sometimes make out: 'Shelley . . . New York . . . edgy . . . *Vogue* magazine'.

At any casting, the client may ask the model to try on a sample of the clothing, or to take her picture with a digital camera or both. But as inevitably happens, if the clients are not interested, they will say 'Thank you', close her portfolio and turn their attention to the next model on the line. It is often a quick, orderly process: introduction, assessment, 'Okay, thank you'.

Sometimes the model is asked, through her interpreter/manager, to do very specific things, like turn profile and smile, or for example we were once asked to jump on a mini-trampoline. Other times she may be asked to do something more general, like walk the length of the room back and forth, or perhaps dance or 'make catalogue poses', which entails a succession of moving arms and legs from bent and crossed positions, as models are seen doing in catalogue pictures. Most models report being embarrassed to make catalogue poses on the spot in front of everyone watching; others are quite skilled at it, and are able to perform an impressive routine of motions and poses on command.

Models' bodily objectification is most blatant at lingerie castings, which are frequent throughout the day and usually involve changing clothes into a sample bra and panty set. A semiprivate space, usually behind a curtain in the corner of the room, is provided for models to change, shielding them from the sight of men in the room. A few women Japanese assistants are on hand to help models with their change of clothes, especially to aid the model into the sample bra. The interaction begins with the female assistant politely asking, 'May I touch?' The assistant then warms her hands, and reaches to the side of the model's breast, under her arm and scoops the flesh firmly to fit into the bra cup. This happens once or twice on each side, however much it takes for the bra cup to appear full. The model is then led from behind the curtain and asked to stand before the clients to inspect how she looks in their lingerie.

Throughout the casting process, models stand speechless and motionless—unless instructed to do otherwise—while clients confer with one another and with the manager in Japanese, which is a language very few foreign models I have ever met speaks fluently nor well enough to understand conversationally. *Kawaii*, meaning 'cute', is often exclaimed repeatedly as clients smile and nod at our pictures. At other times clients evaluate the models before them silently, sitting with their arms folded, heads tilted in deliberation. It is in these few cold moments that models have the chance to let their personalities shine.

Emotional labour, the use of personality and emotional assets like 'charm', is of course a major component of wooing the client in any market. As Micah, the scout who arranges models' contracts, explained to me, this is vital in a foreign market like Tokyo:

> It's personality as well, in any market that matters for modelling but especially in Japan or a foreign market because you don't speak the same language, it's so important to have an outgoing personality that you can see and feel. (Micah, scout)

Models working in Tokyo have a very small window of opportunity to make a good impression, and because they have very limited contact with clients—they are not able to sit and chat and tell jokes, as is the case in New York and London— emotional labour is at best a partial resource.

Standing silent on auction, the goods for sale, the models may have no clue as to how they are really being evaluated, even though decisions appear to be in the making right in front of them. Though models may not understand why they are chosen or dismissed from castings, they can easily detect who among them is most favoured among the Japanese clients.

It is a sure sign of winning the client's favour if a model is asked to try on a sample item of clothing, or to be photographed, preferably both. Meanwhile models in whom the clients show no interest are likely to see clients shake their heads no and hear *daijobu*, which means 'that's okay'.

Models are adept at determining whether or not the casting is 'good', meaning likely to lead to a job for someone, or 'bad', which means it was a waste of everyone's time. When I saw Agnes, eighteen, from Poland, on the street, I asked how her last three castings of the day had gone:

> The last two were crap. The client, it was underwear, they just had us all line up and they looked at one, and were like [she shakes her head no] 'okay thank you, bye, bye!'

Not only do models perceive the 'good' or 'bad' tone of the collective casting, but individually, they are subject to both harsh and flattering assessments. For instance, Anna, a teenager from Russia on her first modelling trip abroad, explained to me in broken English how clients had criticized the circles under her eyes:

> They were like, 'why you have this—' [she motions to light circles under eyes]. They told me to step into the light, and were talking about it right in front of me. I don't know how to call this [she points to the faint bags under her eyes] but they kept saying it!

The signs of election, rejection and critique are publicly broadcast in front of everyone present, and reinforced by their frequent narration by the models. When no one is asked to try on the wedding dress, jewelry or tennis skirt, Irina, an eighteen-year-old Canadian, frequently took to saying with a sigh as we pile back into the van, 'All rejects'. Reassembled in the van, en route to the next casting, the previous casting looms large. Models dissect it, quiz one another and pester their driving manager about it. 'Did they take your picture? . . . Did you try on the clothes?'

Of course, any agent or manager will explain that it's nothing personal if a model does not land the job. Taro explained to me how arbitrarily casting decisions are made: 'It's different for every casting, like fishing, just throw out and see what they like.' In any market in the creative industries, 'nobody knows' what constitutes success. But in the market for Western looks in Tokyo, *nobody knows less* of what's going on than the *gaijin* model hoping to sell her look to Japanese clients.

The agency is exceptionally unhelpful in providing feedback. When I asked my booker, Yasuo, why I was not booking very many jobs, he responded: 'It's up to you to work a lot, so you should try.' But it is decidedly *not* up to models' preference whether they work or not, so what, exactly, should they try to do to increase their chances of securing work? For the foreign model, this question is asked of themselves, their manager and their bookers constantly. But much gets lost in translation, and there is little in the way of a support system from the agency in guiding models towards success. For instance, Sam, a twenty-six-year-old Hungarian who has been modelling in Tokyo for the past five years explained the communication gap between her and her booker: 'I don't like dealing with him because he never understands what I'm saying and half the time I can't understand him either, so what's the point?'

The communication divide is a source of great anxiety. Models constantly ask their managers what was said about them in the casting, sometimes to paranoia levels: Were they talking about me? What did that one say about my legs? Did they say something about my clothing? Models comment freely on things like, 'I hate how you can't tell what they're saying about you.' After one casting in which all nine of us were thanked without further consideration, Sasha, a twenty-four-year-old from Russia, joked: 'That casting was like, line up, execution style, it was like an execution!' She continued:

> That's what I don't like about Tokyo, it's like you're degraded. They treat you like a nobody, line up, no thanks, go home. You know, like you're nothing.

Nor can models figure out what is being rewarded or how. They routinely, almost daily, complain of castings that feel alienating, and even when a casting is warm and friendly, it is not up to them to make it so, as Parker explained:

> The worst is when you go in and they don't say anything, or don't smile or speak, and they just look at you, and they just flip through your book [she mimes shuffling the pages of a book quickly]. I like it when they take a long time to look at your book, and they smile and talk to you.

At another catalogue casting, I overhead models from a different agency: 'In and out, they don't even look at you, just flip four pages in the book, [slams her book shut] thanks, here you go.' She then jutted two fingers in the clients' direction, held down low in a 'V' shape, the British gesture for 'screw you.' Such scenes of objectification and rejection are of course routine characteristics of modelling work more generally, and physical scrutiny is an integral part of the job. But in Tokyo, modelling is not business as usual. Models experience quick and impersonal casting arrangements, language barriers and limited interaction with Tokyo clients. They are therefore not able to 'work it' through their usual channels of resistance like networking and emotional labour. Here they are mere spectacle, or *misemono*.

Resistance

Even in the face of extreme uncertainty and ambiguity, no workers are fatalists. Workers in the cultural industries may throw their hands in the air and admit that all hits are flukes, yet still they attempt to find formulas for success (Bielby and Bielby 1995). So too do models navigate the uncomfortable terrain of the selling themselves in Tokyo. Models strategically attempt to 'save face' (Goffman 1959) by deflecting failure and blame onto their clients and agents through backstage resistance techniques, for instance through racialized othering practices. Such strategies of resistance are what Scott terms 'weapons of the weak', merely symbolic and cultural ammunitions in interactional, indirect form of protest (Scott 1985). Through such 'weapons', models are able to maintain a sense of control and self-respect in an alienating and demoralizing work environment.

To absolve the daily grind of rejection and failure, both collective and individual, models take aim against the Tokyo market, the manners of Japanese clients and what they see as the mismanagement of their agency. These lines of accusation are commonly heard in the agency van, especially late in the day.

Models bemoan what they see as the degeneration of the market, and compare it unfavourably to lucrative years past. For instance, Amanda, a twenty-six-year-old from the USA, has come to Tokyo every year or so for the last seven years, and was one of the most vocal critics of the market when I met her in 2005:

> This trip has been weird for all of us. Last time, it was *amazing*. I got like four really good jobs plus my department store stuff, so it was so good. It's not fair to even compare this trip to last time. Tokyo goes down each year, like the rates go down a little each year.

Despite her pessimistic diagnosis of the market, Amanda returned to Tokyo the following spring. Criticizing the Tokyo market easily flows into a critical discussion of the agency and bookers. Models frequently and collectively discussed the agency's flaws, particularly what they see as Bon's oversupply of models:

> In the van today, Mac was complaining: 'Why the heck are there so many girls in the agency? Is this normal?' Masha added, 'I counted eighteen composites, why so many girls in Bon?'

Each model in the van attending castings indicates a model who does not have a job that day. One rainy afternoon in 2006, each of Bon's two vans was noticeably packed; fourteen girls, the entire population of models at Bon, were attending castings. As we were piling into the vans—seven in each—Sasha, the twenty-five-year-old from Russia, spoke to me with her head down: 'Nobody from the agency is working today. Not one girl! I'm like *embarrassed* to be seen with all these girls.'

Models constantly complain that the agency is poorly managed, and agency employees are subject to ridicule in stories that circulate about, for example the 'lazy' booker or incompetent managers. This is despite evidence that Bon's agents work late into the night and on weekends, and they seem even by American standards to be overworked. By criticizing the agency for mismanagement, models are able to deflect rejection of themselves onto their bookers.

For instance Vic initially took responsibility for her poor booking performance, and took the agency's advice of highlighting her blond hair within the first two weeks of her arrival. But she continued to fare badly on the market, and when discussing her poor booking record of just four jobs in one month, she explained, 'It's not me, I thought it was. I changed my hair, but it didn't help. I'm not coming back here, not with this agency.' It is unclear, and indeed fundamentally unknowable, if the agency, the hairstyle or a random market chance had to do with Vic's relative failure. In the absence of any objective criteria for success or failure, she assigned the agency and agents the blame.

Deflecting blame is just one of many backstage techniques models employ to protect their sense of self-respect and dignity after hours, days and weeks of routine public rejection. It is integral to the collective experience models share, and a lively talking point when models are gathered together in the van. Such anxious conversations behind the scenes highlight the distinction between front and backstage behaviour. In Goffman's classic definition, the backstage is a 'place, relative to a given performance, where the impression fostered by the performance is knowingly contradicted as a matter of course' (1959: 112). In the front stage of their performance, when models are poised before a row of judging eyes, they carefully try to manage the impressions they give to clients. They stand up straight or deliberately slouch to seem effortlessly cool. They try to smile invitingly. They may stand with feet angled apart, posed with a hand on the hip. Such a casting scene might reveal a row of young models looking *kawaii* before a row of older Japanese men and women in suits. But backstage, it is quite a different scene, and an antagonistic one. Beyond the clients' view, models curse their would-be employers, shoot them obscene gestures and make fun of them—in Goffman's terms, they 'save face' amid perceived threat and insult to their own dignity (Goffman 1959).

Those who suffer domination and stand on a lesser footing in unequal encounters are likely to create and deploy 'hidden transcripts', like muttering under one's breath and foot-dragging, as documented by Scott (Scott 1990). Models also use their backstage space collectively as a place to counter the isolation and passivity they experience front stage. Like all workers, models are aware of the need to carefully manage their impressions and emotions before the boss. But sometimes, they reject frontstage rules of etiquette in order to counter directly what they see as rude clients.

For example after one particularly unfriendly casting, I walked back to the agency van with Dani, a nineteen-year-old from Eastern Europe. Dani proceeded to tell me how rude the clients seemed towards her, how the 'fat one was just looking coldly' at her. When this happens, she explains, she doesn't try to smile or even make eye contact with clients. She doesn't even care when they are like that, she says, she doesn't try to impress them at all.

These expressions of contempt for clients' manners reveal a final strategy by which models try to save face. This often takes the form of racialized mockery and scorn for the 'Other'. Late in the evening, at our final casting, five models sat together waiting in the van when Sasha began:

Sasha: I can't do it man. I can't handle it. How are we supposed to do this, with no
food, no break, until 10 at night and they want us to look good for the castings?
Mac chimes in: That's just how the Japanese are, they work really late.
Sasha: No wonder they have so much suicide, fucking idiots.
Everyone laughed, agreeing.

Rather than critique the organization of the market, some models may explain their unlucky fortunes in Tokyo as a result of their clients' and agents' deficient cultural norms and poor manners, understood as specifically Japanese traits. Through racialized jokes and comments, models are able to belittle their employers as the non-Western 'Other', in so doing carving for themselves a little space of autonomy. These small acts of resistance are collectively fashioned and shared among models, the van being a sort of outlet for worker resistance practices.

Models thus are able to deflect the uncertain judging criteria of the market onto the 'rude' Japanese client, who is suspected of being fluent in English but prefers to speak Japanese, as Leah, a nineteen-year-old from Canada, explained after a casting:

This guy [client] spoke English, and he would say stuff to me in English and then speak in Japanese to [the manager], so I know he was saying rude stuff that he didn't want me to know.

Lastly, models emphasize how peripheral Japanese fashion is compared to their work in the Western fashion world. Sasha, for instance was rejected from the casting for a prestigious luxury brand show in Japan, though she had recently modelled for the brand in Paris. In the elevator down to the van, I asked her if she had worked with these clients in the past also, to which she replied, 'No, these people don't cast [the show in Paris]. The Paris people cast. These people are bullshit.'

To counter their lack of control over their work, models view their conditions of heightened objectification as an inherent problem with Japan, a moral failing of Japanese clients. For instance Alya, eighteen and from Russia, noted that the difference between modelling in Japan versus Europe or North America is one of respect:

They showed more respect for the girls. Even in Paris, New York, you go to a casting and they want to talk to you, they ask you where you are from, they are interested in you. Here I feel like a piece of meat. It's just the way they look at you.

Conclusion

It is most likely not the case that clients are uninterested in meeting or speaking to Western models, as Alya claims above. The difference between Western markets and Tokyo is not simply one of respect. It lies primarily in the organization of the market, one which maximizes the model's passivity in an effort to reduce the agency's risk of economic loss on guaranteed contracts, which are necessary to attract international models to the relatively less prestigious market in Japan. This system results in the perceptions among models that Japanese clients are essentially rude and culturally inferior people. Thus, no person is ever entirely powerless, as every individual simultaneously enjoys privilege and suffers domination according to his or her positions in racial, occupational and global hierarchies. Models are powerless as industry outsiders, *gaijin* commodities, and yet they flex their power as Western looks whose value originates in fashion capitals like New York, London and Paris.

Models experience objectification, surveillance and rejection in modelling markets around the Western world. As aesthetic labourers, they are under constant pressure to project an attractive appearance and desirable, energetic persona. To counter the uncertainty, rejection and objectification that come with selling oneself, models embrace the emotional labour involved in their work. They play up their personalities, emphasizing their skills as actors that can woo and network to build rapport with their bookers and potential clients. But in the Tokyo market, where models' emotional labour is restricted by a manager at castings that are efficiently organized yet often painfully impersonal, their usual means of resistance are unavailable. They undergo a commodification process completely removed from their own control; it is a short-term world of work characterized by explicit surveillance and objectification, uncertain criteria for success, enormous competition and daily rituals of public rejection.

Models, as weak actors in the market, take up weapons of the weak—small and indirect forms of protest to counter their own passivity. They deflect blame for their failures onto the Tokyo fashion market, onto their agency and onto their agents. They engage in backstage acts to 'save face' to find autonomy and self-respect on a grossly unequal structural footing. They remind themselves and each other of their power and value as Western subjects, even as they face powerlessness as objects for sale in an alienating marketplace. By expressing contempt for the Japanese 'Other', Caucasian models enact a sense of camaraderie among themselves, and for the length of their contract, resist as best they can being mere spectacle.

Modelling Consumption: Fashion Modelling Work in Contemporary Society

Elizabeth Wissinger

Introduction

What do fashion models do at work? Is it all just smiling for the camera, or walking the runway? When models 'model', what are they selling exactly? Of course they are selling products, but is there more here than meets the eye? In fact, the models' role in encouraging the public's engagement in commodification and branding processes that promote consumption is multifaceted. Most obviously, models lend their image to sell products, incorporating their likeness into the image of a brand. This is an evident feature of the work, and in this respect the modelling industry fuels the desire central to modern consumption in two ways: as an industry it provides the labour force for many clients—big business, fashion houses, advertising agencies and so on—selling goods; it also is centrally important in the experience of being a consumer—by framing consumer experiences and encounters with commodities. In other words, models and model agencies are intermediaries between production and consumption, since our encounters with commodities are heavily mediated by the way they are sold to us through the selection, styling and dissemination of images populated by models. Models also, however, engage in subtle forms of commodifying themselves, to create an image that will sell on the model market. In so doing, they work to appear as if they live 'the life' (Parmentier and Fischer 2007: 23), grooming to produce a fashionable 'look', wearing the most fashionable clothes, going to the most fashionable parties. If they are successful, as in the case of the 'supermodels', they may no longer have to act 'as if '—they will be given the designer clothes, be ferried to parties in limousines and call the shots in their own career. This compulsory self-commodification takes the form of aesthetic, entrepreneurial and immaterial labour that has the side effect of promoting a lifestyle and a particular pattern of consumption in which being in the know, or part of 'fashion', becomes a good in and of itself.

Thus, while at first glance models seem involved only in selling the products they model, they also engage in consumption practices that build their image, and in so doing, they mediate our experiences of commodities, and commodify the experience of being 'in fashion'. These practices involve both aesthetic labour, in which workers must invest in styling their bodies and personalities in order to get and keep work (Entwistle and Wissinger 2006), and entrepreneurial labour, in which workers invest time, energy and funds to foster professional relationships, and build their productive capacity, in return for uncertain rewards (Neff et al. 2005).

The way those in the modelling industry engage in this 'schmoozing' and 'makeover' culture in order to attract and keep paid employment also plays into processes used to brand and sell urban space. When models go out in the latest styles to the hottest nightspots, to project the message of living a lifestyle that fits the image of being a model in order to secure work, these compulsory socializing practices provide fodder for urban venues seeking to up their 'cool' quotient, and thereby augment the value of their brand. Urban nightspots seek to attract those who go out on the 'scene', a form of socializing that is very much part of modelling work, to capitalize on what seems to be a free association of creative and glamorous people, but in reality is an intensely networked realm of production.

By engaging in the sorts of compulsory socializing that modelling calls for, models 'model' a lifestyle that enables 'social interaction and communication' to enter the system of production. In this way, as sociologist Adam Arvidsson claims, social interaction and communication become 'directly productive elements' (2005: 237), in which the product is typically an experience, mood or feeling. This compulsory image management and socializing glamorizes the 'model life', an activity that arguably represents immaterial labour, since it facilitates the creation of the 'social context of production' (2005: 241).

Thus, Part I of this chapter examines how models and model agencies are intermediaries between production and consumption, since our encounters with commodities are heavily mediated by the way these are sold to us through the selection, styling and dissemination of images populated by models. Part II considers how models become commodities themselves, insofar as they embody an image that is bought and sold. From this perspective, the question of consumption is seen in terms of image production; that is how does a model's purchase of beauty services, or luxury goods, contribute to the production of the model's image, i.e. the appropriate self and identity that can be sold in the market for fashion models? Part III looks at how the structure of the modelling industry, calling as it does on models' and other workers in the industry's entrepreneurial labour, depends on socializing and consumption of nightlife 'scenes' as a node of production. Part IV examines how this structure of production in the modelling industry is used in a complex way (by brand managers, for instance) to promote consumption through associating products with modelling, a practice that feeds into a trend towards packaging and selling the experience of being 'in fashion' as a commodity in and of itself.

This chapter is based on data from the fashion modelling industry in New York. The data are taken from a larger study (Wissinger, forthcoming), for which I interviewed thirty-four models (twenty-six female and eight male), twelve modelling agents (or 'bookers' as they are known in the industry), two photographers, two advertising executives, three art directors, two PR agents, one casting agent, one make-up artist and one production assistant, fifty-eight interviews in total. My working definition of 'fashion model' is someone whose job entails posing for photographs destined to appear either in the editorial (e.g. nonadvertising) section of a fashion magazine, or in a brand campaign for a luxury good, such as handbags, make-up or high-end designer clothing. Fashion models also travel the circuit of fashion week shows, from New York, to Paris, to Milan, to walk designers' runways. The models in this study who are not fashion models are either older workers (twenty-five years or older), employed by commercial print and television advertising; or they are fit models, whose bodies are used to fit prototypes of clothes prior to manufacturing. While different types of models were interviewed, the majority in the sample are models who make or did make a living from modelling.

Contacts were made using a snowball sample, and were conducted between 1999 and 2007. Interviewees were asked open-ended questions in order to stimulate a longer discussion, such as how they got into the profession, how they defined their job, what they felt they needed to do on the job, and to relate their experiences of different aspects of the work, in terms of how commercial or mainstream jobs differed from editorial or cutting-edge work, how print differed from runway, and what models have to do in order to get jobs. Interviews were open-ended and unstructured, lasting from one to two hours. The age range for the sample was from sixteen to twenty-eight years old for the models, with one older, semiretired male model in his early forties; the bookers tended to be slightly older, mostly in their thirties and forties. The ethnicity of the sample was predominantly white and of European origin. Both of these facts speak to the youthful composition of fashion more generally, and also to the persistently white bias in fashion modelling, where only recently has it been possible for black, Asian or other nonwhite European models to capture the kinds of campaigns and other contracts sought after in modelling.

While there were about the same number of male and female models in the sample, it should be noted that there are fewer jobs available to male models, and they earn significantly less than their female counterparts. As Joanne Entwistle has pointed out in her study of male models in the 'aesthetic economy' of modelling, this may be due in part to the 'different political economies of male and female modeling', in which big cosmetics contracts and designer campaigns are more readily available to female models, and the overall market for women's fashions is much larger than men's (Entwistle 2002: 320). The higher value of women's 'beauty' and intense scrutiny aimed at female bodily appearance that many feminists have pointed out may also be a factor (Entwistle 2002: 320). In addition, model managers may also accept lower wages for male models because they don't take male models as seriously, claiming they are 'just in it for the girls', or that men model to feed their own vanity (Mears

2011). Despite these differences, both male and female models experience demands exacted by the modelling world.

Part I: Models as Intermediaries

Since the early 1920s, when John Robert Powers founded the first professional modelling agency in the United States, the industry has generally experienced growth. The number of agencies listed in the Manhattan Yellow Pages, for instance, increased more than tenfold, from 8 to 143 between 1935 and 2002. The 2010–11 *Occupational Outlook Handbook* (Bureau of Labor Statistics, US Department of Labor, 2010–11) said that models held about 2,200 jobs in 2008, and the number of jobs in the occupation was expected to increase 14–19 per cent as compared to all occupations through 2018, with fewer job openings than job seekers.

The role modelling played in the post-Second World War boom, in which newly available glossy magazines put slick advertising images into the hands of targeted consumers, was significant. The glamorous images found in *Vogue, Harper's Bazaar, Life* and *Look* magazines showed the way towards the commodification of more and more realms of contemporary life, seducing the public into believing that hope could perhaps be found in a jar, and true love and happiness might be possible if one just made the right purchases.

Insofar as they provide a labour force for constructing the iconography of desire, Joanne Entwistle and I have proposed elsewhere that one way to think about models may be borrowed, loosely, from Bourdieu's idea of 'cultural intermediaries' (Entwistle and Wissinger 2007). Bourdieu initially used this term in *Distinction* (1984) as part of a more general discussion of the supposed expansion of the petit bourgeoisie, to include such occupations as journalist-writers and writer-journalists and the 'producers of cultural programmes on television or radio' (p. 325). In his later work on fields of cultural production, he expanded this term to enable him to talk about a range of occupations involved in the symbolic production of meaning around things such as art and popular culture. These occupations are involved in taste-making or defining, shaping the ways in which we encounter and make sense of cultural artefacts in their work of mediation. According to Bourdieu, understanding the production of the things we consume as 'culture' requires understanding the production of symbolic meanings around goods: these goods are shaped and styled for our consumption by a host of occupations, some of which Bourdieu himself discusses, such as fashion journalists, art and literary agents, for example. Taking their cue from this, recent work from Crewe (2003), Gough-Yates (2003), McFall (2004), Negus (1992, 1999) and Nixon and Du Gay (2002) extends the term *cultural intermediaries* to describe the work of a variety of other occupations—advertising creatives and account managers, men's and women's magazine editors, and music producers and A&R (Artists and

Repertoire) executives. These agents are responsible for translating goods into commodities, moving between the two realms of 'production' and 'consumption', and therefore are responsible for framing or promoting culture within the capitalist marketplace (Entwistle 2009).

It may be rather provocative to describe models as cultural mediators, as one might argue that they are not the authors of symbolic meanings—shaped as they are by the clients they work for and the creative directives of people who style and photograph them. However, there are a few ways in which one can see models performing some of the work of mediation. Bourdieu's later use of the term is suitably vague to enable their inclusion: some models can become self-styled agents of their own symbolic meaning, although this only occurs with a very small number of models, the so-called supermodels who have reached the pinnacle of the industry, and so gain a level of control over their image, an autonomy aspired to by models on the lower echelons (Entwistle 2009).

Kate Moss, for example has succeeded in mediating between producers and consumers: long before she was asked to design a range of clothing for Top Shop, Moss was renowned for selling styles in volume. If she was caught by the paparazzi in a Top Shop T-shirt, it was guaranteed to walk out of the stores thereafter. Reportedly, she noticed her 'ability to create fashion' when she 'would see things that I wore sometimes that designers had copied . . . so I thought, listen, I could do that' (Sykes 2008: 183). Part of the reasoning behind her contract to design for Top Shop comes from precisely this power and influence to shape tastes and sell commodities, not in a formalized fashion campaign or contract, but as an embodied agent of 'style'.

Moss's path to supermodeldom and arbiter of style comprises a complex amalgamation of her appearance, her agency's reputation, the frequency and type of photographs she appeared in, the fashion shows she has done, whether or not she does commercials and where and when she has been seen around town. Most models who reach superstardom have collaborated with an agent or photographer who helped them shape their image. In Moss's case, her image was created in collaboration with photographer Corrine Day, with whom, according to Day's website, she formed a 'long and close relationship' (2007).

Given the history of its formation, it is tempting to see the development of Moss's influential style as the result of shaping by industry experts, but in fact, the relationship between model and mentor is more complex. Models, especially those just starting out, receive guidance about what to wear, how to look, where and with whom to go out. Yet, the onus of the burden is on the model's shoulders to appear as if they just 'are' stylish or glamorous, to naturally embody the kind of careless glamour that fashion images so often project. Instruction and guidance can only go so far. If the model does not bring something of her own flair to the transaction, she will not amount to much in the industry. Comments from an agent at an exclusive 'boutique' agency, which manages only a small number of high-calibre models, highlight the contradiction between the image of the model as totally controlled and her apparent independence when she reaches a certain level, a contradiction that implies that at least some models may have more to do with their own success than initially appears to be the case. For a model starting out, most of the agents I spoke to claimed to control all decisions regarding her image, as typified by this agent's statement:

> It's 98 per cent the manager and 2 per cent the model. We will tell them how to dress for a certain appointment. We tell them how to react to a certain client, how to . . . what parties to go to, where to be seen, what restaurants to hang out at, or I mean everything from where they get their facials to what airlines they fly.

Yet, for models who make it to the top, it is a completely different game. At this point:

> Once she's made, once she's Claudia Schiffer, or Christy Turlington, then she's on her own, well not on her own, but she's involved in every single decision that's made. Once she reaches that level—you manage yourself with your manager. Every single move is made with your manager. You're not being told what you're doing, you're making your [own] decisions.

At the same time, even as she explained the extent to which the manager controls models just starting out, the agent conceded that only those new models who can 'handle it' are sent on appointments to see high-calibre photographers such as Steven Meisel, a trend-setting photographer who most often works for *Vogue Italia* and *W* magazines. Thus, on the one hand, to win bookings with photographers and clients at this level, all the 'little nuances' matter and the amount of 'marketing and image' involved is very high, which requires that inexperienced girls be managed quite closely for these encounters, as this agent pointed out. On the other hand, the manager cannot do it alone. Part of the manager's job is to manage and bring out qualities the model brings to the equation, so that together they can inspire what this agent referred to as the 'very small tiny little community of editorial clients', made up of the photographers, designers and editors who can make a model's career. From this perspective, then, it was not only Kate Moss's savvy management, for example but also her 'cheeky attitude' (Sykes 2008: 183) and development of a trademark 'hi-lo style' (2008: 182) that helped catapult her to the top, and into the role of fashion icon.

For models who have not reached the status of supermodel, their active agency in the process of selling things is more diffuse. It exists within a whole host of networks of consumption, and the images models produce and in which they appear help to circulate a whole host of commodities. In other words, models are nodes in the distribution of the symbolic meaning of things: and this can refer to the way they operate as embodied human agents—wearing particular clothes, styling particular looks in their everyday life as captured by the paparazzi, as Moss does so well—and as component parts of the stylized fashion imagery that circulates, although, in reality, the two are very similar: whether we encounter Moss in a paparazzi shot or a fashion campaign, it is always a highly mediated encounter with an image, not the real person.

Part II: The All-Consuming Image in Modelling

Part of modelling work is to produce a 'look' or 'image' that will sell the model to clients. Where and how they shop, eat, get their hair styled, live, vacation and work are all part and parcel of the process by which a model produces his or her image, all consumption practices that are geared towards producing the model's 'look' for the marketplace. As the boutique agent quoted above pointed out, even the airlines a model flies affect that image:

> Well, yeah, I mean Air France. When you are going to Paris, you are going to get better service when you are coming in as a model than if you flew TWA.

Whether they are making choices dictated by their management, or they have reached the level of making choices for themselves, it is both through their paid work and through their lifestyle that models valorize their image, an image that is constructed on a twenty-four-hour-a-day basis, making it difficult for models to distinguish between when they are on or off the job. This image is the product clients buy in order to sell their products to consumers, and thinking about modelling in this way conflates the often taken-for-granted distinction between 'production' and 'consumption', since models' productive labour is bound up with the ways in which they consume, which in turn produces them as a commodity within the modelling labour market.

Entwistle and I have argued that this work to produce an image may be understood as aesthetic labour (Entwistle and Wissinger 2006), which involves the commodification of self for sale in a highly uncertain labour market. Aesthetic labour is the labour that involves acquiring or maintaining a particular bodily performance at work, whether it is a look that is attractive, or certain attitude or 'professional' demeanour that enables employees to 'look good and sound right' for the job (Warhurst and Nickson 2001: 2). This kind of labour involves a packaging of the body for consumption, in which a certain image is constructed and put out in the marketplace.

Constructing the right image for the marketplace also involves work to produce an appropriate personality and build relationships for work, and thus involves a model's entrepreneurial labour as well (Neff et al. 2005). Models are independent contractors who are employed on a project-by-project basis as part of a team. Freelance workers of this sort engage in entrepreneurial labour when they take the risk of investing large amounts of their time with little promise of a definite payout. Therefore, modelling doesn't just sell commodities; through their aesthetic and entrepreneurial labour, models commodify themselves, producing a self and demeanour that is attractive to hire, and in so doing, help promote the image of a lifestyle, with its own consumption rhythms, which by virtue of its association with modelling helps make it attractive to consumers more generally.

Both aesthetic and entrepreneurial labour demand that workers be enterprising, that they work to create an image that will sell. Managing one's own small enterprise, selling oneself or taking care of one's business involves the aesthetic labour of commodifying one's appearance, in the form of personal grooming and creation of a personal 'style' that clients will find appealing. It also involves the entrepreneurial labour of cultivating potentially lucrative relationships, through engaging in social interaction in the 'right' places with the 'right' people. This section will treat how models commodify their appearance, and the next will discuss how models commodify their personalities.

The aesthetic labour of modelling may involve all manner of bodily work—dieting; working out; tanning or avoiding the sun to preserve one's complexion; looking after one's skin, shaving, waxing, plucking body hair; paying regular trips to the hairstylist, the beauty salon, the gym. Several models I interviewed explained that the work on the self never stops. One model pointed out that even when on vacation from working, she makes sure to take a one- to two-hour jog every day to 'keep things in order'.

In many occupations, aesthetics of the body are important to the labour process and the circulation of value, both the value of the individual body selling itself on the labour market and the value of employees' bodies sold by companies to customers. Thus, aesthetics of the body contribute to capital accumulation in some occupational sectors where the aesthetic body is a commodity, either because it is important to the service sold, or where the body's image is the commodity transacted between employee and client, which is the case with modelling. In labour markets that demand an aesthetically compliant body, the onus is on workers to perform the necessary aesthetic labour and this constitutes an often important part of the production process, while 'on the job' as well as 'behind the scenes', i.e. in time not officially defined as 'work', such as going to the gym or doing anything required to maintain one's body for this work. Thus aesthetic labour involves work on the raw material of the body—shaping it as best one can to fit in with the stringent requirements of modelling.

The body is packaged for consumption in various ways. A female model explains:

> You want to sell them because you're your product; you're the product.
>
> *Your appearance*?
>
> Yeah, your appearance, which is different from who you are, it's hard to remember that it's just your exterior.

The model's image is part of the product that she is. An agent put it succinctly: 'the image is the commodity', and models must engage in specific consumption practices in order to create the right image, which they then sell to clients. They work to produce their image through their self-presentation, which entails specific modes of consumption: one booker has new models look at magazines, and then sends them shopping, so they will be dressed 'right' for clients. They are also sent to an agency-approved salon for a haircut and colour, and are required to get a manicure, a pedicure and buy make-up. A casting agent noted: 'Models actually wear the fashions they model—to get the job they have to look like they know about fashion'. A model who was near the top of the profession for several years remarked:

> You have to look [as if you are at] a certain level, you have to go shopping (so there are certain rules of appearance in terms of your clothes) . . . it's hard to describe what professionalism is.

Another model linked this attention to appearance to the goal of projecting an image of being in demand, saying, 'you have to look like you are making money, you must look like you are working.' She found she had to shop frequently to get the varied and subtle looks called for by the job, and 'forever' found herself 'running into stores at 7 a.m.' on the way to castings to get what she needed to project that image. One model included these demands to look right as part of the job description:

> First you have to distinguish what my job entails which is keeping myself in shape, I consider going to the gym as part of my job, going to the manicurist and pedicurist.

Thus, activities that are normally coded as leisure pursuits, such as shopping, getting a manicure or getting one's hair done, are pulled into the productive domain, when they are aimed at creating the model's 'look' for work.

This compulsion to perform aesthetic labour, combined with the imperative to produce the right image at all times while in public, affects the top models and regular workaday models alike. For those at the top such as Kate Moss, embodying the image involves dressing the part at all times, which can be difficult. She knows that 'any pictures of her help promote her own products', and that 'When I am going out at night, I know I am going to be photographed. But if you're going on the school run and you have to think about looks for the world's paparazzi, it's not so great' (Sykes 2008: 185). While this readiness for public scrutiny seems only to be a problem for celebrities, in fact, lesser-known models are also called on to live as if they are the image they sell, as this model discovered when she pinned up her new bangs (fringe) for a quick trip to her modelling agency. Her agent came running from across the room yelling at her:

> 'Ahhhh! Bangs, bangs!' gesturing toward his forehead saying, 'you can't wear them like that!' and I was really surprised. He didn't like it pinned back, because it was uncool, it wasn't stylish. It was so annoying. If they see you in the street, they say 'you can't do this! You have to blah blah blah' you know? Like you are supposed to be on your job 100 per cent of the time!

This model was learning that modelling entails not only promoting commodities via paid work but also calls for promoting oneself as a commodity by engaging in practices aimed at producing an image that exemplifies the kind of lifestyle choices models' paid work promotes. These practices produce the overall image of models and modelling in ways that mediate encounters with commodities outside of the most obvious features of paid modelling work.

As these examples illustrate, the influence of models goes far beyond their role in selling goods. Models may sell products through stylized fashion imagery they help to create, but their influence and mediating role is greater than simply selling actual goods or services. Complying with the structured demands of the modelling world, they might be said to promote a host of things: aesthetic standards of dress, body and demeanour; a particular 'lifestyle'; and particular patterns of consumption. Models 'model' consumption practices that involve a highly groomed, closely styled image, which is then circulated for sale in the model marketplace. As I argue below, the need to circulate one's image helps create and sustain a particular urban scene and particular consumption habits focused around bars, restaurants, clubs and so on. This 'scene', in part, makes up the model mystique, an image of a lifestyle that is then packaged and sold in the form of television shows, websites, ringtones and other branded products that consumers use to create a sense of community around the idea of fashion, in a form of preprogrammed agency that is profitable for marketers.

Part III: The Value of the Scene

Models not only package themselves by wearing the right clothes or having the right 'look', they also work to present themselves as 'in the know' as part of a community, an important player in the field of modelling. Thus models not only 'model' consumption practices by engaging in aesthetic labour; the entrepreneurial aspects of their work demand that they 'model' forms of nightlife consumption in order to get and keep work. These practices are in turn attractive to venues seeking to capitalize on hype, and all of these activities taken together promote the image of the industry as a centre of glamour and 'cool'. When models and modelling professionals perform entrepreneurial labour, they invest time and energy socializing with others in the industry with an eye towards making possibly profitable associations through building networks. This unpaid time devoted to getting work takes place within what one freelance fashion editor called the 'circuit of scenes'. These scenes comprise the many dinners, parties and other social gatherings that are a major part of 'the life', as many models refer to it (Parmentier and Fischer 2007: 23).

In other words, models produce their image not only in the pictures in which they appear, or how they appear in the street, going shopping, or en route to a photo shoot or fashion show, but also via the energy generated in the various social networks that are a key element of production in the industry. This energy, hype or buzz, created when actors in the field congregate, is attractive to urban nightlife venues, which try to exploit the modelling industry's 'social scene' as a means for creating a potentially profitable image for themselves. Further, brands try to associate themselves with this kind of 'network sociality' (Wittel 2001) in the hope that some of the glamour and attractiveness of the 'scene' will rub off on their product. Finally, the publicity this lifestyle attracts also serves to enlist consumers in the production of its value, as they engage with the fashionable life as a branded experience, spending their free time watching television shows, building websites and fostering a community along preprogrammed lines that shape and guide their apparently autonomous behaviour.

A young model backstage at a New York fashion show was explicit about it: 'fashion parties are about meeting people, not about having fun'. Another model at the same show explained 'I get jobs when I go out into the nightlife. It's unbelievable who you can meet.' When she first started, this model went out seven nights a week because she found she made 'so many connections', but now, having achieved some measure of success, she is more 'moderate—I go out about two to three nights per week'. Going out is usually a model's choice, but a young girl from Slovenia who had been in the industry for about a year said: 'Sometimes even the bookers tell you, you have to go out, this night, because this photographer might be there. Certain parties at a studio you'll have to go to, too.'

Although the less experienced models have to be told what to do, one agent found that as a result of this constant networking, successful models develop what she called a 'sixth sense'—they begin to get a good idea of 'who's who'. A booker tells her models to make it a priority to know all the most important clients, and the best ones do:

> These models come in—I have to give them a little credit. They learn very, very fast. They learn within a few months who's who. They know who the photographers are and they learn how to play the game. They develop a sixth sense of how to be on these appointments and how to react, and how to not be too chatty with their fellow models, and I mean they really get it, they do, and then when they've got a taste of it, they're just like hungry lions, they just want more and more.

Models and other members of the industry 'play the game' on the nightlife scene, engaging in what Elizabeth Currid has called the 'economics of a dance floor' (2007: 87), where workers in creative industries ranging from models, to photographers, art directors, designers and merchandisers meet and inspire one another, and form contacts for potential collaborations, or production teams. Although she does not examine the modelling world in detail, Currid's claim that 'social interactions are essential to the overall production system' (2007: 89) in creative industries is true of modelling as well.

While Currid celebrates this use of urban nightlife spaces by creative people 'as ways to advance their own careers and the cultural economy more broadly' (Currid 2007: 95), she misses how, for models and for other aspirants to the 'hot' jobs in 'cool' industries (Neff et al. 2005), there can be a downside to this form of production. Currid's interviews with the highly successful participants in the creative economy underplay what David Grazian has called 'the darker side of these adventures in compulsory networking and self-promotion', given how:

> the growing instability of the flexible creative economy requires workers to take on the burdens of entrepreneurial labor (Neff et al. 2005) by shouldering more of the risks and overhead costs of developing artistic careers in the first place. (Grazian 2008a: 117)

While Currid herself points out that Dior's fashion designer Hedi Slimane has said he 'plug[s] into the nightlife scene to become inspired' for his collections, she fails to acknowledge that the 'unknown girl on the dance floor' who sparks his creative process (Currid 2007: 6) is most likely an aspiring model who goes out night after night with the hope of making a connection that will be her big break. Models spend their time socializing and conducting their lives with an eye towards making potentially lucrative associations with their peers. Using time and energy for work during what is normally coded as leisure time represents an entrepreneurial aspect of modelling that is important to consider. While going out every night may seem like mere fun, I am interested in how the willingness to engage with this lifestyle in the pursuit of 'cool' feeds into marketing strategies that are capturing social energy for productive ends.

One way to think about this process is to examine how nightlife is made into a workplace in the modelling industry's 'circuit of scenes'. Engaging in the 'scene' of the modelling world, either by direct participation, or by following it in gossip pages or one's favourite 'style' website, can be understood as a kind of immaterial production. According to Maurizio Lazzarato, in immaterial production, 'life becomes inseparable from work' (Lazzarato 1996: 138) and the 'reproduction and enrichment of its productive capacities' becomes an important moment in the production process. Hence, this type of production encompasses a

> series of activities that are not normally recognized as 'work'—in other words, the kinds of activities involved in defining and fixing cultural and artistic standards, fashions, tastes, consumer norms, and, more strategically, public opinion. (Lazzarato 1996: 133)

The fashion crowd, of which models are a part, strive to be the arbiters of taste; they model a form of consumption to which advertisements admonish us to aspire; and when models and their acolytes gather to make the connections which are formative of their 'productive capacity', the fashion crowd engages in a 'series of activities that are not normally recognized as "work"' (Lazzarato 1996: 133), such as going to parties, that are nonetheless an integral part of doing business in this industry.

Adam Arvidsson's work on brands and immaterial labour is useful here for making a connection between the productive social networks Lazzarato describes and consumption. Arvidsson wants to explore, as he explains, the 'productive aspects of consumption', the 'controlling or even exploitative aspects of brands' and 'the new "means of consumption" in general' (2005: 237). Working with ideas from Michael Hardt and Antonio Negri (2000), Arvidsson describes how in the 'post-modern, highly mediatized life world' in which we now live (2005: 242), there has been a 'movement from a Fordist, factory-centred production process to the more diffuse and expanded systems of production that characterize post-Fordism, where social interaction and communication enter as directly productive elements' (Arvidsson 2005: 237).

The work models and their associates do to produce the right 'image' on the 'scene' is one example of this process. This form of immaterial labour takes place when the model or model agent 'draws on knowledge, contacts, and social relations' that they mobilize in the 'network sociality of leisure time' (Arvidsson 2005: 241, quoting Wittel (2001)). By spending their leisure time making connections, the models and their acolytes create a 'scene' that is productive in two ways. When they get together for professional reasons at a party, the fashion crowd nonetheless enjoys itself and produces a typical output of immaterial labour, for example:

> a social relation, a shared meaning, or a sense of belonging; what Hardt and Negri have more recently called a *common*, that feeds into the post-Fordist production process by providing a temporary context that makes the production or the realization of value possible. (Arvidsson 2005: 241, emphasis added)

The 'unpaid social life' (2005: 241) of the modelling world called for by the entrepreneurial aspects of modelling work creates a 'context of consumption', which Arvidsson defines as a 'social relation within which goods make sense' (2005: 242). By engaging in practices that create a 'scene' that appears glamorous or fashionable and thereby generates publicity, workers in the modelling industry help produce a 'common framework' in which goods have value, where getting into the hot nightclub or restaurant, or having the 'it' bag or shoes, or reading and blogging about these practices, will be a meaningful experience, creating a sense of belonging, or being part of, a fashionable life. Arguably, organizational structures such as modelling that create frameworks for tapping into the 'common' as a source of value present the possibility for insidious marketing methods in which consumers can be pulled into creating their own market-driven experiences, experiences that promote patterns of consumption that increase the value of brands.

Part IV: Gilt by Association—Branding and the Fashionable Life

Arvidsson claims that new forms of brand management capitalize on the energies and meanings consumers themselves bring to branded experiences. Marketing commodities in this scenario is achieved through a form of 'biopolitical' control, a form of governance that 'works from below by shaping the context in which freedom is exercised, and by providing the raw materials it employs' (2005: 246). From this perspective, 'what to do with the object' (2005: 246) is not spelled out; rather, 'brands work as platforms for action that enable the production of particular immaterial use-values: an experience, a shared emotion, a sense of community. This way, brands work as a kind of ubiquitous means of production that are inserted within the socialized production process that consumers engage in' (2005: 248).

In particular, when brand managers use the productive capacity of the social scene in modelling to guide and channel responses to particular products and venues, they are using the 'scene' to provide 'an environment, an ambience, which anticipates and programs the agency of consumers' (2005: 245). This programming no longer takes the imperative form of 'You Must!', but rather functions with the softer suggestion of 'You May!' (Arvidsson 2005, quoting Barry 2001 and Žižek 1999: 245). Here, the modelling world is used to produce an ambience for brands, by playing on the layered associations between models and the products their work advertises, the fashionable and attractive ideal they seek to embody, and lifestyle they strive to create the impression of having. By ' "farming out" the diffusion of a branded good, or the construction of a sign value, to a particularly influential or attractive group' (Arvidsson 2005: 248), brand managers on some level cede control of how the process will work, and instead trust that the productive social networks that typify this crowd will produce some valuable associations for their brand.

A typical example of the way models are used to 'farm out' the construction of a sign value for branded settings or products is the model party. This term describes a party ostensibly for models and other workers in the industry. Model parties are thrown by modelling agencies, photo studios, bars, clubs and restaurants. For these parties, agencies spend money to get their models and potential clients into one place, and the agency and the venue for the party benefit from the kinds of interaction enabled by such a setting. A photographer, for example may meet the 'it' girl or boy, befriend the model and so get a chance to photograph him or her on their next job. The models, an agent explained, get exposure in the right sort of setting, 'their names get out there, they make contacts'. If the press comes, 'all the better'; the agencies' and the models' notoriety is built, which produces publicity for all involved.

Clubs and bars want to host these parties to associate themselves with fashion, glamour and beautiful people, an association that might then attract a clientele of a certain calibre. According to a young female booker, 'model parties' enhance the bar or club's image, as well as having an immediate effect on the bottom line, since, in her experience at least:

> female models attract men with money, which brings in a higher bar tab. They'll use any excuse—a model's birthday, a stupid holiday. . . . Deals go down in bars frequently. . . . Brands of alcohol throw these parties too . . . to get the 'right' people there, drinking their product to create the right image.

In one example of the value of attracting the 'right' people to patronize one's business, a nightclub venue in New York City hired a handsome twenty-one-year-old Englishman as 'image director', paying him a weekly stipend to 'create relationships with agents, designers, model agencies, and with the celebs'. Essentially working as what is known in the business as a 'model wrangler', he was to be sent by the club to 'Milan, Paris, and London during their fashion weeks and to the Cannes Film Festival', an investment it made because 'he could be our connection between the A-list and our venue', thereby cementing its market value in the currency of image (Salkin 2008).

This subtle form of branding has the side effect of blurring a perceived reality with what David Grazian refers to as the 'synthetic excitement' (2008b: 86) generated by the 'pseudo event' (2008b: 77) in urban nightlife. Grazian describes the process as 'reality marketing' (2008b: 86) in which 'public relations firms . . . recruit actresses, models, and pop stars to make seemingly casual appearances at their clients' most fashionable hot spots, for a price' (2008b: 78), a practice that infuses their 'branded image with a shot of nocturnal cool' (2008b: 79) to 'legitimate the venue among an even broader crowd of wannabes and hangers-on while attracting the paparazzi and entertainment news media' (2008b: 80). A freelance fashion editor I talked to saw this legitimation process as 'a circuit of "scenes" or power centers; it's very organic, and sometimes it makes a place or a company'; she cited Balthazar, a hot restaurant in New York at the time, as an example of how becoming popular with the fashion crowd can catapult a restaurant to white-hot status. Trying to attract this 'scene' sometimes has its drawbacks, however. As Grazian points out, this crowd's insularity 'drastically limits' the 'ability to reach more heterogeneous, wider webs of consumers who make up the bulk of the city's nightlife market' (2008b: 83). When these consumption practices do make it into the public eye, however, they glamorize a lifestyle, making it attractive in ways that influence far more of our lifestyle choices than merely whether or not to go out at night.

When models 'model' a lifestyle in which life becomes inseparable from work, they glamorize the practice, making it attractive to others (Neff et al. 2005). Further, by actively engaging in the self-commodification required by modelling, a practice that is then publicized as part of a glamorous and fashionable life, models not only make consumption practices—such as following fashion, dressing fashionably, engaging in intensive grooming and patronizing centres of urban nightlife—attractive, they provide the raw materials for the commodification of the fashionable life itself.

Models and those who work with them seem to be living a dream, a dream that disguises their aesthetic and entrepreneurial labour, work that sets the stage for increasing levels of immaterial labour, in which consumers' social networks are pulled towards productive ends, where consumers feel they are freely pursuing what interests them, or creating something that matters to them, while in fact they are creating value for a brand and providing a crucial platform for that brand to realize value. Models not only glamorize products by appearing in advertising images; when they go out on the 'scene' wearing certain styles and socializing with their peers in exclusive nightspots or hip neighbourhoods, they model a lifestyle that does not say 'you must!' but 'you may!' In so doing, they provide raw materials for building what Arvidsson refers to as the 'intertextual, physical and virtual spaces that pre-structure and anticipate the agency of consumers' (2005: 247).

In recent decades, the physical spaces of the 'model life' have made the jump to the virtual world of television and the Internet, in the form of numerous 'reality' television shows about the modelling industry such as *The Agency*, *Make Me a Supermodel*, *America's Next Top Model*, *The Janice Dickenson Modeling Agency* and *A Model Life* in the USA, along with the *Top Model* franchise throughout the world, which at its peak spread to more than 100 markets internationally, including not only England and Canada, but also China, Ghana, Nigeria and Honduras (Banks 2007, 2011).[1] The modelling world, as occupied by workers in the industry, or as depicted in these televised settings, creates a framework of self-expression shaped by modelling and fashion. Consumers contribute to the value of this framework by spending their free time watching the television shows about modelling, or actively participating in online communities associated with them, sending each other phone messages 'from Tyra Banks' via the *ANTM* website[2] commenting on the blogs, voting to elect the 'model of the week', buying 'Top Model' T-shirts and other merchandise or joining Facebook's group called 'Addicted to America's Next Top Model', which had more than 30,000 members in 2009, with the show's fan page reaching more than 4 million 'likes' as of 2011. The model life has been covered in detail on various sites such as www.modelnetwork.com or www.models.com, where participants pick their favourite model, rate runway looks and models' online portfolios, or follow blogs about the 'hottest newcomer', or about fashion weeks around the world. Models and modelling also attract visits to fashion and modelling websites such as www.style. com, www.fashionista.com, or to the discussion of all things fashion at *New York* magazine's The Cut (nymag.com/daily/fashion), as well as YouTube's endless loops of models walking runways.

This level of intimacy with the modelling world shapes consumer agency in both direct and indirect ways. An American fashion publicist observed in one of our interviews:

> people who watch reality television shows about models used to just aspire to be glamorous. Now they aspire to have that specific model look. . . . They have a new familiarity with models and what they are and how they look.

Less directly, the familiarity with models and fashion that these television shows and websites promote doesn't sell particular products, it provides a platform for brands to become part of the modelling world. These spaces of interaction sell fashion, the idea of being fashionable and access to the know-how for emulating the kinds of images models promote, mediating our experiences of them, thereby shaping and guiding consumer agency that seems to be autonomous, but is in fact directed in ways that increase the value of brands.

Conclusion

This chapter has endeavoured to spell out several examples of how models mediate our experience of commodities in ways that are not as straightforward as one might assume, considering that it is their job to pose for photographs and walk runways to create an attraction to and a desire for the clothes or products they are wearing. When models work to produce a desirable image, styling themselves to appear glamorous, or attract attention, they mediate our relationships with the products they use to produce that meaning. As they engage in the system of signs in which glamour or desirability play a part, they also participate in a series of networks in which products, images and people interact, such that images and products are circulated in productive ways. Thus, within these networks, models engage in activities that are productive not only when they are officially 'at work', but also in the quasi-professional social settings that are an integral part of the modelling world. In so doing, models and their peers contribute to the subtle ways branding now gets done, insofar as it plays on meaning by association, in which a mood or feeling can be attached to a product simply by getting it into the hands of a culturally attractive crowd, such as the one found in the modelling world.

By using the social world of modelling to promote their products, brand managers are arguably playing on the model's social role in which they 'model' a form of life that is potentially productive for the brand. Thus, models mediate our experiences with commodities not only when they are posing for the camera, or walking down the runway, but also when they are walking down the street, attending a party or having a coffee at a local café. The structure of modelling work demands that models 'model' a certain kind of life, and in so doing, make it attractive, as something consumers want to participate in or know about. Marketers play on this attraction to the fashionable life, providing it as the raw material that consumers then use to build communities, of fans, or of people who are 'with it' or in the know about fashion. As desire for community is directed towards predetermined ends, consumers produce themselves as attentive audiences, delivering themselves for free as marketable units of attention to be bought and sold in the commercial marketplace. The means offered for belonging in this world are the commodities with which this world is associated, not only via the pictures in advertisements in which models appear, but also in the form of the 'model life', which those in the modelling world work so hard to produce the image of living. In so doing, they model a lifestyle that is then packaged and sold to us as a commodity, an experience that can be had for the price of our attention.

–10–

Fashion Modelling: The Industry Perspective

Introduction

When it comes to fashion modelling, everyone is an 'expert' with some claim to know something about what it takes to be a fashion model. With the exponential increase in the industry's exposure in the last several decades, through fierce public debate regarding concerns about models' size, shape or racial and ethnic diversity in fashion images, or the industry's celebratory treatment by reality TV formats that claim to go 'inside' the industry, models have become a ubiquitous feature in everyday life. In the face of reality TV's claim to expose the inner workings of the industry, a claim which must be treated with some skepticism, as Stephanie Sadre-Orafai's chapter in this collection attests, the editors of this volume interviewed industry practitioners themselves, as the people who actually run the business. We were especially interested in exploring how successful models make it into the spotlight and what contributes to their staying power, what goes into creating a model 'brand', and whether or not the industry will see an era like that of the supermodels again. In a 'round table' discussion with four modelling professionals in London and New York, we therefore began by asking them to consider what occurred during the 'supermodel' era of the 1980s and early 1990s (however defined, as we discuss) and its aftermath.

Participants

Interviewers: Joanne Entwistle (JE) and Elizabeth Wissinger (EW)
Cory Bautista (CB), Agency Director, New York Models
George Speros (GS), Agent, Women's division, New York Models
Doreen Small (DS), formerly Vice President, General Counsel Ford Model Agency, Adjunct Professor at Fordham Law School's Fashion Law Institute
Melissa Richardson (MR), Founder and Owner of Take2 Model Agency in the UK from 1982 to 2010

EW: How long have you been in the industry?

DS: Well I'm new to the industry but my job immediately prior to Ford was in an apparel company, big company called Warnaco, so I've been in the fashion business for about ten years, but in modelling only about four.

CB: I've been in this business since 1988. I started my career in Miami with Ford Models, and before that I was in a production company.

GS: I've been in the industry for probably about fifteen years at least, maybe sixteen to seventeen.

MR: Twenty-eight years—'82 to 2009.

JE: *Melissa, given your longevity in the industry it would be interesting to start with you and try to get some idea of the changes you've seen over this time, which of course covers the period of the supermodels which we'll come back to. Can you possibly tell us what's different from when you started? Would you say there's been a huge amount of change in that time?*

MR: Yeah, huge. Because it was much more parochial in '82, it was much more of a local market and we really didn't have any foreign models when we started, they were all English girls. And it was a much smaller market, so if the girls were pretty, they all really worked. And you could get them jobs quite easily, whether they were great jobs or just catalogue jobs, nearly everybody on our books was working and making a good living, whereas now you get people who just come in to London and do lots of editorial, don't get paid, and then actually never move beyond that point. So I think it was much easier, now girls are coming so fast. In my loo at home I've got a list of the girls we had in about '84. When we'd just started, [there were] about thirty girls on the list. I could tell you about each girl I can remember their face, I can remember who they were, I can remember stuff about them, I can remember jobs they did. If I look at when I closed the agency in 2009, I didn't even know who some of those girls are. I couldn't actually recognize them if they were to walk into a room I have to say 'Hello darling' because I literally did not know their names.

JE: *Is that because you had more, you just had a bigger stable of models . . .?*

MR: We had more. The memory files were getting filled up, I guess. We had 200 on the board. But actually, ratio-wise, they were making less money than those early thirty, and the intimacy, that you knew those girls, I think made it easier to be a good agent because you'd know what that girl was capable of.

JE: *The sheer quantity of models is much, much greater now?*

CB: You know why? It's the electronic accessibility.

EW: *They can find out about it online. Can you say more about accessibility?*

CB: When scouts went out, you used to have to wait a week or two for an image to come, not because there weren't any computers, but because the scouts wanted the right photos for selling the models to the agencies. Polaroids picked up the very worst. Digitals still do that. With video streaming, you know exactly what you're getting into.

It's instant—that's why the world is open, that's why you can find a girl in Riga, Latvia, or you can find a girl anywhere in the world, in Sao Paulo—Sao Paulo's good—and Peru. Sometimes you'll find a girl in a little mountain in Peru.

JE: *Do you think that the web has changed the way we interact with models as well, the blogs and the websites?*

MR: You know, we're just used to consuming images in a very different way and they're just little tidbits rather than, you know, a glossy magazine that was very precious that you might keep—I kept hold of my *Vogues*, sometimes for ages if it was a good cover, they were very valuable precious objects—whereas we can just consume thousands of kinds of celebrity images on the Internet in no time.

DS: Well, blogs and Internet, the Internet in some ways has changed how our clients . . . what the clients want from the models, the kind of usage. So when a client books a model, there's a shoot and then you negotiate how those images are going to be used; on packaging, on point of sale, you know, on labels, in a magazine, on television. So all of that is the subject of negotiation. Increasingly we see that clients want Internet usage because their business models are shifting, their advertising dollars are being spent more on the Internet, they have more eyeballs on the Internet than they do with traditional media, or they have younger eyeballs. They are more interested in getting usage in the electronic media—handheld devices, social networking. On the blog side, I think we have an opportunity to help increase a model's individual profile, to help increase certainly the profile of the agency to let people know who we are and what we're doing and what's current and aggregate some material, these are the models who have been working couture, these are the models who have interesting outside lives, and so we can use our blog to do that. And again, also increase the model's profile to perhaps help increase the opportunities for the models.

EW: *How has the Internet impacted upon the industry?*

MR: All the casting's done by Internet now.

GS: The Internet has completely changed the market. It used to be that girls were scouted—a girl that was stopped on the street was kind of the traditional story—stopped at a coffee shop or something. And now, you have girls from every area of the world, who have personal computers and are sending pictures, many of them at a particularly young age. We're exposed as an industry to so many more models than we were years ago.

EW: *While we're talking about the widespread exposure of modelling to audiences, could you just say a little bit about also how the television shows—America's Next Top Model—have changed the public's perception of modelling or people's relationship to modelling. Do they understand more about it?*

GS: I just think they have brought modelling even more into the public consciousness.

JE: *Can I ask the obvious question—how do these shows fit into the industry? Do they have anything to say about the realities of fashion modelling? They supposedly show you how the industry works. Do they show you some of the elements of the working, sort of day-to-day practice, possibly?*

CB: The TV shows illustrate the ground level of modelling, how a photo shoot happens, etc. The intricacies of modelling are not shown, however. Believe me, I was a judge on one of them, so I know exactly.

MR: They do show you something, sometimes. Yes, like the shoots and things like that.

JE: *Do you mean that they may show how models behave on a shoot and what qualities you might need? Having said that, they've got very little to do with how you really make it in the world of modelling, it's a reality TV phenomenon rather than a fashion modelling phenomenon, is that right?*

MR: Yes, absolutely 100 per cent. But . . . yeah, I mean that's their fifteen minutes of fame isn't it and, you know, my daughter loves to watch those programmes. They actually make me cross because I think it gives people unreal expectations of what the reality is. And it's always a very extreme version of reality. But of course people do do all that stuff they show, like having to fly through the air with their faces coloured pink and wearing harnesses, but they don't do it all in four weeks of starting out. More like once or twice in their whole careers. It's about making good telly.

CB: A reality TV show has got to entertain. Producers will manipulate stories. They have to make great TV for people who don't know anything about the industry. In that sense it's not real. When it comes to the day-to-day, people always want to see drama, they want to see conflict because it sells.

EW: *Some of it is not on camera.*

CB: Right, exactly, the drama that happens off camera is the real drama. True. The presence of a spy camera is between the producers, the models, the agents and the judges.

EW: *So since those shows were on the air then, have you noticed the difference in girls coming in trying to be models, that they have those ideas in their heads now?*

CB: The only reason I appeared as a judge on *Make Me a Supermodel* was to bring New York Model Management exposure. Since I did the show, New York Model Management, which has always been a boutique agency, is now a boutique agency that girls know about, where they want to submit their pictures. We might have been popular with just the scouts that went to see these agencies in small-town areas. Now they're coming to us because they know who we are, so our chances are better because we get to see these girls.

EW: *So you've become a brand . . .*

CB: Right. And so our chances are better because we get to see these girls.

JE: *Our discussion of developments like the Internet, as well as new media formats like model TV reality shows, indicates that these changes have impacted upon the industry today. I wonder if we can reflect back on the supermodel era of the 1980s, when we had just a few big-name models who became household names and were paid millions, can you say why that happened and then consider whether it could it ever happen again, given these developments?*

CB: Well I'll ask you the question first, and then I'll answer it. Define supermodel for me.

MR: Would you consider people like Jean Shrimpton and Twiggy to be supermodels? Because in a way they were, everybody knew their name and they were doing all the big jobs and everything. But that particular thing that we think of as the supermodels, the Christy, Linda, Tatjana Patitz, Elle Macpherson, all those girls, that was really happening around the time we opened the agency I suppose about '82, '83, '84—is that what you've found?

JE: *If you Google it to see how the word circulates, you'll find it has a number of origins, I think people talk about the sixties, and people like Twiggy, as early supermodels—it's referring to well-known models, but here we're using the term the way it gets used in the eighties when models became 'household names'.*

CB: I would answer the question exactly the same way. It all depends on whether you're talking about length of time spent modelling, or if you're talking about its heyday in the eighties. I mean, Janice Dickinson for me was never a supermodel, she's a self-proclaimed supermodel. By my definition, that is not a supermodel.

JE: *A lot of them were American weren't they, the original ones? Though there were some Europeans too.*

MR: Tatjana Patitz was one, Helena Christensen, Naomi Campbell, Kate Moss, but supermodels really came with Linda and Christy and that bunch.

JE: *It's the models who are household names again. You say Gisele and just about anyone, even outside the fashion world, will know.*

CB: Of course, Gisele Bündchen, they know she's from Brazil and they know that she makes millions of dollars a year still, and she's married to Tom Brady. They know she's the whole thing, the whole situation. There have been other models that have trickled down who have a staying power as well.

EW: *Do you think that the supermodel phenomenon could ever happen again?*

CB: Of course it would be more lucrative for us if there were another supermodel era, and I believe fashion is cyclical, so hopefully that will happen.

EW: *Can you say more about why you think that?*

CB: I think the supermodel era would still have been around had it not been for a couple of key issues. The main one was the economy, because these models were so super, and were in such high demand, that their rates continued to go higher and higher. At that time, unlike the stars that we have on covers now, there wasn't much of a celebrity presence. Instead we had these model celebrities. The supermodels were the goddesses, and as such, their rates went higher and higher, and then higher still. Then things dwindled down and designers started thinking, if we pay our photographers to find models each season, then it will become more cyclical. Then models might work for a couple of seasons, but then we find a new face. I think that's what's happened since the supermodel era. Financially it was more frugal [i.e. economical] for these designers to actually have a say in the capping of these supermodel rates. The other thing, quite frankly, is that the American and the European, and even the worldwide market, was getting tired of the same ten supermodels. So something had to change there. And designers began to ask, 'why don't we start going with actresses to see where they can fill in our pages?'

MR: I think that everything is very cyclical and I think it will come back again. But there's a financial element to it and things have changed. When everybody started to scout and scour the world for beautiful faces and bring girls in from all over the place, some of them did really, really well but hundreds, thousands were sent home. And everybody thought they'd make a lot of money. Well, of course, because now there are so many people, the fees have dropped massively and so these girls aren't really making a living wage because they're doing magazines and other work for free, you know.

JE: *As we know, back then the whole supermodel phenomenon was built on these outrageously large sums of money. So financially, something has changed. Can you give us an example of how things have changed?*

MR: We did the Pretty Polly campaign with Saffron Aldridge—it was about 1990—and I think she got twelve grand a day or something for the three days, plus buy-outs, you know. And now it's like six grand, take it or leave it, three years. We were talking UK usage only. And the point is there are so many girls, great bodies, great faces who will work for less. And then there's Facebook: Levis was looking for girls via Facebook and were offering three-hundred quid. And my daughter's nineteen and she's just finished school and gap year and if somebody said to her, 'Do you want to be in a Levis' campaign for three-hundred quid?', she'd think it was a fortune. And I'd say, 'But darling, your image is going to be all over the world for £300'. And she'd say, 'Well, you know, come on mum, how cool is that?' So there's no feeling that your image has value, [among] today's kids, and so it's very difficult for the model agents to keep the prices up. And there's always some model agent coming up under you who's actually just desperate; the girl's got no money, she owes them two grand, the job's two grand, well I can clear the debt, you know. So that's what happens and there's been a lot of undercutting, because as you said, so many agents. So many models.

EW: *Some people argue that once the supermodels got so expensive, even if the world hadn't tired of them, it made economic sense to hire actresses—why not go for Hollywood girls if you are paying Hollywood prices? So that might also have contributed to an increasing use of celebrities.*

DS: Yes, yes. Hollywood is such an American thing. So Gwyneth Paltrow is on the cover of this month's *Vogue*, although you'll see, you know, one of our models, Rose Cordero, was on the cover of French *Vogue*. Also, there's now Chinese *Vogue*, Japanese *Vogue* and so many more of those magazines now.

JE: *Covers used to be . . . one of the stepping stones for a model breaking in, she would shoot her first US* Vogue *or UK* Vogue *or French* Vogue, *and now obviously that has changed hasn't it? Do you have unknown models on the cover of* Vogue *anywhere these days?*

MR: I was talking to Alex Shulman [editor, UK *Vogue*], and she was saying with those supermodels that everybody knew their name and you could put them on the cover of *Vogue* and you would sell exponentially more copies of *Vogue* because they were there and these days she has to put a celebrity on the cover to sell more copies, that's one of the things that rather depressed me about the whole business. Getting covers was, you know, a big part of the agent's job, to get the girl amazing covers. And yeah, it's bloody hard now to get girls on the cover. I mean some magazines do put unknown models on the cover but often it's models like Daria, Natalia, Kate [Moss]; all those more established models, not new models.

GS: You rarely see unknown models on *Vogue* covers (French *Vogue* being the exception). American *Vogue* almost always uses celebrities. It's much different now, many people outside the industry don't even know who the top models are. In the past you had Linda/Christy/Naomi, etc. who had tremendous exposure both outside and in the industry. Today Lara is as close to being a name the way they were, but I don't think many people outside of the industry know who she is, nor do they know a Raquel or Natasha Poly. I mean, they are supermodels within the industry, but my friends growing up would know Brooklyn Decker from *Sports Illustrated* before they would know who Raquel Zimmerman is, who's done fifty stories for French *Vogue*.

EW: *Would it be possible for someone like Raquel to do* Sports Illustrated *so she could become a household name?*

GS: I think an amazing job was done with Carolyn Murphy. She had an amazing (and very long) editorial moment, and then she crossed over and she did a *Sports Illustrated* cover, then Estée Lauder. It's rare that a girl can completely cross over into the other kind of genres.

EW: *How have the fashion industry and the cosmetics industry changed? Do the advertisers have different budgets and requirements today?*

CB: Yes. They have to be more frugal since we are in a recession. Another good point is that fashion, like everything, is changing. Newspapers are changing, catalogues, editorials. Everything is going into the electronic age, which is much more of a tangible communicational medium for the public. Everything is going towards being so instant and having this accessibility of seeing an image. It is said that newspapers are becoming obsolete because everything is going to be accessible to view with instruments like the iPad, or the iPhone: everything's accessible. This changes the fashion industry.

EW: *So it speeds things up?*

CB: Of course, it speeds things up, it makes everything accessible. You might see the same faces because of the accessibility, so then you might have to make it more cyclical. It's the cycle of new faces—oh, who's she? She's a new face. It's all about stimulation and I believe that that's why that supermodel era might not happen again.

GS: I mean the thing is, you're constantly bombarded by images—constantly. When agents are not that busy, we're online all day looking at blogs, we're looking at websites, we're looking at visuals.

EW: *It's true, that wasn't there before . . .*

GS: All this stimuli that you're constantly presented with, and I think that, yeah, at some point it has to level off because it's just sensory overload, information overload. I feel like it's a fast fast motion.

EW: *It's dizzying.*

GS: Yeah that's a good way to put it, it's dizzying after a while.

JE: *Can I ask what makes a model go from model to supermodel? What is it about those in particular, the big ones, that has enabled them to have that staying power and become household names?*

DS: Well they're very good models, all of them are excellent models. All of them have an ability to work with the photographers, with the designers, they understand the concepts, they can create amazing photographs, they project character, they project life and I think that it was an amazing moment in time with so many really, really great supermodels on the scene, apart from their physical gifts. I mean they're genetic anomalies, they're just so amazing. Somebody said Linda Evangelista's a creature. But really, really good models are really able to work it.

MR: They were recognizable, they had a craft, they were, I think they were incredibly professional, you know, they really gave it and they knew how to do it. And the trouble is now, I don't think people—and less and less since the eighties—that people don't get the time to learn the craft. You know, they're shot out there and then they're suddenly doing it. In 1999 when we took on Jacquetta Wheeler, she got discovered by Mario Testino, he booked her for French *Vogue*, she'd never modelled before, she'd done one or two tests. She did French *Vogue*, you know. That's hard. Couture clothes; she was a schoolgirl put into couture clothes. Next thing, she gets the Gucci campaign, she's still at school. She's coming out at half term to shoot the Gucci campaign. So I'm not saying she wasn't great, because she's a great model and she's a terrific girl and hats off to her, but the point is I think that those supermodels had been working a long time.

JE: *They'd been around for a while.*

EW: *And because there wasn't such a fast turnover and they worked for longer, they also had enough time to really learn the business and become super?*

DS: Linda Evangelista was no flash in the pan.

MR: They had time to learn their craft and, you know, they had that whole sort of tight look that they had with their bodies and their faces and their hair. I remember going to a restaurant in New York and there was a whole table of them and just everyone, you know, beautifully dressed, hair amazing. No sort of slopping around in a holey jumper.

JE: *Who are the model makers that create that icon and that household name? I mean the photographers have huge power, and so do the designers.*

MR: Photographers have huge power. I mean someone like Mario or Steven Meisel. They decide they want to use a model for something, and that changes her. I mean it changes her life. And designers. Calvin Klein certainly made Kate Moss didn't he? That was what put her on the map. And I'm going back to the eighties, I mean I suppose the, yes I think the designers had a lot of power, the fashion editors had a lot of power, and I think model agents had quite a lot of power actually in agents' relationships with the photographers. So, you know, people like Frances Grill whose agency was called Click. Flick was the photographic agency. And she had, people like Bruce Weber were her great friends, so she'd say 'Bruce, you know, photograph this girl.' Those people had really strong relationships with photographers and the photographers believed the agents and trusted that they'd got a great look and between them they would bring girls up. The other one was Fabienne Martin, who had FAM agency in Paris, who was slightly later, but she was the one who took really strange-looking girls and made them famous, because she had an intensity and a passion and a sensitivity and artistic quality and photographers really believed her, and designers in fashion houses. So there was more room for personality I think, and suggestibility and creative people working together.

JE: *And the model agent was part of it.*

MR: The model agent could be very powerful in that because people believed that they knew what they were talking about and there were some particularly, the ones I've mentioned—Fabienne Martin of FAM, Frances Grill of Click—this is just like really early eighties—they were all visionary agents and many more. Sarah Doukas at Storm. Well, I think she's a brilliant agent, I think she's a great agent. But she's slightly later, I guess.

JE: *Is there less room for that now in terms of the agents having that control? Is it simply that the market is so big now, it's harder?*

MR: What we used to do was ring up photographers, magazines, saying, 'Oh I've got an incredible new girl, you have to see her'. And they would say, 'Yes, send her in at such-and-such a time'. And then things would go from there. But how many gushes can you do, you know, 'Oh my God, she's so amazing, you've got to see her'. And to sell a girl well you've got to believe that you are giving them something fantastic, whether you're selling them for a cheesy television commercial and you've got quite a cheesy commercial-looking girl, but you think she's got great personality, going to turn up on time, she's going to work really hard, she's going to be charming to everybody. And so even though you're not in love with her look, you would be able to sell her for the television commercial, saying, 'This is your Kraft cheese girl or your Tampax tampon girl' or whatever. And you know, she's going to be great on set, she's going to be completely charming, she's very intelligent, she's going to work really hard. As an agent when you're selling a girl, you've got to believe that what you're saying is true. Sometimes you'd have some girls who, you know, dead edgy-looking, absolutely glorious, big nose, rather druggy, unreliable, but nevertheless, heart-stoppingly beautiful so that when she walks into the room, you know, eyes snap round. You can sell her to a completely different type of client who's going to actually understand what you're talking about there. So yeah, I think that agents do, or certainly did have quite a lot of power. In my best days, I could make people use girls without even seeing them because they would believe. You know, because I'd sent them a few more that they'd understood, they realized I understood what they wanted.

GS: It's not like when a girl starts doing well you give her to all the clients that call for her. People always want what they can't have, so even if a girl has a good relationship with a photographer and he's a top photographer—unless it's a Steven Meisel—there are times that you'll say no for certain shoots, just to keep them kind of wanting the girl, because if they know that they're going to get her, they'll use her for their kind of mid-range jobs, and then for the top-level jobs, they'll get a new girl. Because there is much more competition and more girls up for the same jobs, so you say yes to more jobs than you would in the past on a top girl.

EW: *And that mid-range job would hurt her, if she's becoming a brand?*

GS: Yes.

EW: *Can a model become a brand whatever she looks like?*

GS: Yeah, yeah. It becomes about where is that brand distributed, where is it presented, which photographer is shooting her, etc.? It's a lot about that.

EW: *Could you maybe just speak a little bit to how maybe a model's race or ethnicity affects her ability to become a brand, either as a supermodel, or the muse of a designer, or the face of this or that cosmetic line, and whether it has changed recently? Did it used to be harder as a black model? Is it easier now, or vice versa? I mean we had Naomi Campbell in the supermodel era and there've been very few since and it seems there's just a sort of smaller market for black models.*

MR: Well there's been Tyra Banks and Alek Wek, I mean there have been some, I suppose it was Naomi Campbell really that was the first girl to appear frequently, I think, on the cover of *Vogue*.

DS: I don't know, I can't really say what's on the clients' minds these days. I mean we look for beauty transcending race. We look for great models and the young woman who was on the cover of French *Vogue* is black, from the Dominican Republic. One of the models who left us, Chanel Iman, is African American, Korean American and she's just beautiful and she's doing the Victoria's Secret commercials now. I think that clients may be more and more open to what they need and what works for them and their clothes.

EW: *Is it more open in the commercial markets than it is in couture?*

DS: I think people always go to look and see what will sell. Who's my market, who's buying my clothes, who do I need to relate to, and I need to put models in my catalogue to whom my consumer can relate. And we're a melting pot, so I think models reflect that melting pot and reflect the buying demographic and I think the more savvy the clients are, the more diverse the models, the pool from which they want to draw.

MR: In the UK, we're one of the best countries for using black models, but in France, in fact in Europe it's worse. America has got quite a big black population. I did an Avon ad as a casting director in the late seventies and one in four girls in the ads was black because one in four American people were black or mixed race and Avon was, you know, aware of that.

JE: *One explanation for why there are fewer black models is that a lot of the big campaigns are cosmetic, and there just were not that many black cosmetic brands as there are now. So actually there's a whole kind of work that black models just couldn't book because there just weren't the clients to book them.*

MR: Well, but Tyra Banks did, didn't she, and that other lovely black girl whose name I slightly forget at the minute, but she had green eyes. She had Maybelline or one of those, but they tend to be American.

DS: We keep on seeing more, I see more and more African American models breaking through. A young woman named Joan Smalls who was a catalogue model and has been taken on by the couture houses and the designers and the editors. She's having a really, really good season. Sessilee Lopez, Jourdan Dunn, Rose, you know, I see there are more. There are more and more. Jourdan left but I think she's come back and she's very beautiful, very beautiful. And I think the Asian models, I think we're seeing more, we're seeing girls from different countries. Charlene, for example who was our Supermodel of the Year runner-up, is Philippine and she's so beautiful; she's tall, she has these amazing attenuated limbs and fingers, I mean she's just so graceful and lovely, long neck, you know, just lovely, lovely looking and clothes look perfect on her. So you don't say I need an Asian to fill a slot, it's like, can I get Charlene because she's so perfect and beautiful, you know.

GS: No matter what people say—though I feel like it's eased somewhat—it felt for a long period of time that there was a token black girl, token Asian girl. It's getting better and better though.

EW: *Do you think this tokenism was happening because it was safe, it protected the image from being accused of racism but it also avoided the risk of being overly 'ethnic'?*

GS: Yes.

EW: *Do these black models hold themselves to a Caucasian standard of beauty as the ideal and find themselves wanting as a result?*

GS: Often the black ethnic girls that do well have Caucasian features. This is not the rule and I don't agree with it, but it is the truth for girls like Liya, Chanel, Joan, etc., but I do feel that is shifting. It's great news that Liu Wen and Arlenis are getting Estée Lauder contracts. Shu Pei just signed with Maybelline as well.

EW: *Was that the first time that an Asian girl or a Dominican girl got an Estée Lauder contract? I know that Liya Kebede made news headlines as the first black model doing Estée Lauder . . .*

GS: I'm not sure if it's the first time . . . with Arlenis, the Dominican girl, doing Estée Lauder, I feel like the more things like that happen, hopefully, eventually that'll shift.

EW: *But traditionally, in your experience, has being black been a liability? Can those girls make it as a supermodel or make it as the face of . . . you know, get big contracts to make a lot of money?*

GS: Even though it has gotten better the options are more limited. You often hear 'we already have a black girl in the issue' when a casting is being done.

EW: *Hmm, so it's like they are saying, 'we already took care of that'. We did the representation . . .*

GS: For some I believe that's true. I mean a lot of the Italian and German magazines just will rarely ever use an ethnic girl. But I think it will change a bit when you see more ethnic girls crossing over into advertising—like Joan Smalls in Gucci, the cosmetics we mentioned, etc.

EW: *Here at the agency, the black models that are working, are they working more in commercial work? Not editorial?*

GS: Well, there are two specific kinds of black girls, the girls that are really African, exotic black, really ethnic-looking/super strong, etc.

EW: Like Alek Wek?

GS: Yeah, the Alek Wek types, but the ones that have the more Caucasian features, those are the black girls that make more money, sad to say. The girls that are really ethnic and have a harder look, it's a lot tougher for them financially.

EW: Would you say they have to work harder to make the same level of money?

GS: It's not that, it's just that they don't have access, I think, to the same level of advertising, because their look is not safe, or their look is too specific. So I think that that's why that happens. It's sad and unfortunate.

CB: It all depends on—being a minority myself, I mean I'm Latin American—my point of view is that I'm not sure it had anything to do with financial responsibility equating to not taking chances with ethnic diversity.

JE: Isn't it a risk?

CB: Of course. I mean—I hate to say it because you're not really supposed to— but, the American housewife in Michigan or the middle of this country will relate, perhaps, more to an American blonde-looking girl. I don't know if that's still the mentality. Now that we have an African American president that might have changed, but still there's always the financial thought of the presidents of the advertising agencies and the clients. They could possibly be saying, let's not take a risk with a girl that might not necessarily fill that American dream.

EW: Are there some clients who are less risk-averse? Because if you have pots of money you can take a risk and try something new and different, but if you're struggling with your business you might be less willing to do something that's considered different. Could that affect the client's choice to have a . . .

DS: Maybe. Revlon, it's interesting, it's very diverse, you'll see Halle Berry, you'll see the woman who's on *Desperate Housewives*, Eva Longoria, you know.

CB: In the seventies I think that you could still get along with having a model with a gap tooth, such as Lauren Hutton who showed up on these major campaigns and the covers of *Vogue*. Fashion was still moulding itself in the seventies, and in the eighties, there was so much money, we could get away with anything. It wasn't only made on the catwalk, there were a whole slew of African American girls that were doing major campaigns in the eighties and early nineties.

And then there was a slump. The slump had to do with money and it had to do with the economy, translating into not taking a chance with these advertising agencies and their clients not wanting to take a risk. And I think, in that specific case, ethnicity equals risk.

EW: And is that, I mean after the nineties is when the fashion houses consolidated too, wasn't it?

CB: Absolutely.

EW: Could that consolidation have affected also the adversity to risk, creating more adversity?

CB: Yes, because once you just—or like you said, you used that term—when you have houses coming in and kind of unifying, then it's more of a risk to the global brand for whatever house you're talking about.

JE: Since we're on the subject of diversity in modelling, what are your thoughts on the whole issue of size and shape. Why is the fashion aesthetic so slender and are we seeing any shifts in that?

EW: We were talking yesterday about measurements of models getting thinner, but I had thought, well the supermodels have an image of being more voluptuous than the models of today. So I went and looked up what they reported their bust-waist-hip measurements were and they were still pretty slim. You know, on a voluptuous woman you might think 38, 27, 38 inches or even bigger than that, but the supermodels were reported as 35, 25, 35 inches maximum. But in fashion modelling that actually is voluptuous. So I don't know what's your take on that, what's going on at this moment versus then?

DS: I think it comes and goes. I think Twiggy was tiny and Penelope Tree was tiny and Cheryl Tiegs was round and Christie Brinkley was round.

EW: It's almost like the sixties tiny, the seventies bigger, the eighties maybe . . .

DS: But I think beautiful girls are beautiful girls are beautiful girls and we're not size-ist. I think we have beautiful, beautiful models who are classified as plus but we're hoping to really do away with those kinds of labels. One of our Plus division models has done a number of stories in French *Vogue*, and *V* magazine.

EW: Does she walk runways also?

DS: She walked the Resort show for Karl Lagerfeld just this spring. She's walked with Jean Paul Gaultier. This season she walked ZSpoke for Zac Posen in NY Fashion Week. And so far in Paris, Jean Paul Gaultier and Zac Posen.

JE: *So she's considered voluptuous in the industry?*

DS: She's considered voluptuous.

EW: *So we might be in a swing?*

DS: I think this is a moment of diversity, I think, I don't see it as being so mono-lithic.

EW: *I've heard many people in the industry say: 'Models are skinny because their bodies should not interfere with the clothes.' And, 'Models are skinny because that's what the designers want. They fit the sample size.' Do you think there's anything else going on there? Why do you think models have to be so thin?*

GS: Designers want their clothes to look best, and they look and fall best on tall skinny frames; but it has gotten worse and worse and has been taken to a whole new level the last few years. I know a lot of girls who have experi-enced difficulties with body image and eating issues as a result. It's a really unhealthy ideal that the industry puts out. It trickles to everyone in society as well.

EW: *It seems this new level of slimness is a new aesthetic.*

GS: Look at the early supermodels, the body type is so different. The body of a Christy Turlington or a Claudia Schiffer is so different from a girl you would see in a Prada or a Balenciaga show now, that is a size 0, or size 2 or something. I think it's really a dangerous message both inside the industry and out, and I think when a girl or a woman develops a kind of skewed sense of, 'I'm not thin enough,' it's not healthy. I mean, I know as an agent, there are many girls I've had to talk to about losing weight before the shows, or that they've put on some weight or something, and . . . it's tough. It's a Catch-22 for an agent as well, because you need to give them information you get from clients but you don't want to contribute to a negative body image. 'This client likes you, this one doesn't like you. This client thinks you're great, this client doesn't.' And I think it's important to pass on the information.

EW: *So, fashion, to be fashionable, has to go beyond the ideal that is out there— because we can all get plastic surgery—so, it has to be way out there to be different. It's an interesting thought. Does that seem to resonate at all?*

GS: That ties in a little bit. I think it's related to a lot of people in the industry trying to outdo, or out-create, or beat the pack, beat the masses. I feel like the indus-try's striving to show something, show something different, or more, or less, or something they're not seeing in a mass-consumption kind of way. I think that all ties in, definitely.

EW: *I guess the voluptuous body is more associated with the mass, Victoria's Secret kind of taste.*

GS: Although this season there was a slight hint, of things to come, or hopefully of things to come.

EW: *A shift?*

GS: A shift. Prada ended up showing, using some girls that are more normal body types/Victoria's Secret-type girls, and a couple of girls that actually do Victoria's Secret quite a bit. And then, right after that, a couple of other people like Louis Vuitton used fuller figure girls as well. So I feel like there are signs of a possible shift, or I'm hoping that there are, because, it's like, women *can't get* any skinnier. It's almost humanly impossible—or it *is* humanly impossible and it's not a good message for the industry to put out.

JE: *What about men: we've had a few male supermodels haven't we, like Tyson Beckford?*

MR: Yes, sort of Marcus Schenkenberg and what's he called? Tyson. God, he is beautiful, so beautiful, absolutely shocking.

DS: Male models, we have one of the best male model divisions in the world I think, Ford Men. We represent some of the guys who you see on the runway, in magazines, doing the trendiest high-profile ads: fragrances, grooming products. It can be more difficult for them to be well known. The likelihood of them being a household name, a supermodel, every once in a while there is one, but it doesn't happen that often.

EW: *What about their earnings? Does the work pay as well?*

DS: They're on covers. Models.com has a top fifty men, as it does top fifty women. The Ford blog promotes male models as much as it promotes female models. It's just, I think it's more difficult for a male model to have a breakthrough. I mean Gabriel Aubry, who was Halle Berry's boyfriend for a while and the father of her child, can be a household name because he's also in the tabloid press. Somebody who does Calvin Klein underwear may have a little boost because that's so high profile. But you'd be hard pressed to name a top male model.

EW: *And they're competing with the actors also, just like the female models.*

DS: Actors, yes.

CB: Modelling is one of the few industries, as we all know, where the women make much more money than the men. It is very lucrative for that small pool of male models who do well, that have a universal appeal to all markets, to the global market, but they're few and far between.

JE: *And career-wise, how is it for men?*

MR: It's shorter. Actually, they can have a very long career. I mean there are a couple of really great older models, I can't remember what he's called—the Silver Fox, we used to call him. But a couple of guys in their fifties and sixties; white hair, really tanned, limber bodies, who do great campaigns, I mean there are some incredible older male models. But I don't know, of the boys I had, it was a period of time when that look worked and they made their money but did not have longevity.

CB: There's a higher criteria for the male models I believe. Not only do they have to be good looking, and have to have as perfect a body as possible, but they have to have personality. Women do too, but for men it's more. They have to be able to sell themselves and give that X factor that will convince the client that they want to spend eight hours in front of a camera with them. They have to be able to envelop the entire crew and say, okay, I'm here, I'm not just a male supermodel.

MR: Personality is huge with the guys because most of the—I mean talking at high end—if you're working with Richard Avedon or Bruce Weber who uses a lot of male models, or Steven Meisel or Mario Testino, they tend to use incredibly charismatic, interesting guys. I think they're much more prepared to put up with a sort of slightly dull girl than a dull boy. They want somebody that they can chat to and who's interesting and bright. So I think personality works in a man's favour. I mean I've had boys who were not that perfect looking but had such amazing personalities, the photographers really bonded with them: David Bradshaw when he was doing Prada and Miu Miu and everything, he used to go and play golf with models Edward Ferguson and Ben Jackson and the boys that he was using for Prada, you know, they'd go fishing together and things. So I think it is a really different game, there's less craft in male modelling, more natural styling.

JE: *It's almost like we don't want our men to be too overly styled.*

MR: No, I think we are actually rather alarmed. It's not attractive, I don't think we really . . . we don't like camp very over-styled, I think it makes us a bit uncomfortable.

JE: *We've covered a lot of ground, from the supermodel era and contemporary swings and trends in size, shape, ethnic diversity and the influence of new media. It's been very interesting to talk to you and hear how things work within the industry. Thank you all for participating.*

Notes

Chapter 3: From Artist's Model to the 'Natural Girl': Containing Sexuality in Early-Twentieth-Century Modelling

1. The material on Lucile's models in this section is drawn from primary sources at the Billy Rose Theater Collection, New York Public Library for the Performing Arts, Robinson Locke Collection, Series 2, vol. 278, p. 226; clippings folder for Ziegfeld Follies of 1917; 'Dolores', Robinson Locke [hereafter RL] scrapbooks, Series 3, vol. 368, pp. 191–205, Billy Rose Theater Collection [hereafter BRTC], New York Public Library for the Performing Arts [hereafter NYPL]; for a reference to Dolores's 'somewhat Cockney sister', see clipping from *Town Topics*, 17 March 1921, RL/BRTC/NYPL Series 3, vol. 368, p. 203; RL/BRTC/NYPL Series 3, vol. 127, pp. 196–208; for Wayburn, 'New Wayburn's "Squab Farm" Just off Main Street—The Place Where Chorus Girls Are Taught to Dance and Sing from the Raw Material, and Made Ready for the Footlights', *The World*, Sunday 8 July 1906, in BRTC/NYPL Robinson Locke Series 2, vol. 305, p. 157; Program for Ziegfeld Midnight Frolic, 15 June 1917, in 'Ziegfeld Midnight Frolic 1915–29' microfilm roll, BRTC/NYPL.
2. This paragraph is drawn from a review of the Powers's books at the New York Public Library: John Powers annual books, John Robert Powers publications, New York: Vol. 6 (1930)–v. 8 (1932). v. 6 (1930); Vol. 6 (1930)–v. 8 (1932). v. 7 (1931) and Vol. 6 (1930)–v. 8 (1932). v. 8 (1932).

Chapter 4: 'Giving Coloured Sisters a Superficial Equality': Re-Modelling African American Womanhood in Early Postwar America

1. This chapter was made possible in part by the generous support of the Inaugural Postdoctoral Fellowship in African American Studies in the Department of History at Case Western Reserve University. I would like to thank Dr. Rhonda Y. Williams, my mentor during my fellowship year, for critical feedback on a preliminary version of this chapter. Gratitude is also extended to editors Dr. Jo Entwistle and Dr. Betsy Wissinger for their incisive comments and patient kindness throughout the editorial process. Final comments from Dr. Lynne Pettinger

and Dr. Róisín Ryan-Flood in the Department of Sociology at the University of Essex in England have also happily benefited this work.

2. Watson's closure of the agency in 1956 marked her return to the study of law and the beginning of her vibrant career in politics. In 1977, President Jimmy Carter appointed Watson as Assistant Secretary of State (Consular Affairs). See Carney Smith 1996.

3. Sullivan's data was drawn from fifty cities, throughout America, with significant African American populations (Sullivan 1945).

Chapter 5: Fashion Modelling in Australia

1. This essay is part of a larger study of Australian fashion photography, funded by an Australian Research Council (ARC) Discovery Grant (2004–2006).

2. To date there has been no history of Australian male models published. The first dedicated male modelling agency was set up in 1980, although male models were trained by the Russell Roberts agency in Sydney and parading took place from the 1930s. They appear occasionally in glossy women's magazines during the 1950s and 1960s as compositional adjuncts. The 1960s photographer David Franklin was also a model.

3. Those former models, fashion editors and photographers who gave interviews or personal information to the author are gratefully acknowledged. They include Ann Felton, Caroline Drury, Diane Masters, Janice Wakely, Vivien McDermott (now with her own model agency), Maggie Deas (Margaret Mc-Gurgan), Mary Wilkinson, editor of *Flair*, and the photographers Geoffrey Lee and David Mist.

4. Maggie Tabberer, one of Australia's best-known models, started her career in Adelaide and was taken up by Sydney's David Jones in 1957 (van Wyk 2006: 85).

5. This comes from an interview with Mist by Anne-Marie Van de Ven in 1997.

6. Ten years earlier in 1948, models were paid from 10/6 to one guinea for a garment shot (*Glamour* (Feb. 1948): 38–9). Janice Wakely in her work diary notes (Powerhouse Museum archive) shows she was getting about 15 Australian pounds a day in 1959.

7. Elly Lukas was another mid-century model who later set up a successful modelling agency in Melbourne.

8. By the 1950s, model and deportment schools were springing up in many Australian cities.

9. I would like to acknowledge the considerable amount of unpublished work on Wakely done by Anne-Marie Van de Ven of the Powerhouse Museum, Sydney. This museum houses Wakely's archive.

10. It had, according to Underhill, a circulation of 126,000 copies in 1939.

11. *Flair* ran from 1956 until the 1970s.

12. Amongst these was Jennifer Hocking of Sydney, named *London Daily Express* Model of the Year (*Flair* (Olympic Issue 1956): 56), and perhaps the most successful was Nola Rose, who even modelled in Russia.

13. A hand-coloured photographic spread in the Melbourne magazine *Table Talk* in 1907 advertising hats was an isolated instance of the genre, and perhaps a proto editorial.

14. This comes from an interview with Mary Wilkinson in 2005.

Chapter 6: Performing Dreams: A Counter-History of Models as Glamour's Embodiment

1. This research has been partly funded by a Casals Catalans Research Fund, granted by the Department of Universities, Research and Information Society, Government of Catalonia (2001); and by a Francesca Bonnemaison Research Bursary, granted by Barcelona Provincial Council (2008). My gratitude to Condé-Nast Verlag and Susanne Junker for kindly granting me permission to reproduce their pictures.
   Earlier versions of this chapter were published as 'Modelling Femininity', *European Journal of Women Studies*, 11/3 (2004): 309–26; and 'Charming Power: Models as Ideal Embodiments of Normative Identity', *Trípodos. Llenguatge, Pensament, Comunicació*, 18 (2006): 23–43, http://www.tripodos.com/pdf/18m_SoleyBeltran.pdf.

2. For reasons of space and scope, in this brief historical review I do not consider artists' models nor do I look into the history of male models. See Entwistle (2002) for, to the best of my knowledge, the only existing study on male models, and Soley-Beltran (2010b) for some notes on differences between male and female models concerning body self-identification.

3. In Spanish *la nueva mujer de pura raza*.

Chapter 7: The Figure of the Model and Reality TV

1. Thanks to the members and audience of the panel 'Fashion Reality TV: Fashion as Product, Fashion as Process' at the 2005 American Anthropological Association Annual Meeting, especially Todd Nicewonger and William Mazzarella, for comments on an earlier version of this chapter; the editors, Betsy and Jo, for their incisive feedback on final drafts of this work; and Aisha Khan for her support, insight and endurance in viewing and discussing these shows with me. Portions of this research were made possible by funding from the Wenner-Gren Foundation for Anthropological Research (Dissertation Fieldwork Grant #7493).

2. Throughout the chapter, each show listed will be followed by the original network and year it first aired. While many of these shows lasted only one season, others changed networks, were syndicated on other networks and/or appeared on a limited basis on other networks. Of the twenty-three shows listed, nine are

produced by Viacom, three by CBS Paramount, two by Discovery Communications and one by ABC/Walt Disney.

3. I conducted research at six key sites in the New York fashion industry over a four-year period (2003–2007) where I participated in and observed model casting and development practices. Sites included a leading fashion casting agency (eleven months), a high-fashion boutique women's modelling agency (seven months), a mid-range fashion boutique men's and women's modelling agency (seventeen months), an ethnic women's magazine (two months), a mainstream women's magazine (two months) and an international photo production company (four months).

Chapter 8: Made in Japan: Fashion Modelling in Tokyo

1. All names are pseudonyms in Tokyo who typically range in age from fourteen to twenty-one.
2. I use the colloquialism *girls* because this is the language of participants and it does in fact refer to the majority of female models in Tokyo who are aged fourteen to twenty-one, rarely older.
3. Women only are the focus of this chapter because, like the vast majority of labour markets, modelling is not a gender-neutral phenomenon and women make up a larger presence in the industry globally as well as in Tokyo.
4. Names of agencies are also pseudonyms.

Chapter 9: Modelling Consumption: Fashion Modelling Work in Contemporary Society

1. Data from www.tyrabanks.com (Banks 2007); markets at that time confirmed by *America's Next Top Model* judge, Nigel Barker, in conversation on 14 August 2007. See also http://americantopmodels.blogspot.com/2008/02/international versions.html, for concurrent data, as well as http://www.typef.com/ for more recent data. The popularity of these mediated encounters with the modelling world represents a desire that is particularly acute among young people. The desire stirred by models seems especially pronounced among the thousands of young people who turn out to audition for contests such as the Ford modelling agency's 'Supermodel of the World' or America's Next Top Model. Reportedly, the Ford 'Supermodel of the World' contest selected its finalists from thousands of aspirants in fifty different countries (Espinosa 2008). For the first time ever, one finalist was selected from the some 20,000 hopefuls who submitted their photographs for consideration via the 'Ford Supermodel of the World' Myspace page (Fabrikant 2008). On its most recent thirty-eight-city tour of the USA, the auditions for the television show *America's Next Top Model* drew 1,500 young women in one day, all hoping to win a spot on the show (Wilson 2007).
2. http://www.cwtv.com/shows/americas-next-top-model/about.

Bibliography

Chapter 1: Introduction

Aspers, P. (2001), *Markets in Fashion: A Phenomenological Approach*, Stockholm: City University Press.

Beckford, M. (2007), 'Younger Sister of Skinny Model Dies', *The Standard*, World section, 16 February, http://www.thestandard.com.hk, accessed 19 January 2011.

Berger, J. (1972), *Ways of Seeing*, Harmondsworth: Penguin.

Brown, E. H. (2011), 'Black Models and the Invention of the US "Negro Market", 1945–1960', in D. Zwick and J. Cayla (eds), *Inside Marketing: Practices, Ideologies and Devices*, Oxford: Oxford University Press.

Duff, M. (2006), 'Milan Models to Have Catwalk Code', *BBC News*, 23 September, http://news.bbc.co.uk/2/hi/5374862.stm, accessed 19 January 2011.

Entwistle, J., and Wissinger, E. (2006), 'Keeping up Appearances: Aesthetic Labour in the Fashion Modelling Industries of London and New York', *Sociological Review*, 54/4: 774–94.

Evans, C. (2000), 'Living Dolls: Mannequins, Models, and Modernity', in J. Stair (ed.), *The Body Politic*, London: Crafts Council.

Evans, C. (2001), 'The Enchanted Spectacle', *Fashion Theory: The Journal of Dress, Body and Culture*, 5/3: 271–310.

Evans, C. (2003), *Fashion at the Edge: Spectacle, Modernity and Deathliness*, New Haven, CT: Yale University Press.

Evans, C. (2005), 'Multiple, Movement, Model, Mode: The Mannequin Parade 1900–1929', in C. Breward and C. Evans (eds), *Fashion and Modernity*, Oxford: Berg.

Evans, C. (2008), 'Jean Patou's American Mannequins: Early Fashion Shows and Modernism', *Modernism/Modernity*, 15/2: 243–63.

Gill, R. (2002), 'Cool, Creative and Egalitarian? Exploring Gender in Project-Based New Media in Europe', *Information, Communication and Society*, 5/1: 70–89.

Godart, F. C., and A. Mears (2009), 'How Do Cultural Producers Make Creative Decisions? Lessons from the Catwalk', *Social Forces*, 88/2: 671–92.

Goffman, E. (1979), *Gender Advertisements*, London: Macmillan.

Grabher, G. (2002), 'The Project Ecology of Advertising: Tasks, Talents and Teams', *Regional Studies*, 36/3: 245–62.

Gross, M. (2004), *Model: The Ugly Business of Beautiful Women*, London: Bantam.

Hennigan, T. (2007), 'Extreme Diet Model Dies Six Months after Anorexic Sister', *The Times*, 15 February, http://www.timesonline.co.uk/tol/news/world/us_and_americas/article1386803.ece, accessed 19 June 2011.

Klonick, K. (2006), 'New Message to Models: Eat! A Model's Recent Death and a Ban on Skinny Models from Madrid's Runway Has the Fashion World Spinning', *ABC News*, 15 September, http://www.abcnews.com, accessed 19 January 2011.

McRobbie, A. (2002a), 'Clubs to Companies: Notes on the Decline of Political Culture in Speeded up Creative Worlds', *Cultural Studies*, 16/4: 553–69.

McRobbie, A. (2002b), 'Holloway to Hollywood: Pleasure in Work in the New Cultural Economy?', in P. du Gay and M. Pryke (eds), *Cultural Economy*, London: Sage.

Maynard, M. (1999), 'Living Dolls: The Fashion Model in Australia', *Journal of Popular Culture*, 33/1: 191–205.

Mears, A. (2008), 'Discipline of the Catwalk: Gender, Power and Uncertainty in Fashion Modelling', *Ethnography*, 9/4: 429–56.

Mears, A. (2010), 'Size Zero High-End Ethnic: Cultural Production and the Reproduction of Culture in Fashion Modelling', *Poetics*, 38/1: 21–46.

Mears, A. (2011), *Pricing Beauty: The Making of a Fashion Model*, Los Angeles: University of California Press.

Mears, A., and Finlay, W. (2005), 'Not Just a Paper Doll: How Models Manage Bodily Capital and Why They Perform Emotional Labor', *Journal of Contemporary Ethnography*, 34/3: 314–43.

Morris, A., Copper, T., and Cooper, P. (2006), 'The Changing Shape of Female Fashion Models', *International Journal of Eating Disorders*, 8/5: 593–6.

Mulvey, L. (1975), 'Visual Pleasure in Narrative Cinema', *Screen*, 16/3: 6–18.

Mulvey, L. (1988), *Visual and Other Pleasures*, Bloomington: University of Indiana Press.

Neff, G., Wissinger, E. and Zukin, S. (2005), 'Entrepreneurial Labor among Cultural Producers: "Cool" Jobs in "Hot" Industries', *Social Semiotics*, 15/3: 307–34.

Parmentier, M., and Fischer, E. (2007), 'Working to Consume the Model Life: Consumer Agency under Scarcity', in R. W. Belk and J. F. Sherry Jr. (eds), *Consumer Culture Theory 11,* Research in Consumer Behaviour Series, pp. 23–39. Oxford: Elsevier.

Prabu, D., Morrison, G., Johnson, M.A. and Ross, F. (2002), 'Body Image, Race and Fashion Models: Social Distance and Social Identification in Third-Person Effects', *Communication Research*, 29/3: 270–94.

Quick, Harriet (1997), *Catwalking: A History of the Fashion Model*, London: Octopus.

Sadre-Orafai, S. N. (2008), 'Developing Images: Race, Language, and Perception in Fashion Model Casting', in E. Shinkle (ed.), *Fashion as Photograph: Viewing and Reviewing Fashion Images*, London: I. B. Tauris.

Schell, O., and Ziff, S., directors. (2009), *Picture Me*, distributed by Strand Releasing.

Soley-Beltran, P. (2004), 'Modelling Femininity', *European Journal of Women's Studies*, 11/3: 309–26.

Sypeck, M. F., Gray, J. J. and Ahrens, A. H. (2004), 'No Longer Just a Pretty Face: Fashion Magazines' Depictions of Ideal Female Beauty from 1959 to 1999', *International Journal of Eating Disorders*, 36/3: 342–7.

Thorpe, V., and Campbell, D. (2007), 'Models' Threat to Sue Blocked Size Zero Ban', *The Observer*, 11 February, http://www.guardian.co.uk/uk/2007/feb/11/deniscampbell. vanessathorpe?INTCMP=SRCH, accessed 19 January 2011.

Wilson, E. (2007), 'Health Guidelines Suggested for Models', *New York Times*, 6 January, http://www.nytimes.com/2007/01/06/business/06thin.html, accessed 19 January 2011.

Wissinger, E. (2007a), 'Always on Display: Affective Production in the Fashion Modelling Industry', in P. Clough and J. Halley (eds), *The Affective Turn: Theorizing the Social*, Durham, NC: Duke University Press.

Wissinger, E. (2007b), 'Modelling a Way of Life: Immaterial and Affective Labor in the Fashion Modelling Industry', *ephemera: theory and politics in organization*, 7/1: 250–69.

Wissinger, E. (2009), 'Modelling Consumption: Fashion Modelling Work in Contemporary Society', *Journal of Consumer Culture*, 9/2: 275–98.

Chapter 2: Models as Brands: Critical Thinking about Bodies and Images

Ahern, A. B., K. M.; Hertherington, M. M. (2008), 'Internalization of the Ultra-Thin Ideal: Positive Implicit Associations with Underweight Fashion Models Are Associated with Drive for Thinness in Young Women', *Eating Disorders: The Journal of Treatment and Prevention*, 16/4: 294–307.

Arvidsson, A. (2005), 'Brands: A Critical Perspective', *Journal of Consumer Culture*, 5/2: 235–58.

Arviddson, A. (2006), *Brands: Meanings and Value in Media Culture*, London: Routledge.

Ashmore, R.D.S., M.R.; Longo, L.C. (1996), 'Thinking about Fashion Models' Looks: A Multidimensional Approach to the Structure of Perceived Physical Attractiveness', *Personality and Social Psychology Bulletin*, 22/11: 1083–104.

Bartky, S. (1988), 'Foucault, Femininity, and the Modernization of Patriarchal Power', in I. Diamond and L. Quinby (eds), *Feminism and Foucault: Reflections on Resistance*, Boston: Northeastern University Press.

Bordo, S. (2003), *Unbearable Weight: Feminism, Western Culture and the Female Body*, Berkeley: University of California Press.

British Medical Association (2000), 'Models Link to Teenage Anorexia', *BBC News*, http://news.bbc.co.uk/1/hi/769290.stm, accessed 13 June 2011.

Butler, J. (1993), *Bodies That Matter*, London: Routledge.

Callon, M., Méadel, C. and Rabeharisoa, V. (2005), 'The Economy of Qualities', in A. Barry and D. Slater (eds), *The Technological Economy*, London: Routledge.

Conniff Taber, K. (2006), 'With Model's Death, Eating Disorders Are Again in Spotlight', *New York Times*, 20 November, http://www.nytimes.com/2006/11/20/world/americas/20iht-models.3604439.html.

David, P. M., G., Johnson, M. A. and Ross, F. (2002), 'Body Image, Race, and Fashion Models Social Distance and Social Identification in Third-Person Effects', *Communication Research.*

de Lauretis, T. (1989), *Technologies of Gender: Essays on Theory, Film, and Fiction*, Macmillan.

DeNora, T. (2002), 'The Role of Music in Intimate Culture: A Case Study', *Feminism & Psychology*, 12/2: 176–81.

du Gay, P. (1996), *Consumption and Identity at Work*, London: Sage.

Entwistle, J. (2002), 'The Aesthetic Economy: The Production of Value in the Field of Fashion Modelling', *Journal of Consumer Culture*, 2/3: 317–40.

Entwistle, J. (2009), *The Aesthetic Economy of Fashion: Markets and Value in Clothing and Modelling*, Oxford: Berg.

Foley Sypeck, M. G., Gray, J. J. and Ahrens, A. H. (2004), 'No Longer Just a Pretty Face: Fashion Magazines' Depictions of Ideal Female Beauty from 1959 to 1999', *International Journal of Eating Disorders*, 36/3: 342–7.

Giddens, A. (1991), *Modernity and Self-Identity: Self and Society in the Late Modern Age*, Cambridge: Polity Press.

Gill, R. (2003), 'From Sexual Objectification to Sexual Subjectification: The Resexualisation of Women's Bodies in the Media', *Feminist Media Studies*, 3/1: 100–5.

Gill, R. (2007), *Gender and the Media*, Cambridge: Polity Press.

Gomart, E. and Hennion, A. (1999), 'A Sociology of Attachment: Music Amateurs, Drug Users', in J. Law and J. Hassard (eds), *Actor Network Theory and After*, Oxford: Blackwell/Sociological Review.

Hall, S. (1980), 'Encoding/Decoding', in S. Hall, D. Hobson, A. Lowe and P. Willis (eds), *Culture, Media, Language*, London: Hutchinson.

Harvey, M., McMeekin, A. and Warde, A. (2004), 'Conclusion: Quality and Processes of Qualification', in M. Harvey, A. McMeekin and A. Warde (eds), *Qualities of Food*, Manchester: Manchester University Press.

Hollows, J., and Moseley, R. (eds) (2006), *Feminism in Popular Culture*, Oxford: Berg.

Holt, D. B. (2002), 'Why Do Brands Cause Trouble? A Dialectical Theory of Consumer Culture and Branding', *Journal of Consumer Research*, 29/1: 70–90.

Holt, D. B. (2004), *How Brands Become Icons*, Cambridge, MA: Harvard Business School.

Holt, D. B. (2006), 'Jack Daniel's America: Iconic Brands as Ideological Parasites and Proselytizers', *Journal of Consumer Culture*, 6/3: 355–77.

Jowell, Tessa (2000), *BBC News*, http://news.bbc.co.uk/1/hi/uk_politics/708186. stm, accessed 13 June 2011.

Latour, B. (2007), *Turning around Politics. A Note on Gerard de Vries' Paper. Social Studies of Science 2007*.

Lury, C. (2004), *Brands: The Logos of the Global Economy*, London: Routledge.

Lury, C. (2009), 'brand as assemblage—Assembling Culture', *Journal of Cultural Economy*, 2/1: 67–82.

McKendrick, N. (1959/1960), 'Josiah Wedgewood: An Eighteenth-Century Entrepreneur in Salesmanship and Marketing Techniques', *Economic History Review*, 2nd ser., 12/3: 408–33.

McKendrick, N., Brewer, J. and Plumb, J. H. (1983), *The Birth of a Consumer Society: The Commercialization of Eighteenth-Century*, London: Hutchinson.

Mears, A. (2008), 'Discipline of the Catwalk: Gender, Power and Uncertainty in Fashion Modeling', *Ethnography*, 9/4: 429–56.

Mears, A. (2011), *Pricing Beauty: The Making of a Fashion Model*, Los Angeles: University of California Press.

Mears, A., and Finlay, W. (2005), 'Not Just a Paper Doll : How Models Manage Bodily Capital and Why They Perform Emotional Labor', *Journal of Contemporary Ethnography*, 34/3: 314–43.

Mears, A., and F. C. Godart (2009), 'How Do Cultural Producers Make Creative Decisions: Lessons from the Catwalk', *Social Forces*, 88/2: 671–92.

Miller, D. (ed.) (1997), *Material Cultures: Why Some Things Matter*, London: University College London Press.

Miller, D. (ed.) (2005), *Materiality*, Durham, NC: Duke University Press.

Moor, L. (2003), 'Branded Spaces: "New Marketing" and Consumer Experience', *Journal of Consumer Culture*, 3/1.

Moor, L. (2007), *The Rise of Brands*, Oxford: Berg.

Orbach, S. (1993), *Hunger Strike: Starving amidst Plenty*, London: Faber and Faber.

Parmentier, M., and Fischer, E. (2007), 'Working to Consume the Model Life: Consumer Agency under Scarcity', in R. W. Belk and J. F. Sherry Jr (eds), *Consumer Culture Theory 11,* Research in Consumer Behavior Series, pp. 23–39. Oxford: Elsevier.

Reaves, S., Bush Hitchon, J., Park, S.-Y., and Yun, G. W. (2004), 'If Looks Could Kill: Digital Manipulation of Fashion Models', *Journal of Mass Media Ethics*, 19/1: 56–71.

Riles, A. (2000), *The Network Inside Out*, Ann Arbor: University of Michigan Press.

Ritzer, G., and Jurgenson, N. (2010), 'Production, Consumption, Prosumption', *Journal of Consumer Culture*, 10/1: 13–36.

Shaw, J. (1995), 'Effects of Fashion Magazines on Body Dissatisfaction and Eating Psychopathology in Adolescent and Adult Females', *European Eating Disorders Review*, 3/1: 15–23.

Slater, D. (2002a), 'Capturing Markets from the Economists', in P. du Gay and M. Pryke (eds), *Cultural Economy*, London: Sage.

Slater, D. R. (2002b), 'Markets, Materiality and the "New Economy"', in S. Metcalfe and A. Warde (eds), *Market Relations and the Competitive Process*, Manchester: Manchester University Press.

Slater, D. R. (2011), 'Between Culture and Economy: The Impossible Place of Marketing', in D. Zwick and J. Cayla (eds), *Inside Marketing*, pp. 23–41. Oxford: Oxford University Press.

Warde, A. (2005), 'Consumption and Theories of Practice', *Journal of Consumer Culture*, 5/2.

Wissinger, E. (2007a), 'Modelling a Way of Life: Immaterial and Affective Labor in the Fashion Modelling Industry', *ephemera: theory and politics in organization*, 7/1: 250–69.

Wissinger, E. (2007b), 'Nice Work If You Can Get It: Labor in the New York Fashion Modeling Industry', unpublished PhD thesis, Graduate School, University of New York.

Wissinger, E. (2009), 'Modelling Consumption: Fashion Modelling Work in Contemporary Society', *Journal of Consumer Culture*, 9/2: 275–98.

Wolf, N. (1990), *The Beauty Myth: How Images of Beauty Are Used against Women*, London: Vintage.

Zwick, D., Bonsu, S. K. and Darmody, A. (2008), 'Putting Consumers to Work: "Cocreation" and New Marketing Govern-Mentality ', *Journal of Consumer Culture*, 8/2: 163–96.

Chapter 3: From Artist's Model to the 'Natural Girl': Containing Sexuality in Early-Twentieth-Century Modelling

'12,000 at Trade Fair on the Opening Day' (1922), *New York Times*, 8 August, p. 25.

Ahmed, S. (1994), *The Cultural Politics of Emotion*, New York: Routledge.

Ahmed, S. (2004), 'Affective Economies', *Social Text*, 79, 22/2: 117–39.

'An Almost Perfect Thirty-Four' (1923), *Saturday Evening Post*, 10 November, p. 22.

Bailey, P. (2002), 'Parasexuality and Glamour: The Victorian Barmaid as Cultural Prototype', in K. M. Phillips and B. Reay (eds), *Sexualities in History: A Reader*, pp. 222–46. New York: Routledge.

Bederman, G. (1995), *Manliness and Civilization: A Cultural History of Gender and Race in the United States, 1880–1917*, Chicago: University of Chicago Press.

Brown, E. H. (2000), 'Rationalizing Consumption: Photography and the Commercial Illustration, 1913–1919', *Enterprise and Society*, 1/4: 715–38.

Brown, E. H. (2005), *The Corporate Eye: Photography and the Rationalization of American Commercial Culture, 1884–1929*, Baltimore: Johns Hopkins University Press.

Brown, E. H. (2009), 'De Meyer at *Vogue:* Commercializing Queer Affect in World War I-Era Fashion Photography', *Photography and Culture*, 2/3: 253–75.

Clement, E.A. (2006), *Love for Sale: Courting, Treating, and Prostitution in New York City, 1900–1945*, Chapel Hill: University of North Carolina Press.

Cohen, B.A. (1980), 'The Dance Direction of Ned Wayburn: Selected Topics in Musical Staging, 1901–1923', PhD thesis, New York University.

Dawkins, H. (2002), *The Nude in French Art and Culture, 1870–1910*, pp. 86–115. Cambridge: Cambridge University Press.

Duff Gordon, L. (1932), *Discretions and Indiscretions*, London: Jarrolds.

Du Maurier, G. (1995), *Trilby* (1894), Hertfordshire, England: Wordsworth Editions.

'The Easter Show' (1906), *Dry Goods Economist*, 17 March, p. 101.

Etherington-Smith, M., and Pilcher, J. (1986), *The IT Girls: Elinor Glyn and Lucy, Lady Duff Gordon*, London: Hamish Hamilton.

Evans, C. (2001), 'The Enchanted Spectacle', *Fashion Theory*, 5/3: 271–310.

'Fashion Show as Trade Promoters' (1913), *New York Times*, 19 October, p. XX10.

Fox, S. (1984), *The Mirror Makers: A History of American Advertising and Its Creators*, New York: William Morrow.

Georgen, E. (1893), *The Delsarte System of Physical Culture*, New York: Butterick.

Glenn, S. (2000), *Female Spectacle: The Theatrical Roots of Modern Feminism*, Cambridge, MA: Harvard University Press.

Greer, H. (1952), *Designing Male*, New York: Putnam Books.

Harrington, R.G. (1922), 'The Photographic Portrait Study', *Printers' Ink Monthly*, 5: 106.

Jacobson, M.F. (1998), *Whiteness of a Different Color: European Immigrants and the Alchemy of Race*, Cambridge, MA: Harvard University Press.

Jacobson, M.F. (2000), *Barbarian Virtues: The United States Encounters Foreign Peoples at Home and Abroad*, New York: Hill and Wang.

Judson, J. (1917), 'Illustrator Scouts the City to Get Suitable Models: Lejaren A. Hiller Has Developed Universal Studio for Magazine Work and Card Indexes His Subjects' Faces', *The Sun*, New York, 4 November, p. 10.

Kaplan, J.H., and Stowell, S. (1995), *Theatre and Fashion*, Cambridge: Cambridge University Press.

Kennedy, J.B. (1930), 'Model Maids', *Collier's*, 85 (8 Feb.): 9, 60–1.

Kracauer, S. (1995), 'The Mass Ornament', in T.Y. Levin (trans.), *The Mass Ornament: Weimar Essays*, pp. 75–88. Cambridge, MA: Harvard University Press.

'Lady Duff Gordon, Style Expert, Dies' (1935), *New York Times*, 22 April, p. 17.

Leach, W. (1994), *Land of Desire: Merchants, Power, and the Rise of a New American Culture*, New York: Vintage Books.

'Living Models Make a Hit' (1910), Dry Goods, 10 November, p. 33.

Lowry, H.B. (1920), 'Rude Intrusions of Facts into Fashions', *New York Times*, 1 August, p. 46.

Marchand, R. (1986), *Advertising the American Dream: Making Way for Modernity*, Berkeley: University of California Press.

Mendes, V.D., and de la Haye, A. (2009), *Lucile Ltd: London, Paris, New York, and Chicago, 1890s–1930s*, London: V&A Publishing.

Meyerowitz, J. (1991), *Women Adrift: Independent Wage Earners in Chicago, 1880–1930*, Chicago: University of Chicago Press.

'The Gimbel Millinery Showing Is the Finest in the City', *New York Times*, 30 March 1911, 7.

'Paris Dressmakers Withhold Models' (1912), *New York Times*, 9 April, p. 3.

'The Paris Fashion Show Has Brought a New Epoch' (1915), *New York Times,* 28 November, p. X2.

Peiss, K. (1986), *Cheap Amusements: Working Women and Leisure in Turn-of-the-Century New York*, Philadelphia: Temple University Press.

Peiss, K. (1987), ' "Charity Girls" and City Pleasures: Historical Notes on Working Class Sexuality, 1880–1920', in K. Peiss and C. Simmons (eds), *Passion and Power: Sexuality in History*, pp. 57–70. Philadelphia: Temple University Press.

Peiss, K. (1990), 'Making Faces: The Cosmetics Industry and the Cultural Construction of Gender, 1890–1930', *Genders*, 7: 143–69.

Peiss, K. (1998), *Hope in a Jar: The Making of America's Beauty Culture*, pp. 61–133. New York: Henry Holt.

Powers, J. R. (1941), *The Powers Girls: The Story of Models and Modelling and the Natural Steps by Which Attractive Girls Are Created*, New York: E. P. Dutton.

Schweitzer, M. (2009), *When Broadway Was the Runway: Theatre, Fashion, and American Culture*, Philadelphia: University of Pennsylvania Press.

'Selling "Stouts" in the Showroom: "Team Work" on the Part of Model and Salesman Often Wins over the Buyer' (1916), *New York Times*, 26 November, p. E8.

Studlar, G. (1996), 'The Perils of Pleasure? Fan Magazine Discourse as Women's Commodified Culture in the 1920s', in R. Abel (ed.), *Silent Film*, pp. 263–98. New Brunswick, NJ: Rutgers University Press.

Todd, M. E. (1920), 'Principles of Posture', *Boston Medical and Surgical Journal*, 182/26 (24 June): 645–9, reprinted in M. E. Todd (1977), *Early Writings, 1920–1934*, New York: Dance Horizons.

Troy, N. J. (2003), *Couture Culture: A Study in Modern Art and Fashion*, Cambridge, MA: MIT Press.

'Using the Camera to Illustrate Fiction: Models Pose for Photographs Showing Scenes in the Story—How Two Artists Originated the Plan' (1918), *New York Times Magazine*, 6 January, p. 13.

Vanity Fair (1918), 10/3: 48.

Waller, S. (2006), *The Invention of the Model: Artists and Models in Paris, 1830–1870*, pp. 37–57. London: Ashgate.

Watkins, J. L. (1959), *The 100 Greatest Advertisements*, New York: Dover.

Wissinger, E. (2007a), 'Always on Display: Affective Production in the Modelling Industry', in P. T. Clough and J. Halley (eds), *The Affective Turn: Theorizing the Social*, pp. 231–60. Durham, NC: Duke University Press.

Wissinger, E. (2007b), 'Modelling a Way of Life: Immaterial and Affective Labour in the Fashion Modelling Industry', *ephemera: theory and politics in organization*, 7/1: 250–69.

'Yearn to Be Suit Models: Girls Besiege Garment Firms, Though Hours Are Long and the Work Is Hard' (1924), *New York Times*, 1 August, p. XX2.

Chapter 4: 'Giving Coloured Sisters a Superficial Equality': Re-Modelling African American Womanhood in Early Postwar America

Archival Sources

Barbara Watson Collection, Schomburg Center for Research in Black Culture, Manuscript Division, New York Public Library, New York City, New York.

'Harlem Fashion Show', *Women's World*, 8 June 1950. Radio Transcripts Collection, MG 60, Box 6, Schomburg Center for Research in Black Culture, Manuscript Division, New York Public Library, New York City, New York.

Translations and Newsclippings in Barbara Watson Collection

Dagens Nyheter (a), 'Negress to Study Swedish Women's Clothes: Colored People a Newly Discovered Market', 20 September 1948, Box 9, Folder 12.

Dagens Nyheter (b), untitled, 2 October 1948, Box 9, Folder 12.

Gorandsson, Karin 'Models in Black', *Vecko-Revyn*, 15 October 1948, Box 9, Folder 12.

New York Age, 'Another Step Up', 31 July 1946, Box 10, Folder 1.

New York Post, 'All about the Negro Models', 16 June 1955, Box 10, Folder 1.

Stockholms Tidningen, 'Negro Beauties Trained to Be Proud', 1 October 1948, Box 9, Folder 12.

Svenska Dagbladet, 'Coloured People Should Have Their Own Styles', 1 October 1948, Box 9, Folder 12.

Magazines and Newspapers

Ebony, 'Backstage', November 1945, p. 1.

Ebony, 'Lena Horne Begins a New Movie', March 1946, pp. 14–20.

Ebony, 'Glamor Is Global', July 1946, pp. 18–23.

Ebony, 'Meet the Real Lena Horne', November 1947, pp. 8–14.

Ebony, 'Paris Model', February 1950, pp. 50–3.

Ebony, 'Can Negro Models Make the Bigtime?', September 1954, pp. 100–6.

Ebony, 'The Most Beautiful Woman I've Photographed', June 1951, pp. 56–8.

Ebony, 40th Anniversary Edition, Ebony Interview with John H. Johnson, November 1985.

Jet, 'Paris Model Has Dazzling Wardrobe', 6 December 1951.

Jet, 'Are Negro Women Getting Sexier?', 31 January 1952, pp. 28–31.

Jet, 'The Perfect Negro Beauty', 13 March 1952, pp. 32–8.

Jet, 'Fashion Shows Are Big Business', 13 April 1952, pp. 42–51.

Jet, 'What Is the Perfect Figure?', 26 June 1952, pp. 32–8.

Jet, 'How to Shoot Cheesecake Photos', 10 July 1952, pp. 30–5.

Jet, 'What Makes a Good Model?', 23 April 1953, pp. 38–42.

Our World, 'Color Combinations for Brownskins', April 1949, pp. 50–4.

Our World, 'Paris's Fabulous Negro Model: Dorothea Towles', August 1952, pp. 42–5.

Our World, 'What Makes a Model?', October 1953.

Our World, 'What Happened to the Brandford Models?', February 1954, pp. 30–6.

Our World, 'The Glamazons: Beauty by the Ton', November 1954, pp. 71–4.

'The Personal Equation: Negro Publisher Achieves Success' (1952), Christian Science Monitor, 26 February.

Published Works

Anderson, K. (1996), *A History of Racial Ethnic Women in Modern America*, Oxford: Oxford University Press.

Berger Gluck, S. (1987), *Rosie the Riveter Revisited: Women, the War, and Social Change*, Boston: Twayne.

Bogle, D. (2001), *Toms, Coons, Mulattoes, Mammies, and Bucks: An Interpretive History of Blacks in American Films*, Continuum.

Carby, Hazel V. (1992), 'Policing the Black Woman's Body in an Urban Context', *Critical Inquiry*, 18: 738–55.

Carney Smith, Jessie (ed.) (1996), *Notable Black American Women*, Book 2, Detroit: Gale Research.

Chambers, Jason (2008), *Madison Avenue and the Color Line: African Americans in the Advertising Industry*, University of Pennsylvania Press.

Cohen, L. (2003), *A Consumers' Republic: The Politics of Mass Consumption in Postwar America*, New York: Knopf.

Feldstein, R. (2000), *Motherhood in Black and White*, New York: Cornell University Press.

Gaines, Kevin P. (1996), *Uplifting the Race: Black Leadership, Politics, and Culture in the Twentieth Century*, Chapel Hill: University of North Carolina Press.

Haidarali, L. (2005), 'Polishing Brown Diamonds: African American Women, Popular Magazines, and the Advent of Modeling in Early Postwar America', *Journal of Women's History*, 17/1: 17–37.

Haidarali, L. (2007), ' "Is It True What They Say about Models?": Modelling African American Womanhood on the Eve of the Civil Rights Era', *Atlantis: A Women's Studies Journal*, 32/1: 144–55.

Hartmann, M. S. (1982), *The Home Front and Beyond: American Women in the 1940s*, Boston: Twayne.

Higginbotham, E. Brooks (1993), *Righteous Discontent: The Women's Movement in the Black Baptist Church, 1880–1920*, Cambridge, MA: Harvard University Press.

Hill Collins, P. (2000), *Black Feminist Thought: Knowledge, Consciousness, and the Politics of Empowerment*, New York: Routledge.

Hine, Darlene Clark (1989), 'Rape and the Inner Lives of Black Women in the Middle West', *Signs*, 14: 912–20.

Johnson, J. H. (1989), *Succeeding against the Odds*, New York: Amistad Press.

Landry, B. (1987), *The New Black Middle Class*, Berkeley: University of California Press.

Leach, William R. (1994), 'Transformations in a Culture of Consumption', *Journal of American History*, 71/2: 319–42.

Lears, T. Jackson (1983), 'From Salvation to Self-Realization', in R. Wrightman Fox and T. Jackson Lears (eds), *The Culture of Consumption: Critical Essays in American History, 1880–1980*, New York: Pantheon Books.

McAndrew, Malia (2010), 'Selling Black Beauty: African American Modeling Agencies and Charm Schools in Postwar America', *OAH Magazine of History*, 24/1: 29–32.

Meyerowitz, J. (1993), 'Beyond the Feminine Mystique: The Reassessment of Postwar Mass Culture', *Journal of American History*, 79/4: 1455–82.

Meyerowitz, J. (1996), 'Women, Cheesecake, and Borderline Material: Responses to Girlie Pictures in the Mid-Twentieth-Century U.S.', *Journal of Women's History*, 8/3: 9–35.

Meyerowitz, J. (ed.) (1994), *Not June Cleaver: Women and Gender in Postwar America, 1945–1960*, Philadelphia: Temple University Press.

Peiss, K. (1990), 'Making Faces: The Cosmetics Industry and the Cultural Construction of Gender, 1890–1930', *Genders*, 7: 143–69.

Peiss, K. (1998), *Hope in a Jar: The Making of American Beauty Culture*, New York: Metropolitan.

Shaw, Stephanie J. (1996), *What a Woman Ought to Be and to Do.* Chicago: University of Chicago Press.

Stowe, Harriet Beecher (1852), *Uncle Tom's Cabin: Or, Life among the Lowly*; repr. 1966, New York: Penguin.

Summers, B. (1998), *Black and Beautiful: How Women of Color Changed the Fashion Industry*, New York: HarperCollins.

Tyler May, E. (1999), *Homeward Bound: American Families in the Cold War Era*, New York: Basic Books.

Walker, S. (2007), *Style and Status: Selling Beauty to African American Women, 1920–1975*, Lexington: University Press of Kentucky.

Weems, Robert J. (1998), *Desegregating the Dollar: African American Consumerism in the Twentieth Century*, New York: New York University Press.

Wiese, Andrew (2004), *Places of Their Own: African American Suburbanization in the Twentieth Century*, Chicago: University of Chicago Press.

Wolcott, Victoria W. (2001), *Remaking Respectability: African American Women in Interwar Detroit*, Chapel Hill: University of North Carolina Press.

Chapter 5: Fashion Modelling in Australia

Aspers, P. (2006), *Markets in Fashion: A Phenomenological Approach*, 2nd rev. edn. London: Routledge.

Breward, C. (2003), *Fashion*, Oxford: Oxford University Press.

Burns, J. (2003), 'Steely Chic', *The Age*, 8 August, http://www.theage.com.au, accessed 25 June 2012.

Carew, L., with Masters, D. (2003), *Behind Glass*, Melbourne: Royal Melbourne Institute of Technology.

Conor, L. (2004), *The Spectacular Modern Woman: Feminine Visibility in the 1920s*, Bloomington: Indiana University Press.

Dally-Watkins, J., with Gee, L. (2002), *The Secrets Behind My Smile*, Camberwell, Vic.: Viking.

Entwistle, J. (2002), 'The Aesthetic Economy: The Production of Value in the Field of Fashion Modelling', *Journal of Consumer Culture*, 2/3: 317–39.

Featherstone, G. (2005), 'Helmut Newton's Australian Years', *La Trobe Journal*, 76 (Spring): 105–23.

Healey, R. (2005), *Dressed to the Eyes: The Fashion of Hall Ludlow*, Exhibition curated and catalogue essay written by Robyn Healy, Melbourne: Royal Melbourne Institute of Technology Gallery.

Jobbins, J. (2006), *Shoestring: A Memoir*, Sydney: Joy Jobbins.

Le Guay, L. (1957), 'The Modern Trend in Photography', in Oswald L. Zeigler (ed.), *Australian Photography*, Sydney: Ziegler Publications.

Leong, R. (1997), 'Sydney's Most Fashionable Europeans', in Roger Butler (ed.), *The Europeans: Emigré Artists in Australia 1930–1960*, Canberra: National Gallery of Australia.

McQueen, H. (2004), 'Colour: Emblem of Change, Catalyst of Commerce', Paper presented at the Antipodean Modern Symposium, Curtin University, Perth.

Maynard, M. (1995), ' "The Wishful Feeling about Curves": Fashion Femininity and the New Look in Australia', *Journal of Design History*, 8/1: 43–59.

Maynard, M. (1999), 'Living Dolls', *Journal of Popular Culture*, 32/1: 191–205.

Maynard, M. (2001), *Out of Line: Women and Style in Australia*, Sydney: University of New South Wales Press.

Maynard, M. (2007), ' "Lady Be Beautiful": Selling Corsets in the 1920s', *Journal of Australian Studies*, 91: 145–53.

Maynard, M. (2009), 'What Is Australian Fashion Photography?—A Dilemma', *Fashion Theory*, 13/4: 443–60.

Mist, D. (2005), *Exposed: A Life behind the Camera*, Leichhardt: A&A Book Publishing.

Mitchell, L. (1994), *Christian Dior: The Magic of Fashion*, Sydney: Powerhouse Museum.

Nile, R. (ed.) (1994), *Australian Civilisation*, Melbourne: Oxford University Press.

Palmer, D. (2005), 'Tracing the Origins of Australian Fashion Photography', *La Trobe Journal*, 76 (Spring): 87–102.

Quick, H. (1992), *Catwalking: A History of the Fashion Model*, London: Reed International.

Reekie, G. (1993), *Temptations: Sex, Selling and the Department Store*, Sydney: Allen and Unwin.

Ripper, M. (1941), 'A Talk About Our Fashion Future', *Australian Women's Weekly*, 29 March, p. 32.

Rudique, L. (1949), 'The Mannequin Story', *Fashion*, June, p. 19.

Safe, G. (2008), 'Glimpses of Models' Lives', *Australian*, 13 August, p. 24.

Soley-Beltran, P. (2004), 'Modelling Femininity', *Journal of European Studies*, 11: 309–26.

Thompson, E. (1994), 'Cringers', in Richard Nile (ed.), *Australian Civilisation*, Melbourne: Oxford University Press.

Tolmach, R., and Scherr, R. L. (1984), *Face Value: The Politics of Beauty*, London: Routledge and Kegan Paul.

Underhill, N. (1991), *Making Australian Art 1916–49*, Oxford: Oxford University Press.

Van de Ven, A-M. (2010), *Creating the Look: Bernini and Fashion Photography*, Sydney: Powerhouse Publishing.

Van Wyk, S. (ed.) (2006), *The Paris End: Photography, Fashion and Glamour*, Melbourne: National Gallery of Victoria.

Verstraeten, G. (1966), 'Henry Talbot: A Pro-profile', *Australian Photography* (Dec.): 20–5, 46.

Whitfield, D. (2006), '*La Mode Française* Australian Style', in S. Van Wyk (ed.), *The Paris End: Photography, Fashion and Glamour*, Melbourne: National Gallery of Victoria.

Chapter 6: Performing Dreams: A Counter-History of Models as Glamour's Embodiment

Ballerino Cohen, C., Wilk, R., and Stoelje, B. (1996), *Beauty Queens on the Global Stage: Gender, Contests, and Power*, London: Routledge.

Benn de Libero (1994), 'This Year's Girl: A Personal/Critical History of Twiggy', in S. Benstock and S. Ferris (eds), *On Fashion*, pp. 41–58. New Brunswick, NJ: Rutgers University Press.

Barthes, R. (1977), Elements of Semiology, New York: Hill & Wang.

Baudrillard, J. (1993) 'The Evil Demon of Images and The Precession of Simulacra', in T. Docherty (ed), *Postmodernism. A Reader,* pp. 194–199. UK: Harvester Wheatsheaf.

Beevor, A. and Cooper (1994), *A. Paris After the Liberation, 1944–1949,* London: Hamish Hamilton.

Bellafante, G. (1995), 'The Runway Girls Take Off', *Time*, 17 April, 66–7.

Berger, J. (1972), *Ways of Seeing,* London: Penguin.

Blanchard, T. (1995), 'Supermodels Reject Paris Catwalk 'Pin-Money'', *The Independent,* 29 January.

Bordo, S. (1993), *Unbearable Weight: Feminism, Western Culture and the Body.* Berkeley: University of California Press.

Butler, J. (1990), *Gender Trouble: Feminism and the Subversion of Identity*, London: Routledge.

Castle, C. (1977), *Model Girl*, London: David and Charles.

Colebrook, C. (2006), 'Introduction', Special issue on Beauty, *Feminist Theory*, 7/2: 131–42.

Colebrook, C., and Felski, R. (eds) (2006), 'Beauty', *Feminist Theory*, 7/2: 273–82.

Craik, J. (1994), *The Face of Fashion: Cultural Studies in Fashion*, London: Routledge.

Dixon, J., and Dixon, P. (1963), *Fashion Modelling*, London: Robert Hale.

Douglas, M. (1990), *Natural Symbols. Explorations in Cosmology,* UK: Penguin.

Dudgeon, B. (1994) 'To be Perfectly Plain', *The Guardian,* 5 May, Style Supplement, pp. 14–15.

Elgort, A. (1994), *Arthur Elgort's Model's Manual*, New York: Grand Street Press.

Elias, N. (2000), *The Civilizing Process: Sociogenetic and Psychogenetic Investigations*, US: Blackwell.

Elle (2009), 'Con Ñ de Doña' (268): 153–9, Spain: Hachette.

Elle (1993), 'The Rise of the Nasty Girl', (September): 20–1, United Kingdom: Hachette.

Emery, A. (2007), 'Klum Shot', *ARENA*, 17 September, Emap, pp. 152–63.

Entwistle, J. (2002), 'The Aesthetic Economy: The Production of Value in Fashion Modelling', *Journal of Consumer Culture*, 2/3: 317–39.

Evans, C. (2001), 'The Enchanted Spectacle', *Fashion Theory*, 5/3: 271–310.

Falcón, L., and Hijar, M. (1982), '¡Hágase la moda! Y surgieron las modelos', *Actual Magazine*, 8: 72–5.

Featherstone, M. (1988), *Consumer Culture and Postmodernism,* London: Sage.

Fink, L. (2000), *Runway*, New York: Powerhouse Books.

Finkelstein, J. (1991), *The Fashioned Self*, Philadelphia: Temple University Press.

Foley, M. H. (1989), 'Professional Female Models: Body Esteem and Causal Attributions', PhD thesis, Arizona State University.

Fressange, I. (2002), *Profession Mannequin*, Paris: Hachette.

Frisell Ellburg, Ann (2008), *Ett Fåfängt arbete. Möten med modeller I den svenska mode-insdustrin*, Stockholm-Goteburg: Makadam Förlag.

Gross, M. (1996), *Model: The Ugly Business of Beautiful Women*, New York: Warner Books.

Gundle, S. (2008), *Glamour: A History*, Oxford: Oxford University Press.

Hartman, R. (1980), *Birds of Paradise: An Intimate View of the New York Fashion World*, New York: Delta.

Helcké, J. (2003), 'Magazines in Everyday Life: Negotiating Identity, Femininity and Belonging in Lifestyles Magazines for Minority Ethnic Women in France and the UK', *New Media, Technology and Everyday Life in European Conference*, London School of Economics, 23–26 April.

Hudson, J. (1994), 'Black Models: The Cover Gap', *International Herald Tribune*, 29 March, p. 8.

Irvine, S. (1994), 'Less Than Perfect', *Vogue* (UK) (Jan.): 9–10.

Jeal, N. (1994), 'Super Weird', *Elle* (UK) (Nov.): 25.

Jones, L.A. (1993), *Naomi: The Rise and Rise of the Girl from Nowhere*, London: Vermilion.

Juliano, D. (2002), *La Prostitución: el Espejo Oscuro*, Barcelona: Icaria.

Keenan, B. (1977), *The Women Wanted to Look Like*, London: Macmillan.

Koda, H., and Yohannan, K. (2009), *Model as Muse: Embodying Fashion*, New York: Metropolitan Museum of Art and Yale University Press.

Lakoff, R.T., and Scherr, R.L. (1984), *Face Value: The Politics of Beauty*, New York: Routledge.

Lecturas (2003), 'Natalia Vodianova de vendedora de frutas a modelo mejor pagada del mundo', *Lecturas*, 7 November, pp. 90–1.

Lehndorf, V., and Hubertus Ilse, A. (2006), 'Self-Portraits 1992–1996', Exhibition Catalogue, Helmut Newton Foundation, Berlin.

Lehndorf, V., and Trulzsch, H. (1986), '*Veruschka'. Trans-figurations*, New York: Thames and Hudson.

Lipovetsky, G., and Roux, E. (2004), *El lujo eterno. De la era de lo sagrado al tiempo de las marcas*, Barcelona: Anagrama.

Livingstone, J. (1987), 'Paris Is Burning', *Dangerous to Know* (Copyright and distribution—1994), Miramax Films: New York.

Lomas, C. (2000), ' "I Know Nothing about Fashion. There's No Point in Interviewing Me": The Use and Value of Oral History to the Fashion Historian', in S. Bruzzi and P. Church-Gibson (eds), *Fashion Cultures: Theories, Explorations and Analysis*, pp. 363–70. London: Routledge.

Marie Claire, (2003), 'Editorial', (September): 115–45, Spain: Hachette.

Marshall, C. (1978), *The Cat-Walk*, London: Hutchinson.

McKay, A. (1995), 'Kitten of the catwalk', *Scotland on Sunday*, 23 April, p. 3.

Mears, A., and Finlay, W. (2005), 'Not Just a Paper Doll: How Models Manage Bodily Capital and Why They Perform Emotional Labor', *Journal of Contemporary Ethnography*, 34/3 (June): 317–43.

Moncur, S. (1991), *They Still Shoot Models My Age*, London: Serpent's Tail.

O'Hagan, S. (2010), 'Corinne Day: She Added Grit to the Glamour of Fashion Photography', *The Observer*, Sunday 5 September, http://www.guardian.co.uk/artanddesign/2010/sep/05/corinne-day-photography-kate-moss, accessed 25 September 2010.

O'Neill, J. (1985), *Five Bodies: The Human Shape of Modern Society*, London: Cornell University Press.

Perkins, L., and Givhan, R. (1998), *Runway Madness*, San Francisco: Chronicle Books.

Phaidon Press (1998), *The Fashion Book*, London: Phaidon Press.

Quick, H. (1997), *Défilés de mode. Une histoire du mannequin*, London: Hamlyn.

Raymond, J. (2002), *No Lifeguard on Duty: The Accidental Life of the World's First Supermodel*, New York: HarperCollins.

Reed-Danahay, D. (ed.) (1997), *Auto/Ethnography. Rewriting the Self and the Social*, New York: Berg.

Rudolph, B. (1991), 'The Supermodels', *Time* (September): 62–68.

Shrimpton, J. (1990), *Jean Shrimpton: An Autobiography*, London: Ebury Press.

Soley-Beltran, P. (1995), 'High Exposure: A Study of Modelling and the Postmodern Self', Cultural History dissertation, Aberdeen University.

Soley-Beltran, P. (1999), 'Supermodelos como emblema cultural', *Historia, Antropología y Fuentes Orales*, 22: 105–11.

Soley-Beltran, P. (2004a), 'Modelling Femininity', *European Journal of Women Studies*, 11/3: 309–26.

Soley-Beltran, P. (2004b), 'Modelos de Feminidad', *La Moda desde el género, Emakunde*, Instituto Vasco de la Mujer, 55: 18–21.

Soley-Beltran, P. (2006), 'Charming Power: Models as Ideal Embodiments of Normative Identity', *Trípodos. Llenguatge, Pensament, Comunicació*, 18: 23–43, http://www.tripodos.com/pdf/18m_SoleyBeltran.pdf, accessed 25 June 2012.

Soley-Beltran, P. (2008), 'Fashion Models as National Products: A Coloured Look', *Ending International Feminist Futures?*, Unpublished paper presented at Conference at University of Aberdeen, 24–25 October.

Soley-Beltran, P. (2009), *Transexualidad y la Matriz Heterosexual: un estudio crítico y empírico de la teoría performativa de género de Judith Butler*, Barcelona: Ediciones Bellaterra.

Soley-Beltran, P. (2010a), 'Auto/Ethnography of Fashion Modelling: Who Is the Object?!', *El cuerpo. Objeto y Sujeto de las Ciencias Sociales*, Institució Milà i Fontanals, Centro Superior de Investigaciones Científicas, Barcelona, 28–31 January 2009, pp. 239–52.

Soley-Beltran, P. (2010b), Research Report 'Body, Gender and Identity: Towards a Critical Pedagogy of the Social Construction of Body Ideals', Barcelona: Office for the Promotion of Equality Women-Men, Diputació de Barcelona, http://www. diba.es/dones/descarrega/soley.pdf, accessed.

Stearns, P. N. (2002), *Fat History: Bodies and Beauty in the Modern West*, New York: New York University Press.

Steele, N. (1985), *Fashion and Eroticism: Ideals of Feminine Beauty from the Victorian Era to the Jazz Age*, Oxford: Oxford University Press.

Tatler (1993), 'Moss Gloss', October: 28–30.

Telva (1994), 'Adios al Barroquismo', February: 86.

Versace, Gianni (1997), *Marcus Schenkenberg: New Rules*, New York: Universe.

Warner, M. (1985), *Monuments and Maidens: The Allegory of the Female Form*, London: Weidenfeld and Nicolson.

Chapter 7: The Figure of the Model and Reality TV

Banet-Weiser, S., and Portwood-Stacer, L. (2006), ' "I Just Want to Be Me Again!": Beauty Pageants, Reality Television and Post-Feminism', *Feminist Theory*, 7/2: 255–72.

Carnegie, C. V. (1996), 'The Dundus and the Nation', *Cultural Anthropology*, 11/4: 470–509.

de Moraes, L. (2004), 'No More Miss America Pageantry for ABC', *Washington Post*, October 21.

Entwistle, J. (2002), 'The Aesthetic Economy: The Production of Value in the Field of Fashion Modelling', *Journal of Consumer Culture*, 2/3: 317–39.

Entwistle, J., and Wissinger, E. (2006), 'Keeping up Appearances: Aesthetic Labour in the Fashion Modelling Industries of London and New York', *Sociological Review*, 54/4: 774–94.

Guider, E. (2005), 'Klum Fitted for "Model" ', *Variety*, August 11.

Haraway, D. (1997), *Modest_Witness@Second_Millennium.FemaleMan©_Meets_ OncoMouse™*, New York: Routledge.

Hartigan, J. (2005), *Odd Tribes: Toward a Cultural Analysis of White People*, Durham, NC: Duke University Press.

Heller, D. (2007), 'Introduction: Reading the Makeover', in D. Heller (ed.), *Makeover Television: Realities Remodelled*, New York: I. B. Tauris.

Hirschberg, L. (2008), 'Banksable', *New York Times Magazine*, June 1, pp. 38–45, 58, 62–3.

Kissell, R. (2006), 'Prime Week for NBC, CBS', *Variety*, December 12.

Kissell, R. (2008), 'Networks Spread Wednesday Wealth', *Variety*, May 8.

Lew, I. (2008), 'CBS Paramount Inks New Format Deals', WorldScreen.com, January 30, http://www.worldscreen.com/articles/display/14564.

Linder, F. (2007), 'Life as Art, and Seeing the Promise of Big Bodies', *American Ethnologist*, 34/3: 451–72.

Lowe, L. (2006), 'The Intimacies of Four Continents,' in A. L. Stoler (ed.), *Haunted by Empire: Geographies of Intimacy in North American History*, Durham, NC: Duke University Press.

Magder, T. (2004), 'The End of TV 101: Reality Programs, Formats, and the New Business of Television', in S. Murray and L. Ouellette (eds), *Reality TV: Remaking Television Culture*, New York: New York University Press.

Mao, D. (2003), 'The Labour Theory of Beauty: Aesthetic Subjects, Blind Justice', in P. R. Matthews and D. McWhirter (eds), *Aesthetic Subjects*, Minneapolis: University of Minnesota Press.

Martin, D. (2005), 'Reality Rocks Cable: VH1 Steps up for "Model," "Tommy Lee" Reruns', *Variety*, June 6.

Miller, T. (2008), *Makeover Nation: The United States of Reinvention*, Columbus: Ohio State University Press.

Miss America (2007), 'TLC Gives Miss America a Makeover in Original Reality Series "Miss America: Reality Check" ', Press Release, 5 December.

Miss America (2008), 'In Its Premiere Weekend, More Than 19 Million Viewers Tune in for Miss America', Press Release, January 30.

Ouellette, L., and Hay, J. (2008), *Better Living through Reality TV: Television and Post-Welfare Citizenship*, Malden, MA: Blackwell.

Ouellette, L., and Murray, S. (2004), 'Introduction', in S. Murray and L. Ouellette (eds), *Reality TV: Remaking Television Culture*, New York: New York University Press.

Raphael, C. (2004), 'The Political Economic Origins of Reali-TV', in S. Murray and L. Ouellette (eds), *Reality TV: Remaking Television Culture*, New York: New York University Press.

Schneider, M. (2006), 'CW Imports Brit "Mode" ', *Daily Variety*, December 4.

Stun Creative (2008), 'Miss America Live', TV commercial, produced by Mark Feldstein and Brad Roth.

Taylor, J. S. (2005), 'Surfacing the Body Interior', *Annual Review of Anthropology*, 34: 741–56.

Trebay, G. (2005), 'Who Is America's Next Top Model, Really?', *New York Times*, November 6.

V Magazine Blog (2007), '48 Hours Later', December 5, http://www.vmagazine.com/blog.php?m=200712.

Weismantel, M. (2001), *Cholas and Pishtacos: Stories of Race and Sex in the Andes*, Chicago: University of Chicago Press.

Wissinger, E. (2004), 'The Value of Attention: Affective Labour in the Fashion Modeling Industry', PhD diss., City University of New York.

Wissinger, E. (2007), 'Always on Display: Affective Production in the Modeling Industry', in P. T. Clough (ed.), *The Affective Turn: Theorizing the Social*, pp. 231–60. Durham, NC: Duke University Press.

Wissinger, E. (forthcoming), *Always on Display: Fashion Models, Work, and Consumer Culture*, New York: New York University Press.

Chapter 8: Made in Japan: Fashion Modelling in Tokyo

Anderson, Leon (2006), 'Analytic Autoethnography', *Journal of Contemporary Ethnography*, 35: 373–95.

Aspers, Patrik (2005), *Markets in Fashion: A Phenomenological Approach*, London: Routledge.

Bielby, William T., and Bielby, Denise D. (1994), 'All Hits Are Flukes—Institutionalized Decision-Making and the Rhetoric of Network Prime-Time Program-Development', *American Journal of Sociology*, 99: 1287–1313.

Bourdieu, Pierre (1993), *The Field of Cultural Production: Essays on Art and Literature*, New York: Columbia University Press.

Brenner, Jennifer B., and Cunningham, Joseph G. (1992), 'Gender Differences in Eating Attitudes, Body Concept, and Self-Esteem among Models', *Sex Roles*, 27: 413–37.

Carrier, James G. (ed.) (1995), *Occidentalism*, Oxford: Clarendon Press.

Caves, Richard E. (2000), *Creative Industries: Contracts between Art and Commerce*, Cambridge, MA: Harvard University Press.

Creighton, M. (1995), 'Imaging the Other in Japanese Ad Campaigns', in James G. Carrier (ed.), *Occidentalism*, Oxford: Clarendon Press.

Creighton, M. (1997), 'Women, Media and Consumption in Japan', *Journal of Japanese Studies*, 23: 238–42.

Currid, Elizabeth (2007), *The Warhol Economy: How Fashion, Art, and Music Drive New York City*, Princeton, NJ: Princeton University Press.

Darling-Wolf, Fabienne (2001), 'Gender, Beauty, and Western Influence: Negotiated Femininity in Japanese Women's Magazines', in Elizabeth L. Toth and Linda Aldoory (eds), *The Gender Challenge to the Media: Diverse Voices from the Field*. Cresskill, NJ: Hampton Press.

Entwistle, Joanne (2002), 'The Aesthetic Economy: The Production of Value in the Field of Fashion Modelling', *Journal of Consumer Culture*, 2: 317–39.

Entwistle, J., and Wissinger, E. (2006), 'Keeping up Appearances: Aesthetic Labour in the Fashion Modelling Industries of London and New York', *Sociological Review*, 54: 774–94.

Goffman, Erving (1959), *The Presentation of Self in Everyday Life*, Garden City, NY: Doubleday.

Goldstein-Gidoni, O. (2001), 'The Making and Marking of the "Japanese" and the "Western" in Japanese Contemporary Material Culture', *Journal of Material Culture*, 6: 67–90.

Hirsch, Paul M. (1972), 'Processing Fads and Fashions—Organization Set Analysis of Cultural Industry Systems', *American Journal of Sociology*, 77: 639–59.

Hochschild, Arlie Russell (1983), *The Managed Heart: Commercialization of Human Feeling*, Berkeley: University of California Press.

Hodson, Randy (2001), *Dignity at Work*, Cambridge: Cambridge University Press.

Kalleberg, A. L., Reskin, B. F., and Hudson, K. (2000), 'Bad Jobs in America: Standard and Nonstandard Employment Relations and Job Quality in the United States', *American Sociological Review*, 65: 256–78.

Kawamura, Yuniya (2005), *Fashion-ology: An Introduction to Fashion Studies*, Oxford: Berg.

Kondo, Dorinne K. (1997), *About Face: Performing Race in Fashion and Theater*, New York: Routledge.

McRobbie, Angela (2004), 'Making a Living in London's Small Scale Creative Sector', in Dominic Power and Allen J. Scott (eds), *Cultural Industries and the Production of Culture*, London: Routledge.

Mears, Ashley (2008), 'Discipline of the Catwalk: Gender, Power and Uncertainty in Fashion Modeling', *Ethnography*, 9: 429–56.

Mears, Ashley (2011), *Pricing Beauty: The Making of a Fashion Model*, Berkeley: University of California Press.

Mears, Ashley, and Finlay, William (2005), 'Not Just a Paper Doll—How Models Manage Bodily Capital and Why They Perform Emotional Labor', *Journal of Contemporary Ethnography*, 34: 317–43.

Menger, P. M. (1999), 'Artistic Labor Markets and Careers', *Annual Review of Sociology*, 25: 541–74.

Neff, Gina, Wissinger, Elizabeth, and Zukin, Sharon (2005), 'Entrepreneurial Labor among Cultural Producers: "Cool" Jobs in "Hot" Industries', *Social Semiotics*, 15: 307–34.

Negus, Keith (1999), *Music Genres and Corporate Cultures*, London: Routledge.

Rosenberger, Nancy R. (1996), 'Fragile Resistance, Signs of Status: Women between State and Media in Japan', in Anne E. Imamura (ed.), *Re-Imaging Japanese Women*, Berkeley: University of California Press.

Scott, Allen John (2000), *The Cultural Economy of Cities: Essays on the Geography of Image-Producing Industries*, London: Sage.

Scott, James C. (1985), *Weapons of the Weak: Everyday Forms of Peasant Resistance*, New Haven, CT: Yale University Press.

Scott, James C. (1990), *Domination and the Arts of Resistance: Hidden Transcripts*, New Haven, CT: Yale University Press.

Soley-Beltran, P. (2004), 'Modelling Femininity', *European Journal of Women's Studies*, 11: 309–26.

Thompson, John B. (2005), *Books in the Digital Age: The Transformation of Academic and Higher Education Publishing in Britain and the United States*, Cambridge: Polity Press.

Velthuis, Olav (2005), *Talking Prices: Symbolic Meanings of Prices on the Market for Contemporary Art*, Princeton, NJ: Princeton University Press.

Witz, A., Warhurst, C., and Nickson, D. (2003), 'The Labour of Aesthetics and the Aesthetics of Organization', *Organization*, 10: 33–54.

Chapter 9: Modelling Consumption: Fashion Modelling Work in Contemporary Society

Arvidsson, A. (2005), 'Brands: A Critical Perspective', *Journal of Consumer Culture*, 5/2: 235–58.

Banks, T. (2007, 2011), www.TyraBanks.com, accessed 4 February 2007, and www. typef.com, accessed 14 July 2011.

Barry, A. (2001), *Political Machines: Governing a Technological Society*, London: Athlone.

Bourdieu, Pierre (1984), *Distinction: A Social Critique of the Judgment of Taste*, Cambridge, MA: Harvard University Press.

Bureau of Labor Statistics, US Department of Labor (2006–2007) *Occupational Outlook Handbook*, 2006–07 Edition, 'Demonstrators, Product Promoters, and Models', http://www.bls.gov/oco/ocos253.htm, accessed 14 July 2011.

Crewe, B. (2003), *Representing Men: Cultural Production and Producers in the Men's Magazine Market*, Oxford: Berg.

Currid, E. (2007), *The Warhol Economy: How Fashion, Art, and Music Drive New York City*, Princeton, NJ: Princeton University Press.

Day, Corrine (2007), 'Corinne Day Biography', http://www.corinneday.co.uk/bio. php, accessed 14 July 2011.

Entwistle, J. (2002), 'The Aesthetic Economy: Fashion Modeling and the Production of Culturally Valued Bodies', *Journal of Consumer Culture*, 2/3: 325–47.

Entwistle, J. (2004), 'From Catwalk to Catalogue: Male Fashion Models, Masculinity and Identity', in H. Thomas and J. Ahmed (eds), *Ethnographies of the Body*, pp. 55–73. London: Blackwell.

Entwistle, J. (2009), *The Aesthetic Economy of Fashion: Markets and Value in Fashion Modelling and Buying*, London: Berg.

Entwistle, J., and Wissinger, E. (2006), 'Keeping up Appearances: Aesthetic Labor in the Fashion Modeling Industry', *Sociological Review*, 54/4: 774–94.

Entwistle, J., and Wissinger, E. (2007), 'Modelling Consumption', Paper presented at the Present and Future of Consumer Studies Conference, Barnard College, New York, 10 August.

Espinosa, R. (2008), 'Ford Names New Supermodel of the World', *Fashion Wire Daily*, 17 January, http://www.fashionwiredaily.com/first_word/fashion/article. weml?id=1682, accessed 19 July 2011.

Evans, C. (2001), 'The Enchanted Spectacle', *Fashion Theory*, 5/3: 271–310.

Fabrikant, M. (2008), 'Ford Supermodel Presents Supermodel of the World Global Model Search', *The Paramus Post*, 11 January, http://www.paramuspost.com/ article.php/20080111202404847, accessed 4 February 2008.

Firat, F., and Dholakia, N. (1998), *Consuming People: From Political Economy to Theaters of Consumption*, New York: Routledge.

Gilbert-Rolfe, Jeremy (1999), *Beauty and the Contemporary Sublime*, New York: Allworth Press.

Gough-Yates, A. (2003), *Understanding Women's Magazines: Publishing, Markets and Readerships*, London: Routledge.

Grazian, D. (2008a), Book review of Elizabeth Currid, *The Warhol Economy: How Fashion, Art, and Music Drive New York City*, in *Journal of Planning Education and Research*, 28: 116–22.

Grazian, D. (2008b), *On the Make: The Hustle of Urban Nightlife*, Chicago: University of Chicago Press.

Gross, Michael (1995), *Model: The Ugly Business of Beautiful Women*, New York: W. Morrow.

Hardt, M., and Negri, A. (2000), *Empire*, Cambridge, MA: Harvard University Press.

Kilbourne, J. (1999), *Killing Us Softly 3* (DVD). Northampton, MA: Media Education Foundation.

Lazzarato, M. (1996), 'Immaterial Labor', in P. Virno and M. Hardt (eds), *Radical Thought in Italy: A Potential Politics*. Minneapolis: University of Minnesota Press.

McFall, L. (2004), *Advertising: A Cultural Economy*, London: Sage.

Maynard, M. (1999), 'Living Dolls', *Journal of Popular Culture*, 32/1: 235–40.

Mears, A. E. (2007), 'Pricing Looks: The Gendered Production of Value in Fashion Modeling', Paper presented at the Gender and Work panel of the Annual Meeting, American Sociology Association, New York.

Mears, A. E. (2008), 'Discipline of the Catwalk: Gender, Power, and Uncertainty in High Fashion Modeling', *Ethnography* 9/4: 429–56.

Mears, A. E. (2010), Size Zero High-End Ethnic: Cultural Production and the Reproduction of Culture in Fashion Modeling', *Poetics*, 38/1: 21–46.

Mears, A. E., and Finlay, W. (2005), 'Not Just a Paper Doll: How Models Manage Bodily Capital and Why They Perform Emotional Labor', *Journal of Contemporary Ethnography*, 34/3: 317–43.

Neff, G., Wissinger, E., and Zukin, S. (2005), 'Entrepreneurial Labor among Cultural Producers: "Cool" Jobs in "Hot" Industries', *Social Semiotics*, 15/3: 307–34.

Negus, K. (1992), *Producing Pop: Culture and Conflict in the Popular Music Industry*, London: Edward Arnold.

Negus, K. (1999), *Music Genres and Corporate Cultures*, London: Routledge.

Nixon, S. (2003), *Advertising Cultures*, London: Sage.

Nixon, S., and Du Gay, P. (2002), 'Who Needs Cultural Intermediaries?', *Cultural Studies*, 16/4: 495–500.

Parmentier, M., and Fischer, E. (2007), 'Working to Consume the Model Life: Consumer Agency under Scarcity', in R. W. Belk and J. F. Sherry Jr (eds), *Consumer Culture Theory 11*, Research in Consumer Behaviour Series, pp. 23–39. Oxford: Elsevier.

Quick, H. (1997), *Catwalking: A History of the Fashion Model*, London: Octopus.

Ritzer, G. (1999), *Enchanting a Disenchanted World*, Thousand Oaks, CA: Pine Forge Press.

Salkin, A. (2008), 'Hard at Work, the Model Whisperer', *New York Times*, 10 February, http://nytimes.com, accessed 19 July 2011.

Soley-Beltran, P. (2004), 'Modeling Femininity', Spectacular Women, *European Journal of Women's Studies*, 11/3: 309–26.

Sykes, P. (2008), 'View from the Top', *Vogue* (August): 182–6.

Warhurst, C., and Nickson, D. (2001), *Looking Good, Sounding Right: Style Counselling in the New Economy*, London: Industrial Society.

Wilson, E. (2007), 'Waiting to Show Model Behavior', *New York Times*, 26 March, http://nytimes.com, accessed 19 July 2011.

Wissinger, E. (2007), 'Modeling a Way of Life: Immaterial and Affective Labor in the Fashion Modeling Industry', *ephemera: theory and politics in organization*, 7/1: 250–69.

Wissinger, E. (forthcoming), *The Modeling Life: Fashioning Our Attention from Gibson Girls to Glamazons*, New York: New York University Press.

Wittel, A. (2001), 'Towards a Network Sociality', *Theory, Culture & Society*, 18/6: 51–76.

Žižek, S. (1999), 'You May!', *London Review of Books*, 18 March, pp. 3–6.

Index